ADVENTURE EDUCATION

Adventure education is a form of experiential learning typically associated with activities involving risk, from cooperative games such as raft building to high-adventure activities such as rock climbing. *Adventure Education: An introduction* provides a comprehensive introduction to the planning, delivery and evaluation of adventure education, with a strong emphasis on professional practice and delivery.

Written by a team of leading adventure educators who draw upon an extensive experience base, the book explores the most important strategies for teaching, learning and implementation in adventure education. The book is fully illustrated throughout with real-world case studies and research surveying the key contemporary issues facing adventure education practitioners. It includes essentials for the adventure educator, such as risk management and tailoring activities to meet specific learning needs, as well as providing an insight into contemporary uses for adventure programmes. With outdoor and adventure activities more popular than ever, this book is essential reading for any student, teacher or practitioner looking to understand adventure education and develop their professional skills.

Matt Berry is a lecturer at the University of Chichester, where he teaches on both the Adventure Education and the Physical Education degree programmes. Matt is a keen whitewater kayaker and he has been active in adventure education through teaching and research for fifteen years, with a special interest in teacher and coach education.

Chris Hodgson is a lecturer at the University of Chichester, where he teaches Adventure Education and Physical Education. He has been involved in the delivery of adventure education for over twenty years. Professional experience includes the delivery of adventure programmes to a wide range of participants, from young children through to adults and from performance-based adventure sports programmes through to management training as well as personal and social education.

ADVENTURE EDUCATION

AN INTRODUCTION

**EDITED BY MATT BERRY
AND CHRIS HODGSON**

Routledge
Taylor & Francis Group

LONDON AND NEW YORK

This edition first published 2011
by Routledge
2 Park Square, Milton Park, Abingdon, Oxon, OX14 4RN

Simultaneously published in the USA and Canada
by Routledge
711 Third Avenue, New York, NY 10017

Routledge is an imprint of the Taylor & Francis Group, an informa business

British Library Cataloguing in Publication Data
A catalogue record for this book is available from the British Library

Library of Congress Cataloging in Publication Data
Adventure education : an introduction / edited by Matt Berry and Chris Hodgson.
p. cm. – (Models and milestones in adventure education)
1. Adventure education–Study and teaching. I. Berry, Matthew II. Hodgson, Chris.
LC1038.A35 2011
371.3'84–dc22
2010047306

ISBN13: 978–0–415–57183–8 (hbk)
ISBN13: 978–0–415–57185–2 (pbk)
ISBN13: 978–0–203–85675–8 (ebk)

Typeset in Zapf Humanist and Eras by Keystroke, Station Road, Wolverhampton
Printed and bound in Great Britain by T J International Ltd, Padstow, Cornwall

CONTENTS

CONTRIBUTORS

Pete Allison is Deputy Head of the Institute for Sport, Physical Education and Health Sciences at the University of Edinburgh. He is a fellow of the Royal Geographical Society and founder of the *Journal of Adventure Education and Outdoor Learning*. He has also served on the board of directors of the Association for Experiential Education.

Marcus Bailie is Head of Inspection at the Adventure Activity Licensing Service. Previously, he worked as an instructor at Plas y Brenin (the National Mountain Centre), where he had specific responsibility for mountain leadership, and as director of Tiglin (the Irish National Adventure Centre).

Simon Beames is a lecturer at the University of Edinburgh. His outdoor instructing experience has mainly been gained in North America and Asia, where he has worked with Outward Bound, Project DARE, the YMCA and the Hong Kong International School.

Matt Berry is a lecturer at the University of Chichester, where he teaches on both the Adventure Education and the Physical Education degree programmes. He is a keen whitewater kayaker and has been active in adventure education through teaching and research for fifteen years, with a special interest in teacher and coach education.

Pete Bunyan is Head of the Department of Adventure Education at the University of Chichester. Previously, he ran the PGCE in Outdoor Education at the University of Exeter.

Ed Christian is a lecturer at the University of Chichester. He has worked with young people excluded from mainstream education for the Devon Youth Service and has taught at Skern Lodge, Devon, where he had responsibility for working with disaffected young people.

Suzanne Everley is a lecturer at the University of Chichester, where she specialises in participants' perceptions of physical education and physical activity.

Johannes Felter is a research student at Liverpool John Moores University. He has taught Religious, Moral and Philosophical Studies in combination with Outdoor Education for ten years at various schools and centres.

Joseph Gibson is Outdoor Education Coordinator for Sense Scotland, where he specialises in work with participants with dual sensory impairments.

Paul Gray is a lecturer at the University of Central Lancashire, where he teaches on both the Outdoor Leadership and Adventure Sports Coaching degree programmes. Previously he was Operations and Centre Manager for numerous adventure education companies throughout the UK and Europe.

Chris Heaney is a lecturer at the University of Chichester. Previously, he was Managing Director for Life Gateway – a provider of experiential educational and respite services for looked-after children – prior to which he was a course director for Outward Bound in Utah, USA.

Chris Hodgson is a lecturer at the University of Chichester, where he teaches Adventure Education and Physical Education. He has been involved in the delivery of adventure education for over twenty years. Professional experience includes the delivery of adventure programmes to a wide range of participants, from young children through to adults and from performance-based adventure sports programmes through to management training as well as personal and social education.

John Kelly is a lecturer at the University of Chichester, where he specialises in physiology and competitive adventure sports. Previously, he was a physical training instructor for the military and worked in cardiac rehabilitation for the National Health Service.

Jane Lomax is Programme Coordinator for Sports Coaching and PE at the University of Chichester. Her previous experience includes management training and snow sports instruction.

Aaron Marshall is a research student at the Institute for Sport, PE and Health Sciences, the University of Edinburgh, where he specialises in experiential education as a framework for character formation.

Julia Potter is a lecturer at the University of Chichester. She specialises in children's health and fitness in relation to lifestyle and physical activity.

Tim Stott is Professor of Physical Geography and Outdoor Education at Liverpool John Moores University, where he teaches earth science, geomorphology, weather and atmospheric processes, mountains and upland landscapes, natural hazards and applied geomorphology, fluvial processes and outdoor pursuits (kayaking, mountain leadership, orienteering, skiing).

John Telford recently completed a longitudinal sociological study of residential outdoor education for which he gained a Ph.D. at the Institute for Sport, PE and Health Sciences, the University of Edinburgh. He has fifteen years' experience of working with adults and children in various contexts, ranging from residential outdoor education centres to community projects to higher education institutions.

Malcolm Thorburn is a lecturer in Physical Education at the University of Edinburgh. His research interests include knowledge representation in practical learning environments, and the goals of physical education in schools.

INTRODUCTION

Chris Hodgson and Matt Berry

Recent years have seen a sustained growth in interest in outdoor and adventure-based learning. From a discipline with a relatively short history we are now part of a world which sees adventure ever more prominent in media, lifestyles and mainstream education. Even television programming is rich with images of adventure and themes that we can see are linked to adventure and outdoor education philosophies. This is interspersed with advertisements that also often borrow from typical adventure themes and portray the characteristics commensurate with desirable traits and healthy living. In some ways it may seem strange that we ever have to justify adventure-based programmes since it is so often implied that there is an automatic benefit from participation. However, whilst superficially this may all appear good, it is still necessary to differentiate between real, meaningful education with profound benefits for participants and society, and activities that seem adventurous in nature but offer little quality learning potential. Otherwise, we may miss an opportunity to achieve broader educational goals and enrich the lives of participants. Of course, it is always possible to learn from an adventurous experience in an incidental or accidental way, but adventure education essentially should have clear purposes and seek to move learners actively in a direction that is likely to meet their specific needs.

The purposeful use of adventure has now reached the point where there is a significant degree of interest in studying the subject at academic and professional levels. This is reflected in the large number of opportunities to study adventure and outdoor-related disciplines at post-sixteen, undergraduate and postgraduate levels in the UK, the USA, Australia, Canada, New Zealand and elsewhere. Such a development would not have seemed likely even as recently as the 1980s.

This book is intended to appeal to a range of readers from varying backgrounds. Primarily we expect that students studying at undergraduate level will find it particularly useful as a guide to the processes and practical aspects of adventure education that will support their intellectual understanding of our ever-developing discipline. We also expect that professional adventure educators will find that the book supports them as they develop an understanding of what we do and why we do it, which can go hand in hand with knowledge of technical skills. If we want credibility as professionals in education, it is imperative that we move beyond purely sports- and technical-based knowledge, which is already well catered for by the governing body and activity instructor award schemes. As yet, this educational knowledge base and skills set have not had the recognition and emphasis that they deserve. This may be due partly to our preoccupation with safety-based skills, which, although vital, do not constitute the complete understanding that is necessary to plan and deliver educational experiences. Organisations like the UK-based Institute of Outdoor Learning are now making inroads in this area with an accreditation scheme that aims to recognise and validate an educational skills set that is equal to technical and safety skills. This book can provide a valuable resource for professionals hoping to develop their educational skills.

The philosophy of our approach is that we aim to complement existing texts within the field of adventure and outdoor education. Rather than see ourselves as an exclusive group, or our approach as an alternative to other forms of education, we feel we belong to a large and diverse community of educational professionals. As such, we need to embrace the lessons that we can learn from these colleagues and related educational disciplines. We also have a responsibility to engage with these disciplines. This is a two-way process with mutual benefits for all concerned. Whilst mainstream education has much to gain from experiential disciplines of education, we can also make use of decades of research and development in more formal education methods. Importantly, we see our role as complementary to other educational experiences, rather than an alternative. Whilst it may be theoretically possible to learn all we need to know in adventure education, practicalities dictate that adventure education often performs a vital but supporting role in a fully rounded education.

In the past, some adventure educators have been very concerned about the label we attach to ourselves. This means some professionals refer to themselves as 'facilitators' and actively avoid terms like 'teacher', believing that the latter somehow limits their engagement with clients. In this book, we see rounded educators as changing the emphasis of their delivery to suit the needs of the learner. We have not attached a strong value to one label and we do not see a hierarchy in such descriptors as 'facilitator', 'teacher', 'instructor', 'educator' and 'guide'. In fact, we have often used these terms interchangeably or have assumed that a single person can fulfil all of these roles – although not necessarily at the same time! We do not assume that any such titles automatically mean formal qualifications or a particular educational standpoint or setting.

We hope you enjoy this book, which has been written by a diverse and very experienced team. It would probably have been impossible for one person to have articulated all of the ideas found here, so we feel the number of contributors is one of the book's key strengths.

In Chapter 1 Pete Bunyan presents his view of the theorists and models that have shaped the way in which most of us understand adventure education. This is a good starting point for anyone wishing to engage in adventure as an educational tool. Pete is particularly interested in the development of self-esteem through adventure.

2

In Chapter 2 Matt Berry looks at how we might justify the approaches that we take in planning adventure experiences. He presents a summary of what we know participants can gain, and the chapter concludes with some practical approaches to planning. Matt believes that we need to make the best possible use of the experiential learning philosophy. As a science teacher, adventure sports coach, adventure educator and now university lecturer, he draws on wide learning experience.

In Chapter 3 Chris Hodgson and Marcus Bailie examine risk management from the perspective that risk is a defining feature that needs to be respected and is vital to the learning experience. The chapter takes a practical approach to these issues and asks the reader to examine their standpoint on safety and justifiable risk, dynamic risk management and participants' responsibilities. Chris is an adventure sports coach with a broad experience base within coach education and now higher education, while Marcus performed a number of roles in national mountain training centres before becoming head of the inspection team for the UK's statutory adventure activities licensing scheme.

In Chapter 4 Matt Berry presents the learning philosophies central to experiential and adventure education. This chapter explores the nature of 'experientiality' and draws upon other teaching and learning strategies that adventure educators may find useful at a practical level.

In Chapter 5 Jane Lomax presents the notion that adventure educators coach as well as facilitate. She draws upon established theories and research within sports coaching and suggests the potential advantages of using coaching concepts to enhance learning opportunities. As a highly experienced sports psychologist and coach, Jane has used many of these concepts in her working life.

In Chapter 6 Malcolm Thorburn and Aaron Marshall explore why and how we might go about evaluating learning in adventure education. They argue that we need to make genuine efforts to demonstrate efficacy or success if we wish to be taken more seriously as professional educators.

In Chapter 7 Suzanne Everley explores how we might encourage reflection to enhance learning from experience. She presents the idea that participants' reflections can assist us in evaluating the impact of an experience in order to inform us about future practice.

In Chapter 8 John Kelly and Julia Potter cover the use of adventure as a targeted intervention for the prevention of the lifestyle-based illnesses that are becoming increasingly common in the Western world. In the future, adventure educators may well find themselves working alongside health professionals to address this issue.

In Chapter 9 Ed Christian explores what we mean by the commonly used but largely misunderstood term 'disaffection'. He uses his considerable experience of working with young people to explore the causes of disaffection and the role that adventure education can play in addressing this significant issue.

In Chapter 10 Pete Allison and colleagues discuss the benefits and history of overseas youth expeditions. This has been a main component of many UK adventure education programmes and it seems to be a growing phenomenon.

In Chapter 11 Pete Allison and another set of colleagues present the idea that adventure education can be a powerful mechanism to explore ethics, values and moral behaviour.

In Chapter 12 Joseph Gibson outlines the growing field of inclusive adventure, with specific reference to disability. He presents some basic guidance on inclusive philosophy and provides real-world examples and practical advice on working with participants with disabilities. Joe is an expert in the field of adaptive adventure, with more than fifteen years' experience of and research in the provision of adventure experiences for participants with profound sensory impairments.

In Chapter 13 Paul Gray, Chris Hodgson and Chris Heaney suggest how we might develop as adventure educators through the use of personal profiling, goal setting and targeted activities. They argue that if we wish to pursue meaningful careers, we need to plan more robustly for our own futures as learners.

Finally, in the conclusion, we consider possible directions that the adventure education sector might take. Whether charitable, private or public sources of funding drive our work, we suggest that it will become increasingly important that we strive to be seen as a profession. Moreover, managers and practitioners should embrace stronger links between research and practice, and should take every opportunity for ongoing professional development within a philosophy of lifelong learning.

Chris Hodgson and Matt Berry

CHAPTER ONE

MODELS AND MILESTONES IN ADVENTURE EDUCATION

Pete Bunyan

Our lives are filled with images of adventure; everywhere we look there are links to activities in the outdoors. Adventure seems to be associated with healthy living, success and fulfilment; it has an image that is readily used by businesses and marketing companies to endorse and sell their products. Whitewater kayaking has recently been used to sell indigestion medication, and it seems that you cannot drink certain brands of Australian lager without a surfboard under your arm. Images of adventure enter our lives at an early age, our parents read us *The Adventures of Robin Hood* and we sit spellbound watching *Harry Potter*. Adventure seems to be associated with 'good', 'challenge', 'endeavour', 'success' and 'achievement'. It is virtuous to go off adventuring, pitting oneself against nature to become a better person.

Today, people talk freely about adventure, and modern technology allows you almost to be there when a mountain is conquered or when the Atlantic is crossed in record time. After Hillary and Tenzing had summited Everest at 11.30 on the morning of 29 May 1953, it took days or even weeks for the rest of the world to hear about it. The world is very different today. Adventure is easily accessible and available; the Institute for Outdoor Learning (IOL, 1998) now regularly publishes listings of centres and establishments where groups and individuals can engage at a variety of levels in diverse and challenging activities. In an article aptly titled 'Adventure in a Bun', Loynes (1996) goes as far as to say that the provision of adventure has become a highly marketable commodity. Opportunities for adventure are now commonplace; the user can purchase adventure in almost any shape or form with known outcomes. Loynes likens this explosion of adventure opportunities to the growth of the McDonald's burger chain. Like the 'Big Mac', adventure is the same wherever you order it, you know what you are getting, and you are not disappointed with the outcome.

The *Outdoor Source Book* (IOL, 1998) states that there are over 1,500 centres providing adventure experiences in the United Kingdom alone. Moreover, numerous 'sole providers' increase the opportunity to become involved in adventure experiences. Along with this increased provision and diversification of adventure opportunities, there has been an evolution of the practices used to facilitate these experiences. Notable individuals have significantly influenced how people experience adventure today. Their influence may have been through their philosophy of adventure, through the development of models or concepts, or through the challenging of existing ways of operating as an adventure facilitator. This chapter concerns itself with the principal people and models that have influenced adventure education, the way it is provided and the way it is experienced by an increasing number of participants who benefit from it.

Developments in adventure education have not taken place in a linear or sequential way. They have always been influenced by the prevailing economic climate, government legislation and an array of human factors, such as recreation and leisure patterns. Growth has sometimes been slow, sometimes rapid, and it has never occurred in isolation.

The models and people who have influenced the way we experience adventure education today are considered thematically in this chapter. You will see that many of these themes are ongoing, with endpoints unlikely to be achieved – and even undesirable – for some things.

ADVENTURE – WHO BENEFITS?

Most of us who work in adventure education believe that adventure activities are both enjoyable and beneficial. And some of us have moved beyond 'because of the buzz' as an explanation for why we enjoy it and keep going back for more. But is it the same for those people who are not routinely involved with adventure? During what has become known as the 'Golden Age of Adventure', the human race finally overcame many of the natural challenges that it had faced, such as the summiting of Everest and the first nonstop circumnavigation of the world. John Hunt (1953: 231) who led the successful Everest expedition, explained how the human outcomes of adventure were perceived at that time: 'Comradeship, regardless of race or creed, is forged among high mountains, through difficulties and dangers to which they expose those who aspire to climb them, the need to combine their efforts to attain their goal, the thrills of a great adventure shared together.' Adventuring was considered 'good' for all those involved, with terms such as 'character building' often attached to it, irrespective of the outcome. Kurt Hahn, the man who established both the Outward Bound movement and Gordonstoun School, very much identified both institutions' value with the character development that could take place as the youth of society undertook adventurous activities. Today, this 'it's got to be good for you' attitude is not so widely accepted. It has been replaced by a generally accepted belief that engagement in adventurous activities has the *potential* to enhance individuals, groups or society in general.

Chris Bonnington (2000) recognises that adventure experiences can affect individuals differently. He recalls how he returned to the hostel exhausted and soaked to the skin, having experienced the most exciting day's climbing of his life. However, his climbing partner returned to London the next day, vowing never to climb again. Today, we probably have to accept that there are as many negative stories about encounters with adventure as

6

Pete Bunyan

there are positive ones. Those providing adventurous activities for others need to accept that individuals react differently and that personal growth outcomes, if experienced at all, will be uniquely different for each individual.

THE UNANSWERED QUESTION

The 'Can the mountains speak for themselves?' debate was first addressed in print by Thomas James in 1980, but the argument had been around for many years before that. Whilst this debate still continues today, it would be true to say that most people are a little more informed and educated about it now. It concerns the way in which adventure experiences are presented to others. A lot of complex philosophical assumptions are associated with this issue, but the two extremes of the argument are simple to understand. Unfortunately, people frequently forget that they are merely considering two ends of a continuum, and that there are numerous positions in between. The two extremes of this continuum are: 'The Mountains' and 'Facilitation'.

It is argued that 'The Mountains' provide a rich learning experience that, if managed and sequenced appropriately, will provide an opportunity for personal growth. At the other end, it is argued that experiences are educationally meaningless without 'Facilitation', and that the provider plays a central role in the outcomes of the individual's experience. James Neill (2007) perfectly explained the two perspectives in the following example: 'Sea kayaking with a group around a remote island I notice something happening within the group, what should I do? Do I say nothing and let the group take away what they want from the experience, or do I step in and help the group make sense of what has occurred?' Many of us have faced a similar dilemma. Superficially, it comes down to whether we should disrupt the natural flow of events occurring within the group. A deeper discussion focuses on whether the facilitator has the right to determine what an individual takes away from the experience. At the Mountains end of the continuum, the argument would be that adventurous encounters are individually experienced and the outcomes are unique to that individual. Alternatively, at the Facilitation end of the continuum it is argued that adventurous activities are complex and often novel, and individuals need help to understand them. You will have heard of such terms as 'reviewing', 'funnelling' and 'frontloading' that describe some of the processes that facilitators use to help make sense of the participant's experience. Those at the Mountain end would also argue that they have not been trained to 'council' activity outcomes, and that time could be spent more profitably in participation.

In reality, most facilitators place themselves naturally between the two extremes but vary their position in accordance with the intended session outcomes they are trying to achieve and the ability of the learners to reflect independently. For example, when facilitating activities on a stag weekend, very little time is spent talking about the effects of anxiety on a high ropes course. However, when working with a managerial group, reviewing and transfer form essential parts of the experience.

7

INDUSTRY OR SECTOR? PROCESS OR 'SAUSAGE MACHINE'?

Having made some general comments about the varying ways individuals, groups and society are affected by participation in adventurous activities, and having considered the diverse continuum of ways in which facilitators approach delivering adventurous activities, it is now important to think about the structure of adventure facilitation in more detail. Over the past decade there have been subtle changes in the terminology used to describe where and how outdoor and adventurous activities take place. Whilst this change in terminology might appear trivial and insignificant, it does signify an evolutionary change in the approach that is taken towards the delivery of adventurous activities. In moving from the term 'Outdoor Industry' to 'Outdoor Sector' there was a recognition that a 'one-size-fits-all' approach did not optimise the value of participating in outdoor (adventurous) activities. Similarly, there was recognition that outdoor activities could provide a powerful educational medium and that providers of it were recognisable professionals. This places more emphasis on the facilitator to shape and structure the adventure experience so that it unlocks potential as a learning environment.

Parcham (1975: 15) provides an insight into how many practitioners viewed learning through experience before this change took place: 'experiential learning is like a black box, where we put people in one end and they come out better at the other end . . . we don't really know what happens inside the box but it works'. The idea that an adventure experience is like a journey through a mystical box is a useful starting point for describing many of the ways in which adventure facilitation has changed over the past few decades. Parcham's 'Black Box' model has now been reshaped and called the 'Input–Process–Output' model (Figure 1.1).

We recognise today that individuals and groups from diverse backgrounds are involved in a wide variety of adventure activities. These differ in their expectations, previous experiences and abilities. We also recognise that adventure is currently used to attain a diversity of learning outcomes. For instance, dinghy sailing could be used equally effectively to target a range of outcomes, from practical boating skills to enhancement of communication or self-esteem. In fact, one of the challenges that face adventure facilitators is to clarify which learning outcomes are justifiable. So-called 'outcome' research has been undertaken to provide evidence about which learning outcome can be associated with participation in adventurous activities. This is becoming particularly important in an economic environment where adventure facilitators are being asked to be ever more accountable.

Figure 1.1 Input–process–output model

8

Pete Bunyan

The model (Figure 1.1) emphasises that to achieve the learning outcomes targeted by groups and individuals, the facilitator must consider the 'processes' that underpin their experience. For instance, they must consider how the experience is structured, the roles of both the individual or group and themselves, and the important things that they should experience. So-called 'process' research is trying to determine the contents of the process box so that facilitators can more informatively create experiences where diverse groups and individuals can attain the learning outcomes that they have targeted with more certainty.

So what have we learned so far? What do we know about the processes that underpin the adventure experience?

THE DYNAMIC ADVENTURE ENVIRONMENT

Prior to the 1990s there had been sparse and fragmentary attempts to explore the adventure process. These often consisted of poorly conceived research that lacked appropriate methods and measurement tools. Frequently, such research merely attempted to justify the value of adventure experiences to those outside adventure education. In 1995 Barrett and Greenaway published *Why Adventure*, a summary of previously published research, in an attempt to clarify the findings and provide a stimulus for future research. Importantly, this book acknowledged that, while there was some knowledge of the short-term effects of adventure, very little was understood about the long-term effects. This was due in part to the fact that the long-term effects of adventure were difficult to measure, and this problem was compounded because these effects were inextricably bound up with the effects of participation in non-adventurous activities.

Previous research had also recognised the complexities that surrounded the place and structure of the adventure experience. It highlighted five critical ingredients that alone were essential in fostering personal growth, such as self-esteem. However, when these five ingredients were considered together, they 'dynamically' provided an environment that was potentially more powerful in enhancing personal growth. Barrett and Greenaway termed this the 'dynamic adventure environment' (Figure 1.2). These five critical ingredients (overcoming a fear, being in a supportive group, having an appropriate leader, being involved in physical exercise, and activities taking place in a natural environment) prompt two further questions that research and professional debate have tried to answer. First, how much of each of these critical ingredients is needed? Take, for example, 'activities taking place in a natural environment'. Could it be argued that experiences on a climbing wall, artificial ski slope or whitewater course have less effect than equivalent experiences that take place out of doors? Or could it be that this ingredient has a marginal effect and that in some instances the venue has very little effect?

Second, if each ingredient is individually considered, how, precisely, should it contribute to the adventure experience? What exact role should the leader play? How should the

9

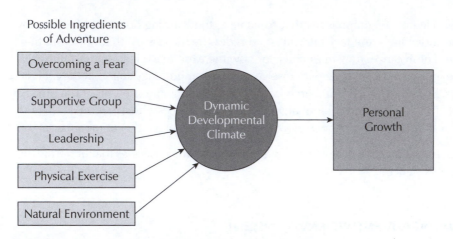

Figure 1.2 The dynamic adventure environment model

group offer support? These are important questions that adventure facilitators have begun to answer. However, we are still far from achieving definitive answers.

Overcoming a fear

By definition, adventures include an element of risk and uncertainty. As I mentioned at the beginning of this chapter, many participants say they enjoy adventurous pursuits 'because of the buzz'. They enjoy the emotions that are tied up in setting their own abilities against the demands of such activities as climbing, kayaking and sailing. Instinctively, we think of these as purely physical risks, but they could equally be of a cognitive or an affective nature. Our minds can play tricks on us. I have often heard people during their first kayaking session talk about drowning as if it were a probable outcome. Logically, why would the facilitator ever put anybody at risk of drowning? However, after their first capsize (intended or not), the paddler feels a sense of accomplishment through the challenge of returning to the surface after exiting their kayak underwater. I have also seen people not wanting to take part in a session because they felt at risk from underperforming in front of their friends and peers. So, in some activities, a person will need to pitch their abilities against a social risk.

If you were to ask adventure facilitators to name somebody who has influenced the way adventure activities are presented to groups and individuals, they would frequently cite Simon Priest. He has made a significant contribution over the past decade in forging theory to practice links by using cleverly constructed models and phrases to bring theoretical concepts into everyday language. For example, in 1991 he produced a list of ten facilitation guidelines – the 'Ten Commandments'. These were deliberately written in a snappy format to mimic the biblical Ten Commandments. Facilitators are much more likely to remember 'Thou shalt not teach Norma normal' than some long explanation of how to construct individual experiences. Amongst Priest's other significant contributions to our understanding of adventure facilitation was the 'Adventure Experience Paradigm'. His initial model (Martin and Priest, 1986), like most of the models we now use to guide our practice, was a collection of theoretical ideas that have subsequently been verified through real-life observation. The model explains how different levels of individual competence and risk interplay to achieve different levels of adventure (Figure 1.3).

The model suggests that the outcome of an adventure experience is determined by the balance of a person's competence and the risk (potential to lose something of value) to which they are exposed. Different combinations of risk and competence give rise to different experience outcomes. For instance, when the competence is high and the risk is low, the participant experiences 'Experimentation & Exploration'. An example of this would be an accomplished kayaker practising her skills on flat water. The experience is of value, but it does not result in a sense of adventure. If the same paddler progresses to a situation where the outcomes are less certain and their skills are more challenged, there is more risk and the paddler begins to feel more adventurous.

The model and practical experience tell us that there are two recognised situations where risk begins to challenge the individual's competence ('Adventure' and 'Peak Adventure'). During Peak Adventure, competence and risk are perfectly matched. Priest (1990: 157) commented that this is when one is 'testing one's limits on the razor's edge'. Peak Adventure has also been associated with such physiological states as 'peak performance' and such psychological states as 'flow'. When competence is no longer sufficient actively to manage the risk, two further states can be reached: 'Misadventure' and ultimately 'Devastation &

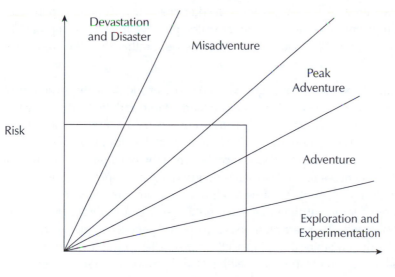

Figure 1.3 The adventure experience paradigm

Disaster'. Misadventure can be a positive experience for the individual, as it often signifies to them the extent of their competence. For instance, an uncomfortable swim down a boulder field following a capsize might still have meaningful outcomes for the paddler. When the risks greatly outweigh competence (Devastation & Disaster), there are unlikely to be any advantageous outcomes from the activity. In this situation, physiological and/or psychological damage is likely to occur; and even if this is avoided, luck will obviously have played a big part, so there are no gains to the participant.

This model has highlighted many important points for facilitators. Primarily, it has shown that, if experience is facilitated in the same way for every individual, they will experience different outcomes because they have different perceptions of their own competence and the risks to which they are being exposed. The facilitator must therefore recognise people as individuals in their planning and structuring of experiences. For example, when facilitating a sailing experience, it is appropriate for individuals to have different sail sizes and to sail at varying degrees of closeness to the wind. This will allow the facilitator to manage the risk–competence interaction much more closely.

The model has prompted facilitators to look carefully at the diversity of tasks that they include in their activities. In structuring experiences that balance risk and competence, facilitators are now much more able to recognise the clues that indicate if they have this. For example, at the top of an abseil, should an individual perceive that they are not competent to complete the challenge, the facilitator might readily recognise a narrowing of focus towards self-preservation that is a classic trait of individuals moving into the Misadventure sector of the model. This should prompt a restructuring of that individual's experience so that it becomes set to a more appropriate level for them. However, it would be true to say that we are still a long way from 'individualising' the adventure experience. Today, similarly competent members of groups are often put together so that appropriate experiences can be provided to broad bands within a group, rather than the group as a whole.

Whilst the Adventure Experience Paradigm has allowed us to look at the structure of adventure experiences in a fresh way, it has been criticised. Martin and Priest (1986) suggest that personal growth through adventure is likely to occur when competence and risk are matched. But other authors (e.g. Boniface, 2000) have argued that, for personal growth to occur, there needs to be a small gap or 'dissonance' between the perceptions of individual competence and the risk encountered. They have theorised that if competence and risk are balanced, the individual remains at the same level; but if the amount of risk requires the individual to be more competent than they have previously demonstrated, there is the potential for personal growth. There are numerous examples of people completing the same task rather than taking on something that is just a little more challenging and moving forward as an individual with increased competence, self-belief and possibly even self-esteem.

An understanding of the relationship between competence and risk in facilitating and participating in adventurous activities is critical if appropriate outcomes are to be achieved.

12

Pete Bunyan

The Adventure Experience Paradigm allows us to visualise this relationship, the potential outcomes and its appropriateness for individuals.

Facilitative leadership

The Dynamic Adventure Environment model (Figure 1.2) identifies the importance of the leader in participating in adventurous activities. In fact, it would be difficult to think about any adventurous pursuit without considering the role of the leader, as he or she is often considered to have the pivotal role in the success of an adventurous activity. However, on many occasions, the failure to achieve a target has been attributed in some way or another to the leader. The Channel Four documentary *Seven Go Made in Peru* (1996) shows how a poorly conceived expedition, inappropriately led by a self-appointed leader, can fail to meet expedition targets and the expectations of group members.

Leadership, as an area of study, has its roots in industry, where the outcomes of 'good' leadership are increased production and productivity. Despite its importance, there is very little agreement on what exactly makes a good leader. We have, however, moved on from the images of leadership that were associated with some of the major expeditions and conquests of the Golden Age of Adventure. These images were usually of men, with abundant testosterone and facial hair, overtly confident in their own decisions and commanding in their management of other individuals. Whilst we might be highly critical of this mode of leadership today, we need to consider whether their highly significant accomplishments were due to their type of leadership, or whether they were achieved *despite* the groups being led in this way. Perhaps, when we judge today's leaders against those of the past, we are not comparing 'like with like'. I would argue that advances in equipment, technology, training and our knowledge of group dynamics have fundamentally changed the nature of the demands placed on leaders in the outdoor sector. Any discussion about leadership needs to bear in mind the context of where and when it is taking place. The role of the leader should reflect the intended outcomes of the experience, the group that is participating, and the environment where the activity is occurring.

There is an age-old argument that asks whether leaders are 'born' or 'nurtured'? The so-called 'trait' or 'situational' approach to leadership is probably best satisfied by suggesting that good leaders are born with certain traits that allow them to use learned skills in challenging situations. Think about some of the leaders you have encountered in your adventurous activities. What typified them as leaders? How did they attain the attributes that they have? One of the earliest pieces of research on leadership considered how leaders achieved their power or influence over others in the group (French and Raven, 1968). This research recognised that some leaders were successful because they were 'charismatic' and 'charming', and these attributes had a significant effect on those they led. Returning to the nature versus nurture argument, it is obvious that such a trait cannot be coached or achieved through some national governing body award.

The diversity of demands placed on a leader was recognised in a simple model formulated by Adair (1983), who recognised that the leader was concerned with 'achieving a task', 'building and maintaining a team' and 'developing the individual' (Fig 1.4). This model was developed by Adair in relation to military leadership at Sandhurst and was adapted by the outdoor sector because it was easy to understand. Furthermore, it highlighted the demands placed on a leader.

Adair explains that the model demonstrates that the leader must continue to attend to all three key areas. Whilst they might focus on one circle at any one time, this must not be at the expense of the other two. Critics of the model generally agree that it highlights the principal areas of leader concern, but comment that it fails to acknowledge that the circles often coincide. For example, the *task* might be for a person to walk on a precise compass bearing, but this also represents the development of the *individual*. Similarly, the *task* might be for a group to navigate to a point at night using the 'leapfrog' method, but this might aid *team* development. Furthermore, current opinion questions whether it is possible to satisfy all three leadership concerns during one experience. The portion of the model where all three areas of concern overlap is very small, representing very little opportunity. There are larger areas (opportunities) to achieve intended outcomes when considering just two areas of concern, and the greatest opportunity when only one area is considered. Perhaps some of the inconsistency seen in adventure-related research stems from this very point. Results may vary due to the complexities of the learning outcomes that the facilitators were trying to achieve.

One of the most important contributions to the understanding of leadership in the outdoors was made by Priest and Chase (1989), when they introduced the 'Conditional Theory of Outdoor Leadership' (COLT). This model echoed some of the developments that were taking place in the teaching of physical education (Mosston and Ashworth, 1989) by recognising that learning outcomes should be linked to leadership style. For example, in snowboarding, a 'creativity' learning outcome is unlikely to be achieved if the facilitator adopts a 'command' or 'telling' leadership style. It is more likely to be achieved through a

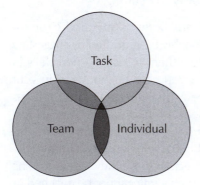

Figure 1.4 Adair's circles

14

cooperative approach where the learner is given the freedom to explore within a learning environment that has been carefully constructed by the facilitator.

Priest and Chase simplified the relationship between leadership style and learning outcome by categorising the former on a continuum between 'autocratic' (telling, command, facilitator-led) and 'abdicratic' (delegated, client-led), with a 'democratic' (negotiated, consulted) style between these two extremes (Figure 1.5).

The continuum explicitly recognises the contributions that the facilitator and learner make to the adventure experience, but it also implicitly recognises who is the 'gatekeeper' to the knowledge and development that will take place. In the autocratic style, the leader is the focal point of the group and the source of knowledge, and they grant access to the experience. In the democratic style, there is recognition that the group has knowledge and must jointly agree on how the decisions and experience will unfold.

The model similarly uses a continuum to describe the facilitators' natural 'orientation' towards the type of learning outcomes they wish to achieve. One end is characterised by the desire to achieve 'task' outcomes, such as reaching the summit of a peak or correctly pitching a tent. The opposite end recognises 'relationship' outcomes, such as developing empathy, cooperation and trust. Between these two extremes, there is a recognition that whilst they might be dominant in one type of outcome, some practitioners are able to work towards outcomes of a different dimension. Priest and Chase suggest that we will naturally place ourselves as facilitators at an appropriate place on this continuum (Figure 1.6).

The most important part of the COLT Model is its recognition that the relationship between leadership style and orientation is dramatically influenced by the conditions in which facilitators work. Priest and Chase highlight five 'conditional' factors that influence the relationship between leadership style and orientation: environmental dangers, individual competence, group unity, leader proficiency and decision consequence. These singularly and in combination affect the leader's intentions and facilitation. Again, the model uses a continuum to describe 'favourability' (high–low). In highly favourable conditions (good weather, unified and proficient group, experienced leader and so on), the facilitator utilises the most appropriate leadership style to achieve the identified learning outcomes. As the

| Autocratic | Democratic | Abdicratic |

Figure 1.5 Leadership style

| Task | Relationship |

Figure 1.6 Leader orientation

conditions deteriorate, the model acknowledges that facilitators become progressively more autocratic and focus on getting the task done. When the conditions are low in favourability, only facilitators at the extreme relationship end continue to use abdicratic approaches to achieve their learning outcomes. All of us have experienced situations where the leader has taken over when the weather suddenly deteriorated or there was an injury in the group. At that point, the goal of the experience usually changes to keeping the group together and returning home safely.

The COLT model represents a significant step forward in the way facilitators understand and construct experiences for others. It has also prompted an acknowledgement that facilitators operate effectively using different leadership styles. Subsequently, we have acknowledged that female facilitators are far more democratic than their autocratic male counterparts, and they are equally or more effective at achieving relationship-orientated outcomes.

Supportive group

There can be no doubt that the group influences the outcomes of an adventure experience. Shared experiences are an important foundation for good working relationships. I particularly enjoy climbing or high mountain walks with close friends. The Dynamic Adventure Environment (Figure 1.2) places particular importance on the role of a 'supportive group' in achieving personal growth through adventure. It is obvious that a collection of individuals meeting for the first time cannot achieve as much as a similarly skilled but 'well-established' group of people who have experience of working together as a team.

One of the widely accepted models of the way individuals come together to form effective groups was outlined by Tuckman and Jensen (1977). They theorised that groups progressed through five distinct phases (see Table 1.1).

This model has been refined over the past thirty years. At first, it had very little practical significance, other than it acknowledged that groups did not immediately function

Table 1.1 Stages of group development

Stage	Characteristic
Forming	Discomfort, superficial relationships, restricted communication modes, feelings of self-doubt, self-esteem threat.
Storming	Relationships established, participants begin to establish themselves and their roles, possible conflict and polarisation.
Norming	Behaviour and roles accepted, establish group identity, sense of group belonging, acceptance.
Performing	Group has task and social health, good interaction amongst group members.
Adjourning	Closure, termination of relationships, mourning.

16

effectively, if at all. The original model did not recognise that groups did not spend equal amounts of time in some stages. In fact, some groups seem to miss all stages because they pass through them very fleetingly. A real understanding of Tuckman and Jensen's work is achieved when it is considered in conjunction with the 'Reflexivity' model put forward by West (1994). He recognises that groups serve both 'task' and 'social' functions (Figure 1.7).

The Reflexivity Grid allows us to explore the task and social functions of groups in two ways. Primarily, groups have four combinations of basic characteristics corresponding to the four quadrants of the model. West goes so far as to give each of these basic groups a name: for example, a group that is high in both task and social attributes is 'fully functioning'. If you are interested in group dynamics, it is worth studying the Reflexivity Grid in more depth. I have used it to plot a group's perception of their functioning and to develop strategies for development. Second, in the context of the five stages of group development, the grid prompts us to accept that task and social functioning have different priorities for a group during the five stages, which means that different demands are made on the facilitator. For example, in the 'forming' stage, the facilitator is more likely to be autocratic and focused on getting the group to engage in a task, setting appropriate goals in light of how familiar and comfortable the group members feel with each other. As they progress

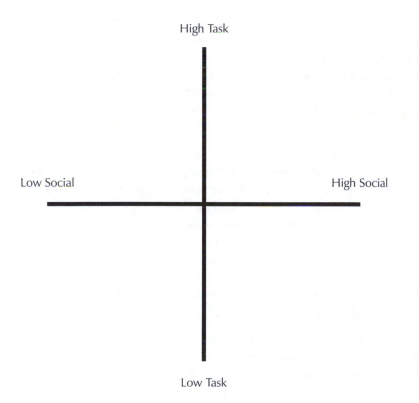

Figure 1.7 Reflexivity grid

into the 'storming' stage, the facilitator should recognise that social functioning is of prime importance, they should direct the group towards the task, and they might facilitate the group activity in a more democratic way. In the 'performing' stage, the group is functioning well – they have established roles and responsibilities and accept one another. At this time, the facilitator might chose to become abdicratic in his relationship with the group, allowing them to develop their task and social functioning naturally. Success at this point would be identified by the group itself enhancing (amongst other things): motivation, ownership, self-esteem and self-actualisation.

This is facilitation at its best. Meeting the needs of a group by recognising its stage of development and choosing a complementary leadership style are advanced facilitation skills. An understanding of some of the more complex models that explain this process is something to work towards as your experience of group dynamics and facilitation broadens and you become familiar with working with diverse groups in different environments (see Attarian and Priest, 1994).

PEOPLE WHO HAVE CONTRIBUTED TO OUR UNDERSTANDING

So far in this chapter we have considered the major models that have influenced the way adventure is facilitated today. We have used the Dynamic Adventure Environment model (Figure 1.2) as a framework for developing an understanding of risk, leadership and the need to be in a supportive group. In addition to such models, though, a number of individuals and agencies have had dramatic effects on the way in which adventure is now facilitated. The remainder of this chapter is devoted to a discussion of their contributions to our understanding of adventure facilitation.

We have already encountered the 'Can the mountains speak for themselves?' debate. One of the bedrock arguments that is used to support the 'touchy-feely' philosophy is the need to help participants make sense of the complex adventure experience. One of the mechanisms frequently used to aid this is 'frontloading'. This simply means providing 'hangers' on which the participants might place their experiences by explaining to them what the important learning outcomes are. For instance, prior to a gill scramble, the facilitator might highlight that the experience will focus on developing cooperation and trust in each other. They might also explain how the activity will be constructed to achieve these outcomes. Frontloading the experience in this way does not exclude other outcomes, but it maximises the potential achievement of the identified outcomes.

Frontloading is often used in conjunction with 'reviewing' – revisiting the experience during or after its completion. Over the past ten years, reviewing has become the bandwagon that almost every facilitator has jumped aboard. Some facilitators even believe that you are not facilitating 'correctly' if you do not review an experience. The principles of reviewing are primarily attributed to the work of Roger Greenaway, who was originally based at

18

Brathay Hall in the Lake District. Greenaway's many publications and website (http://www.reviewing.co.uk/) provide an insight into how revisiting the activity can enhance the experience of the participants. He is keen to point out that reviewing is not merely evaluating the experience, and suggests that it can make an experience more worthwhile. He states that reviewing has five recognisable purposes (Greenaway, 1993):

1   To energise the learning process.
2   To enrich the experience.
3   To make sense of the experience.
4   To make connections.
5   To develop learning skills.

Whilst Greenaway is persuasive in arguing that reviewing can be utilised as a tool for enhancing personal and group development, he is realistic when recognising that some activities speak for themselves. His list of five purposes contains some very good reasons for including reviewing in an adventure experience: in a competitive market, what facilitator would choose not to 'make sense of the experience' or 'enrich' it in some way? But a degree of credibility blackmail has developed around reviewing: it seems you *must* do it if you want to be a good facilitator.

As you might imagine, reviewing has attracted considerable research attention. But facilitators can still draw on little more than anecdotal evidence in order to reassure themselves that reviewing enhances the adventure experience. There are considerable methodological problems associated with the type of research that might deepen our understanding of the true value of reviewing as a facilitation tool. Consequently, to date, the evidence is scant and inconclusive either way.

Greenaway suggests a four-stage reviewing process that is often represented as a cyclical model (Figure 1.8). In essence, this model asks participants to explain what happens during the 'experience', then to 'express' what they felt about what went on, then to 'examine' their emotions and finally to 'explore' them in a holistic or whole-life context.

One of the strengths of Greenaway's work is his consideration of review methods. He questions whether all-talk review methods are effective in many contexts, recognising that individuals express themselves effectively in many different ways. His book, *Playback* (Greenaway, 1993), provides a comprehensive list of diverse review methods, including action, poetry, drawing, movie-making, writing newspaper articles and singing. It is inevitable that you will have taken part in some sort of review if you have ever facilitated an activity.

Greenaway has had a significant impact on adventure facilitation. His work has been power-ful in shaping what is happening in the outdoor sector today. However, many questions associated with reviewing remain unanswered.

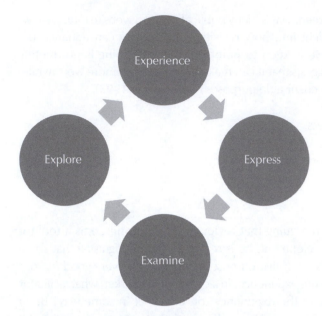

Figure 1.8 Greenaway's reviewing model

The diversification of the outdoor sector and the increase in the number of individuals and groups experiencing adventure activities have bought with them questions of justification. For instance, is there any evidence that the outdoor sector actually achieves what it claims to achieve? An interesting aspect of these debates is what constitutes 'evidence'. Does it have to be measurable or can it be more anecdotal or story-based? How much credibility should we give to the comment of a social worker or teacher who says a child has been able to form more stable relationships with authority figures since they had an adventure experience? Inevitably, this aspect of the debate will continue and opinion will remain divided.

There have been several attempts to summarise the research that has focused on the processes and outcomes of adventure participation. The most creditable of these was completed by Hattie, Marsh, Neill and Richards (1997). Whilst their analysis focused entirely on empirical research, it is still cited more than any other, and it has been a catalyst for improved adventure-related research. One of the problems in reviewing adventure-related research stems from trying to combine studies that have used different instruments for measuring the outcomes of adventure participation. For example, take self-esteem, a commonly targeted activity outcome: there are over 2,000 measures in existence. If evidence from different studies is combined to give more conclusive results, a common unit of measurement needs to be found. Hattie *et al.* used a statistical technique known as 'meta-analysis' to overcome this problem. This creates a common unit called an 'effect-size' (ES) for each study, allowing all of them to be combined and comprehensively evaluated. The process is similar to the European Union's creation of a common currency (the euro), which enabled more effective trade between member countries. Hattie *et al.* achieve credibility by calculating 1,728 effect-sizes for the combining of 151 unique samples from 96 separate studies. Their analysis demonstrated that the average programme outcome was 'moderate', and that there were at least 'weak' continuing effects several months after the adventure participation. In comparison to similar school-based activities, participation in adventurous activities was at least equal if not better. Amongst the programme variables that were considered, there was evidence that the effect increased with the length of the experience. Similarly, adventure-based activities were more 'potent' than city-based or other wilderness-based activities. There was also evidence to support 'single-sex' courses, and the effects of adventure seemed to be more pronounced as the participants got older.

Hattie *et al.*'s study is not the easiest paper to read, but at the very least you should dip into it for the highlights. It also makes some very sensible advice for those who wish to avoid the mistakes of the past in the area of adventure research.

It is important to acknowledge the work of James Neill, who has worked tirelessly to forge the links between academic theory and practice. You will have noticed that he was one of the authors of the meta-analysis above, but he is probably best known for two significant contributions to adventure facilitation. First, his excellent website Wilderdom (http://www.wilderdom.com/) provides a library of research reports and facilitation activities. Many of these contributions have been generated through his work as a university professor who facilitates adventure activities for his undergraduate students. Neill's second contribution is his development of the 'Life Effectiveness Questionnaire' (Neill *et al.*, 2003). The LEQ is one of a handful of questionnaires specifically developed for use in the adventure context. Until very recently, research in the outdoor sector has been plagued by problems associated with utilisation of measurement instruments that have been borrowed from other knowledge areas, such as business and education. Neill has provided much-needed validity to the broad range of learning outcomes through his questionnaire. A full account of its development is given on his website, and it is becoming increasingly refined as more researchers and practitioners use it and as their studies gain a wider audience.

Finally, some consideration must be given to the ongoing contribution to the outdoor sector that is being made by the Institute for Outdoor Learning (IOL). The IOL aims to encourage 'outdoor learning by developing quality, safety and opportunity to experience outdoor activity provision and by supporting and enhancing the good practice of those who work in the outdoors' (IOL, 2010). It promotes the professional development of facilitators and also employs governmental lobbying to secure resources for future learning. Moreover, it is growing in importance as a result of its facilitator 'accreditation scheme'. This four-stage scheme recognises the professional development and achievements of facilitators in the outdoors. Through the achievement of 'benchmark' statements, facilitators are accredited at nationally recognised levels: from RPIOL (Registered Practitioner) through APIOL (Accredited Practitioner) and LPIOL (Leading Practitioner) to Fellow, the IOL's highest award. The scheme was developed in conjunction with practitioners working in the outdoor sector, and many employment positions in the outdoors now require at least APIOL accreditation from applicants.

Whilst the IOL would be keen to point out that its scheme complements the national governing body awards, it achieves its credibility by taking a much more holistic view of facilitators' professional attributes, such as reflection and their contribution to the outdoor sector. As the IOL grows in importance and it accreditation scheme becomes more established, the outdoor sector will benefit significantly through increasing development and accreditation opportunities.

SUMMARY

This chapter has provided a personal view of the models and people who have helped shape adventure facilitation from the Golden Age of Adventure to our current consumer-driven market place, where adventure opportunities are abundant. Another author might share some of my views but would also have their own perspective on what has shaped the way adventure is experienced by others. We live in exciting times. Changes in our understanding of personal growth through adventure will no doubt prompt us to consider again how facilitation might be best undertaken.

REFERENCES

Adair, J. (1983) *Effective Leadership: A Self Development Manual*, London: Gower Press.

Attarian, A. and Priest, S. (1994) The Relationship between Stages of Group Development and Styles of Outdoor Leadership, *Journal of Adventure Education and Outdoor Leadership*, 11: 13–19.

Barrett, J. and Greenaway, R. (1995) *Why Adventure*, Coventry: RAP.

Boniface, M. (2000) Towards an Understanding of Flow and Other Positive Experience Phenomena within Outdoor and Adventurous Activities, *Journal of Adventure Education and Outdoor Leadership*, 1: 55–68.

Bonnington, C. (2000) *Boundless Horizons*, London: Weidenfeld & Nicolson.

French, J.R.P. and Raven, B. (1968) The Basis of Social Power, in Cartwright, D. and Zander, A. (eds) *Group Dynamics*, Evanston, IL: Row Peterson.

Greenaway, R. (1993) *Playback*, Edinburgh: Callander.

Hattie, J., Marsh, H.W., Neill, J.T. and Richards, G.E. (1997) Adventure Education and Outward Bound: Out-of-Class Experiences That Make a Lasting Difference, *Review of Educational Research*, 67: 43–87.

Hunt, J. (1953) *The Ascent of Everest*, London: Hodder & Stoughton.

IOL (1998) *The Outdoor Source Book*, Penrith: Adventure Education.

IOL (2010) IOL website. Available online at: http://www.outdoor-learning.org/.

James, T. (1980) Can the Mountains Speak for Themselves? Available online at: http/:www.wilderdom. com/mountains.html.

Loynes, C. (1996) Adventure in a Bun, *Journal of Adventure Education and Outdoor Leadership: Finland Welcomes the World*, 13 (2): 52–57.

22

Pete Bunyan

Martin, P. and Priest, S. (1986) Understanding the Adventure Experience, *Journal of Adventure Education and Outdoor Leadership*, 3: 18–21.

Mosston, M. and Ashworth, S. (1989). *Teaching Physical Education*, Columbus, OH: Merrill.

Neill, J.T. (2007) Wilderdom. Available online at: http://www.wilderdom.com.

Neill, J.T., Marsh, H.W. and Richards, G.E. (2003). *The Life Effectiveness Questionnaire*, Sydney: University of Western Sydney.

Parcham, A. (1975) *Notes on the Evaluation of Outdoor Experience Programmes*, Ambleside: National Conference on Outdoor and Experiential Education.

Priest, S. (1990) The Semantics of Adventure Education, in Miles, J. and Priest, S. (eds) *Adventure Education*, State College, PA: Venture.

Priest, S. (1991) The Ten Commandments of Adventure Education, *Journal of Adventure Education and Outdoor Leadership*, 8: 8–10.

Priest, S. and Chase, R. (1989) The Conditional Theory of Outdoor Leadership, *Leisure Studies*, 10: 163–170.

Tuckman, B.W. and Jensen, M.A. (1977) Stages of Small Group Development Revisited, *Group and Organizational Studies*, 2: 419–427.

West, M. (1994) *Effective Teamwork*, Exeter: Wheatons.

CHAPTER TWO

PLANNING ADVENTURE EDUCATION

FAIL TO PREPARE, PREPARE TO FAIL

Matt Berry

INTRODUCTION

Research has demonstrated that a wide variety of beneficial outcomes can be gained from participating in adventure programmes (Hattie *et al*., 1997). As a result, it is difficult to determine precisely what individuals will take from their experiences in adventure education. Despite this difficulty, most adventure educators rise to the challenge of planning activities that aim to meet the needs of the participants. Many students and practitioners in adventure education find that whilst they are able to develop plans that meet the organisational outcomes, such as activity, equipment and venue, they find that planning activities that meet the specific learning needs of participants is much more challenging. It is also common for adventure educators beginning their careers to focus on personality characteristics that seem commensurate with effective teaching, such as being approachable, charismatic and enthusiastic, rather than on key skills, such as imaginative planning and strategies to improve opportunities for learning. This situation mirrors the current issues found in adventure education research, where the present focus is on how adventure education outcomes are achieved. Planning in order to meet particular outcomes in adventure education has become the subject of much recent attention, particularly because adventure educators continue to find themselves working with an increasingly wide range of participants, combined with the increasing need to provide evidence that programmes are worthwhile.

This chapter aims to introduce some important concepts in planning adventure education by examining the historical context and the development of research regarding the delivery of adventure education whilst also offering more practical guidance in planning.

THE DEVELOPMENT OF PLANNING IN ADVENTURE EDUCATION

Historical approaches to delivering adventure education share common goals with all other types of experiential education. All rely on an engaging activity that is intended to lead to a wide variety of learning outcomes. Adventure education, as a type of experiential education, engages learners through the use of such activities as rock climbing and canoeing. Because there is inherent risk associated with these activities, thorough planning is essential. However, the planning has often focused on organisational factors, such as staffing, venue and equipment, and this emphasis can overshadow the specific needs of the participants. Whilst organisational factors obviously must be considered, there is a risk that the participants, whatever their background, pass through a homogenised package of activities without sufficient attention being paid to their individual learning needs and development. Credible research evidence supports a broad-brush approach (e.g. Hattie *et al.*, 1997), but as adventure education continues to evolve and demand greater professional status, it is important that we aim to understand better how its outcomes might be achieved.

Early research in the field tended to focus on *what* the beneficial outcomes were rather than *how* they were achieved. This perspective is typified by Walsh and Golins (1976), who even argued that there was a need to keep the Outward Bound programme 'mysterious'. The current and more widely held view (as proposed by McKenzie, 2000) is that research into how the various characteristics interact to achieve programme outcomes, rather than simply what the outcomes are, would help adventure educators design and implement more effective adventure education programmes. Even without research evidence, many adventure educators have been surprisingly skilled in creating effective learning opportunities. There are concerns, however, that adventure educators have too often turned to personal philosophy and blind faith in order to justify these opportunities: 'To date, the vast majority of programmes have been sustained by an act of faith. We can choose to continue walking along a path of faith; however, this will require praying harder than ever that schools, teachers, parents and funding bodies don't dare question the evidence of that faith' (Neill, 1997: 6). Here, Neill not only demonstrates the desire for a stronger rationale for approaches to adventure education but highlights the fact that a number of important stakeholders (in addition to the participants themselves) are interested in the outcomes derived from adventure programmes.

Adventure educators therefore have a real challenge beyond simply creating a series of engaging activities that incorporate risk. They need to be able to use those activities in a very purposeful way. Whilst retaining skill and creativity when developing engaging adventurous programmes, adventure educators must have a sound rationale for the approaches they take. This could mean incorporating knowledge from research or joining organisations that share good practice. It is important, therefore, that adventure educators and adventure education researchers develop a healthy acceptance of each other, and it is to be hoped that they increasingly become one and the same.

With an increasing number of students graduating from specific adventure- and outdoor education-oriented degree courses, a stronger research base might well develop across a wider range of adventure education contexts. The relationship between research evidence and planning would then become increasingly clear, which would enable us to become more effective in meeting the needs of all participants.

TRENDS IN RESEARCH – UNPACKING THE BLACK BOX

The difficulty in finding ways to meet outcomes in adventure education is best summarised by the 'Black Box' theory. This has been used by many fields in addition to adventure education, including philosophy, psychology and science. Despite its simplicity, it serves to describe the complex nature of events that occur in fields where it is difficult to explain the causes of particular outcomes. In psychology, for example, we can only speculate about what has occurred in the brain when we observe changes in human behaviour. In adventure education, we might hope to see changes in attitudes and behaviour as an *output*, but obviously we cannot peek inside the brain to check exactly what has happened. I think the black box also hints at the sceptical view that we might never fully identify the underlying mechanisms and structures that lead to specific changes.

Early research in adventure education largely aimed to identify 'outputs' of adventure programmes by looking at what individuals gleaned from participating in these programmes. In this way, it could be demonstrated that adventure education was an effective means of facilitating some kinds of personal development. Research from this phase tended to rely on anecdotal accounts from adventure educators and participants who advocated the effectiveness of adventure programmes. Over time, more valid and reliable approaches to research were implemented and a body of credible empirical evidence began to grow. By the time Hattie *et al.* conducted their meta-analysis in 1997, they were able to draw upon ninety-six other studies that had aimed to identify what positive changes (outputs) took place in individuals and groups during adventure education programmes. At that point, this very important work provided the clearest evidence of what adventure education did, illustrating a broad range of positive potential outcomes from participation in adventure education programmes. Of the eighty-nine outcomes presented in the analysis, there were examples from self-esteem, which is widely accepted as a person's overall judgement of the self; physical fitness, derived from the physical nature of some of the activities and the duration of the programme; and cognitive areas, such as academic ability.

However, Hattie *et al.* (1997) pointed out that we should take only limited comfort from a conclusion that adventure education programmes can be effective. Under closer examination, the details reveal a different picture. The authors stated that only some adventure programmes were effective, and even then only for some outcomes, and it was probable that only individual parts of each programme were influencing these outcomes. The meta-analysis showed that adventure education is clearly a powerful medium for developing a wide range of learning and personal development outcomes, but Hattie *et al.* warned that future research needed to look at what aspects were responsible for producing (or, more importantly, not producing) these outcomes.

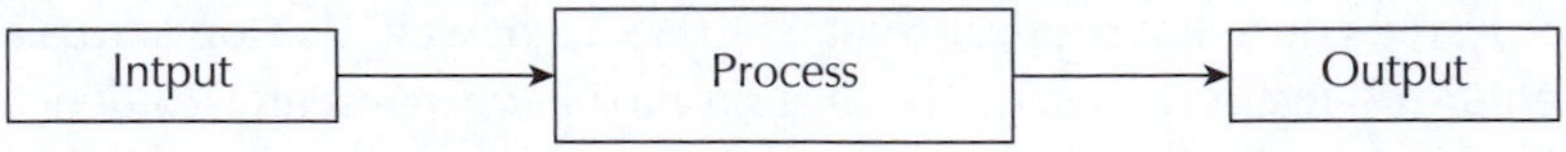

```
┌──────────┐        ┌──────────┐        ┌──────────┐
│  Intput  │ ─────▶ │ Process  │ ─────▶ │  Output  │
└──────────┘        └──────────┘        └──────────┘
```

Figure 2.1 Black box theory

26

Current research into adventure education tends to try to identify how it works rather than whether it works. Therefore, the focus is to try to understand relationships between the component parts of an adventure education programme and particular outcomes. This is an area of developing research from which McKenzie (2000) presents a useful review of the relevant literature. This draws upon both evidence-based and theoretical material in order to summarise how components of adventure education might contribute to the achievement of particular outcomes. It serves not only as a summary but is used in this chapter as a means of grouping programme characteristics that would be helpful in planning purposeful adventure education.

ADVENTURE EDUCATION PROGRAMME CHARACTERISTICS AND OUTCOMES

Unfortunately, investigating the relationship between programme characteristics and outcomes is not simple. Researchers have devoted much time and energy in attempting to establish links between adventure education outcomes and what caused them. Ewert and Sibthorp (2009) explain that this is a problem for all types of experiential education because these variables tend to be difficult to control. This is because the adventure educator simply cannot control such variables as the weather. There are also concerns about applying scientific research designs to inappropriate learning situations – treating learners like pigeons in behavioural experiments. This approach tends to lead to overly simplified and inaccurate conclusions. That said, however, adventure educators can at the very least begin to stack the odds in their favour by planning to meet desirable outcomes by drawing upon either existing evidence or established and critically reviewed theoretical frameworks. McKenzie (2000) draws upon such evidence and theory relating to how programme outcomes are achieved whilst also identifying gaps and offering suggestions for closing these gaps in the knowledge base. This review forms the basis of numerous subsequent studies but also categorises programme characteristics in a way that is helpful to us as we think about planning to enable participants to reach desirable outcomes.

Several programme characteristics are thought to influence programme outcomes:

- the participant;
- the group;
- instructors (facilitators);
- physical environment;
- activities; and
- processing.

Adventure educators account for specific programme characteristics in their planning by referring to these main factors that contribute to achieving programme outcomes. Research conducted in these areas is by no means complete, but the key ideas from both evidence

27

and theoretical perspectives can serve to strengthen the rationale you have for your chosen approaches to adventure education facilitation.

The participant

The participant is the most important factor to consider when planning any adventure education activity. Research conducted within adventure education contexts remains inconclusive in determining trends that enable us to see what works best for different participants. However, some research has been conducted on age, gender and background. We know that participants will bring existing knowledge, skills and prior experience with them, and we also know that these should significantly influence the planning process. Ewert and Sibthorp (2009) categorised such factors as prior knowledge and experience, age, gender and background as precursor variables that can influence outcomes.

Prior knowledge and experience will affect the nature and type of activity you select in order that the level of challenge is appropriate both physically and intellectually. Fundamentally, adventure education is a branch of experiential education and it should therefore centre upon the use of activities that are both engaging and compelling. If activities lack appropriate challenge they will be neither compelling nor engaging. Problem-solving exercises often fit into this category, particularly if participants find the problem too contrived or the solutions too easy. *Demographics*, such as age, sex and socio-economic status, can be predictors of what participants learn in adventure education. For example, research on participant age has shown that the short-term effects of adventure were greater for adults than for youth (Hattie *et al.*, 1997), whereas Witman (1995) found that the use of ropes courses was less valued among older participants.

Literature from outside adventure education can also prove useful in the planning of adventure education experiences. For example, Piaget's (1937) theory of cognitive development illustrates that children pass through particular stages in their intellectual development. Therefore, activities focusing on personal and social development that rely on some form of metaphorical transfer may not offer the opportunities for development that the facilitator intended. Although there are no clear boundaries between the stages of cognitive development, it is widely accepted that there is a relationship between age and the ability to make meaning from metaphor. The trust-fall activity may aim to demonstrate the ability to 'let go and leave old habits behind', but a more literal interpretation would consist of the need for people to work as a team so that the participant does not fall to the floor. In contrast, activities that focus on technical skills, such as map-reading and orientation, may not work out as expected because very young pupils may be incapable of applying spatial representations found in certain map-related tasks (Reese, 1994).

Research on gender suggests that the effects of programmes across a wide range of outcomes are equally effective for males and females (Hattie *et al.*, 1997). Witman (1995) investigated what males and females thought of various activities, and found that females tended to value

Matt Berry

activities focusing on trust, whereas males valued those relating to power and dominance. Preferences aside, Hattie *et al.* (1997) found that, across all studies that included gender-differentiated data, there were no significant differences in outcome achievement between males and females. It should also be stressed here that although some general trends in preferences were found, this does not necessarily dictate what activities should be used. Sex-role stereotyping, for example, would be influential here, and it would be counter-productive to plan purely on the basis of gender. Educationally, it would be more useful to plan activities and interventions for mixed groups that challenge sexual stereotyping rather than reinforce it. It is important to consider group composition in light of numbers of males and females. Maintaining a gender balance often offers more opportunities for facilitators to question and challenge attitudes and behaviours that are counter-productive.

With reference to background, the Hattie *et al.* (1997) meta-analysis found no significant difference between delinquents, managers and 'normal 'participants when comparing achievement across eighty-nine outcomes. It is worth considering, however, that a participant's past experiences within certain contexts will determine levels of expectation. High expectations can provide the necessary motivation for participants to gain maximum benefit from the adventure education programme. There could therefore be a considerable difference in motivation levels between those who have been *sent* and those who have *chosen* to participate.

The ways in which individuals respond to their experiences depends upon their previous experience. The individual's background obviously plays a significant part here, and none more so than their culture and ethnicity. Although speculations and pieces of research can be cited, the reality is that it is still early days in terms of developing a mature understanding of cultural issues and adventure education. Fundamentally, treating everybody the same way does not mean treating everybody as if they are the same.

The group

Many outcomes from adventure education will be influenced by the characteristics of the group. The interaction between group members is likely to be a key factor in influencing outcomes. Personality, for example, is thought to be shaped by our interaction with others. As McKenzie (2000) points out, little adventure education research has attempted to identify how the characteristics of a participant's group influence the impact of an adventure education programme. However, numerous authors have made sensible suggestions from a theoretical basis. Kimball and Bacon (1993) suggest that the strong feelings of mutual dependence often fostered during challenging situations help create a bond between participants that can be linked to the achievement of shared outcomes. This is also linked to reciprocity, where the group begins to realise the dependency they have on each other and also that each member has something to offer. To this end, Witman (1995) found that helping others, realising the importance of caring about oneself and others, and getting

29

support from other participants were three of the four characteristics that were most valued by participants.

Autonomy is also thought to be linked to programme outcomes. Conrad and Hedin (1981) and Paisley et al. (2008) found that group autonomy has a strong pedagogic value and explain that personal development outcomes are related to participants' perceptions of autonomy. Interestingly, Paisley et al. also found that rates of injury, evacuation and near miss were no different during autonomous expeditions than when participants were accompanied. They point out that careful planning and preparation are essential in order to ensure facilitators can plan for appropriate levels of challenge. Naturally, the age of the participant should be considered in relation to degree of autonomy, with increasingly autonomous elements being introduced for appropriate ages. For example, in the UK, the Duke of Edinburgh's Award Scheme introduces elements of autonomy for bronze-level expeditions at 14 years of age.

Group size has been shown to impact upon outcomes. Numerous studies from other fields have investigated this relationship, but research has yet to be undertaken to determine what works best in adventure education. Riggins (1986) reports that there is a positive correlation between small group size and learning effectiveness in a classroom setting. Interestingly, Hattie et al. (1997) point out that the smaller group sizes commonly found in adventure education may be a main determining factor for success. Walsh and Golins (1976) suggest that a group of between seven and fifteen participants would most likely bring about sufficient diversity and conflict but would be small enough to avoid cliques and enable conflict resolution. The amount and intensity of physical activity in relation to group size has been given some attention in physical education research. Carron (1990) found correlations between group size and social and physiological outcomes, with overall trends tending to show poorer outcomes for larger groups. This is of particular interest to those of us involved in adventure education because of current concerns regarding health, and obesity in particular (see Chapter 8).

Finally, group size has been shown to be linked to the notion of 'productivity'. One study in the late nineteenth century showed that during a tug of war each participant contributed less effort as more group members were added. Research interest in group dynamics tends to be dominated by the business world rather than adventure education, probably due to the financial rewards for success, but findings tend to support the idea of an optimum group size. However, this will vary and will be dependent upon the nature of the task. The best way to think of optimum group size is to consider opportunities for participation. More learning is likely to occur if we plan activities that allow opportunities for everyone always to be engaged.

Matt Berry

Instructors

Adventure and outdoor education settings tend to use a variety of terms, including 'teacher', 'coach', 'instructor' and 'facilitator', interchangeably. Whatever the title, it is commonly accepted that the staff are any organisation's greatest asset. However, this is true only if they are effective at what they do both individually and collectively. Of all the factors contributing to the effectiveness of adventure education programmes, the characteristics of instructors have received the most attention from researchers. Participant or observer ratings have been used to determine instructor effectiveness, whilst specific relationships between outcomes and facilitation have been somewhat neglected. Despite obvious problems with this approach, the findings are still useful because they generally show that there is a correlation between perceived effectiveness and levels of education and experience. Meanwhile, significant relationships are not usually found between instructors' effectiveness and their leadership opinions, vocational interests, age or gender. Males and females can be equally effective in facilitating outcomes, but it is worth considering the idea of the so-called 'hidden curriculum'. This theory proposes that participants can pick up stronger messages through *who* facilitates the learning rather than *what* that facilitator says or does. In other words, a female leading a climbing session delivers a stronger message than a male who asserts that females can climb well or be good leaders.

The interpersonal interactions of instructors seem to have generated most research interest, with the most significant factor being the relationship between the expectations of the instructor and student growth (Dyson, 1995; Riggins, 1986). Instructors with high yet attainable expectations of participants can create a 'self-fulfilling prophecy'. Setting high yet attainable expectations is deemed important in all branches of education and should inform the planning process. It should not be confined solely to participants, but should apply to the instructor, too. Adventure educators who have a genuine interest in their own professional development regularly reflect on their own practices and consider how they might improve what they deliver and the means through which they deliver it. There remains an emphasis on formally recognising only *technical* skills that have been assessed through governing body awards for activities. This is in contrast to recognising and benchmarking skills that demonstrate an ability to facilitate broader, more personal educational outcomes. The Institute for Outdoor Learning has gone some way to rectifying this through an accreditation scheme that uses reflective practice and goal-setting to help practitioners focus on their skills in facilitating learning.

The physical environment

The physical environment is a key factor that contributes to an experience being viewed as 'adventurous'. Kurt Hahn, one of the founders of adventure education, extolled the virtues of an unfamiliar physical environment and the naturally occurring challenges that it presented. Surprisingly, then, despite the pivotal role thought to be played by the physical environment in achieving adventure education outcomes, little research has explored this relationship. Fortunately, though, there is no shortage of theoretical material on this subject. Walsh and Golins (1976) suggest that the contrast provided by an unfamiliar environment can enable participants to gain fresh perspectives on their familiar, home environments. An unfamiliar environment may also create a sense of neutrality as none of the participants is on 'home turf', so all may be more prepared to experiment.

It is thought that the physical environment assists in the creation of a 'constructive state of anxiety, a sense of the unknown and a perception of risk' (Nadler, 1993: 61). This newness can create situations in which participants need to work hard to overcome the environmental demands placed upon them, obliging them to develop new psychological strategies. Paisley *et al.* (2008) reported that participants commonly remarked that adverse situations also forced them to work harder towards group goals. Finally, it is thought that a new environment can act as a catalyst for behavioural change because participants feel that they can begin to develop a fresh sense of identity.

Although any new environment might provide these benefits, wilderness-type environments would seem to have particular potential to do so. I use the term 'wilderness-type environment' here because it is debatable whether there are any true wilderness areas left in the UK. However, there are many non-urban environments that most participants would perceive as relatively wild. With respect to outcomes, there are obvious links between

Figure 2.2 Wilderness-type environments are thought to provide natural rather than contrived consequences necessary for challenge, mastery, success and failure

Matt Berry

being in a wilderness-type environment and the opportunities that it presents to gain new knowledge about that environment and develop personal connections with nature. Most literary interest in adventure education has been concerned with the role played by the wilderness-type environment in enhancing personal attributes. In a study by Goldenberg, McAvoy and Klenosky (2005), participants listed the environment as an important factor in developing such personal values as self-fulfilment, enjoyment and a sense of accomplishment.

However, despite a wealth of recent interest in programmes that use the term 'wilderness therapy', there is still little research exploring the relationship between outcomes, wilderness environments and other unfamiliar environments. Indeed, the very notion of wilderness is debatable. In terms of adventure education, though, wilderness-type environments are thought to provide natural consequences that participants are less likely to consider as unfair when compared to more contrived challenges, such as problem-solving and initiative exercises. Most likely, wilderness-type environments offer a better chance to host activities that participants find more engaging, compelling and risky due to the awe, wonder and countless variations in physical features that nature can provide.

Wilderness, then, is a powerful medium for change. But facilitators should not rely on it alone to develop useful outcomes. Activities must also play a significant role in developing participants' outcomes.

Activities

Activities common to adventure education programmes include rock climbing, kayaking, mountain walking, expeditions/campcraft and problem-solving/initiative exercises. However, there are many other equally appropriate activities, such as caving, sailing and surfing. This is because it is the *qualities* of the activities, rather than the activities themselves, that influence outcomes. It is commonly thought that these qualities contribute to cognitive dissonance (Festinger, 1957), sometimes referred to as 'adaptive dissonance' in adventure education. This theory is based on the idea that individuals have an inner drive to hold beliefs and attitudes in harmony (consonance). So when we hold two thoughts or beliefs that appear inconsistent with each other, a state of tension occurs. This tension is uncomfortable and we are motivated to reduce it. A common example is a smoker who reflects that his habit causes cancer. He might try to resolve the conflict by giving up, rejecting the evidence that smoking is bad for him, or rationalising this by saying, 'I don't want to live a long, dull life!'

In adventure education, similar conflicts exist between the perceived risk of the activity and the ability to complete the task. Participants are faced with conflicting thoughts: for example, 'That climb looks scary and I will fall' versus 'I'll probably be OK because the hand holds look good and the rope will hold me even if I slip.' The participant will be unwilling

33

to accept both outcomes at the same time and is therefore often motivated to resolve the dissonance by attempting the climb. It is believed that each act of achieving success and mastering the skills associated with the activity can lead to participant growth, and this has been the focus of numerous studies (e.g. Dyson, 1995; Witman, 1995).

Given the centrality of activities in creating adventurous experiences, there has been surprisingly little research linking specific activities to outcomes. But whilst no studies have attempted to determine the specific merits of individual adventure activities, some at least have looked at activities more broadly and could influence planning. We should aim to provide activities that offer opportunities to create dissonance or a 'constructive state of anxiety'. The likes of rock climbing, kayaking and expeditions have stood the test of time, perhaps because they often generate situations in which cognitive dissonance might occur and because they also offer the right blend of challenge, mastery and success necessary for a range of affective outcomes (Hattie *et al.*, 1997). High ropes activities are also popular because they allow participants the potential for cognitive dissonance while being relatively easy to facilitate: staff can be trained relatively cheaply on site, especially when compared to the time and money needed to become qualified in other adventure activities. There has been a shift towards more site-based activities over recent years in the UK, most likely because of their cost-effectiveness and ease of implementation, rather than their educational outcomes.

Expeditions have traditionally been the cornerstone of many adventure programmes. Mostly they have been based on walking, but expeditions using canoes, boats or horses are not uncommon. In terms of levels of engagement, real problem-solving and decision-making, expeditions arguably offer the greatest potential for achieving the complete range of cognitive, affective and psychomotor learning outcomes. This is particularly evident when there is a degree of autonomy for the participant. Many studies have investigated specific benefits from expeditions, with Bunyan and Gibbs (1997) finding significant positive changes in self-esteem in participants who completed an independent, fifty-kilometre backpacking expedition. Sibthorp *et al.* (2008) also state that an expedition is a powerful medium for developmental outcomes, having found evidence of strong relationships between developmental outcomes and participants' perception of autonomy. However, expeditions, particularly independent ones, no matter how short in duration, are heavily time and resource dependent and often require significant logistical input from the facilitator. This may explain why they have become less common in many UK settings over recent years, despite their clear merits.

The volume of research evidence for the relationship between specific activities and adventure education outcomes is developing slowly and presents a mixed picture. However, critical thinking, some research and theoretical underpinnings have helped us develop a sensible rationale for the selection of activities that give the best chance of creating meaningful adventure experiences that meet the learning needs of participants.

Matt Berry

Figure 2.3 An independent expedition is a powerful medium for developing a broad range of physical, emotional and cognitive outcomes

Processing

Processing can be defined as the sorting and ordering of information that enables participants to make sense of their experiences. It is thought to make a significant contribution to the achievement of outcomes and is frequently used alongside such terms as 'reflection', 'reviewing' and 'debriefing'. The act of reflection that is necessary for processing is believed to occur naturally, as we learn from our successes and failures. The theoretical foundations for processing largely come from Kolb's (1984) model of experiential learning, which states that experience alone does not necessarily result in learning; rather, reflection upon the experience turns experience into learning. According to Kolb, this reflection may not have to be a group process, activity or discussion; it may be an introspective act in which the learner alone integrates new experiences with the old. In this way, reflection should enable learners to look for patterns that unite previously isolated incidents. However, some would argue that participants do not always see the full value of the activity and are therefore unable to 'join up' these isolated incidents. The role of the facilitator in this case is to enable participants to draw more from the experience than perhaps they would when reflecting on their own. This would then necessitate structured, facilitated processing or reviewing.

There has been a long-running debate regarding the relative merits of self-directed reflection by 'letting the mountains speak for themselves' or by providing structured, facilitated reflection sessions. Of course, some individuals probably have a better predisposition to reflect on experience than others. Many students I work with seem capable of drawing a great deal from experiences through introspection, but there are also some who feel that they glean more from experience when they take part in structured sessions due to the framework offered by a facilitator, as they are often prompted to consider events from more than one perspective.

There is precious little data at present to demonstrate the effectiveness of structured processing, but it is common in most adventure and outdoor education programmes. It is broadly accepted that it is a very important factor in learning from experience, and facilitated reflection is widely practised. The role of debriefing aims to allow participants to revisit actual events with some accuracy, draw out meaning and facilitate positive change. More therapeutic goals, such as reducing dysfunctional behaviour, are believed to require more sophisticated forms of processing.

THE CHALLENGE OF CONFOUNDING VARIABLES

Confounding variables are difficult to control when trying to determine the effectiveness of an adventure experience or programme. For example, it is difficult to control what relationships will develop among participants and between facilitators and participants; and it is equally difficult to control how individuals will interpret experiences, despite the greatest efforts for consistency from facilitators. Some researchers argue that the interplay between programme components contributes most to influencing outcomes, and basic pre-test/post-test experiments attempt to simplify this complex relationship.

Despite the ever-present confounding variables that make it difficult for researchers to determine what caused specific positive changes within individuals, it is clear that adventure education is effective in making positive contributions to participants' development across a wide range of outcomes. Although there has been some useful research into what is likely to be effective, there is a need for more to determine what works best in adventure education for participants with specific needs. This would be extremely useful in making programmes maximally effective for all participants.

PRACTICAL APPROACHES TO PLANNING

This emphasis on outcomes and their position in the planning process differs from the way some experiential educators go about planning for learning. The latter would start with planning the experience first, with the meaning and learning from the experience being drawn out during some form of reflective process afterwards. This reflection may be structured by the facilitator or carried out naturally by the participant through introspection. Some experiential educators refer to this process of starting with what you hope the

Matt Berry

participants will gain from the experience by the end as 'backward design' (Rheingold, 2009). However, one could easily argue that this method is in fact 'forward design' because the participant is the most important factor and the outcomes, once established, then trigger the rest of the planning process. What follows next is the generation and selection of learning activities that are thought to give the best chance of meeting those outcomes.

Adventure educators who come from a more formal teaching or coaching background might find the 'outcomes first' approach comes naturally to them. However, in experiential education, there are concerns about using this approach. One concern is that we may become 'obsessed' by the outcomes and therefore too prescriptive in our subsequent facilitation. The danger here is that we may not read situations as they unfold and therefore fail to capitalise on significant events as they happen. Rather, the facilitator ends up simply telling participants what they got out of the experience in order for progress to be demonstrated quickly (and possibly falsely). This shift of emphasis away from the participant can render them less likely to achieve any permanency in learning – probably because they will not have developed a particular skill themselves. More importantly, if this 'hijacking' of learning is repeated, the significance of the individual in the activity can be eroded, leading to less interest and engagement for the rest of the activity, or even the whole programme.

Some experiential educators also fear that focusing on outcomes first could lead to approaches that are more dictatorial and too similar to negative classroom experiences that may have impacted on the participant in the past. With an overemphasis on outcomes, the learning opportunities offered by the experience are lost, and whatever knowledge skills or attitudes that could be developed may be short lived, less meaningful or indeed completely absent.

The development of relevant and appropriate outcomes is still very important. They act as a good guide for what participants should gain from the activity. But outcomes need not be set in stone. It is important that we recognise the need to modify outcomes if they seem unrealistic once we get to know the participants better. This is true if outcomes are too ambitious or too easy, thus serving to facilitate underachievement. However, experience tells us that it is much easier to adapt an existing plan than to develop one from scratch on the spot. Referring back to the black box, and accounting for the challenge of confounding variables, we can stack the odds of success in our favour by developing sensible goals for participants and having an informed rationale for our decisions to bring about beneficial changes.

Although there is a lack of specific research evidence, we can refer to literature and research outside adventure education – for example, from psychology, physiology and mainstream education. Such work can help us provide a stronger rationale for our approaches to adventure education planning, delivery and evaluation. Adventure educators should consider the following questions when taking account of research, relevant literature or their own critical thinking and experience to develop a rationale for their approach:

- Who are the participants and what characteristics, knowledge and skills do they already possess?
- What are the specific needs of those participants based on conversations with them and/or those who are responsible them?
- What are the general aims?
- What more specific outcomes are desirable and achievable?
- What specific activities are most likely to bring about the achievement of those outcomes?
- What blend of activities will most likely bring about the achievement of those outcomes?
- How should those activities be organised to optimize their effectiveness?
- How will participant progress be evaluated?

Planning what we do is a fundamental part of the job, but it's an interesting factor because despite the fact that we all agree on its importance, we rarely share ideas on how best to go about it. With regard to forwards and backwards design, I think I sit somewhere in the middle really. Although I always start with the needs of the group and the individuals within it by meeting with them and those responsible for them, I will also draw upon my experience of what activities I think work best in a general sense in terms of challenge and enjoyment. I then tend to think about the specific abilities within the group and what kind of previous experiences they might have, in terms of specific skills in the activity as well as intellectual and social abilities, in order to refine specific details like venue, distances they can travel, whether they could work in pairs and so on.

I might have a group of thirteen–fourteen-year-olds from a mainstream school, so in this case I have thought of the group first. But I also know that a caving experience would really develop confidence and autonomy and also encourage them to rely on each other, which I think thirteen–fourteen-year-olds tend to be pretty poor at, on the whole. In a way, I think of both the outcomes and the activity at the same time, but this probably comes from many years of experience. Anyone setting out or looking to develop their skills as an adventure educator needs to work closely with the group to get a feel for what skills and attributes need developing. In this way, activities can be really tailored to what the participants not only want but need.

Chris Pierce, Head of Outdoor and Adventure Education at
Oxfordshire's Woodlands Outdoor Education Centre, Glasbury, South Wales

Matt Berry

INTENDED OUTCOMES IN ADVENTURE EDUCATION

A common suggestion aimed at increasing the effectiveness of an adventure programme is to set clear outcomes in the planning stage. Effectiveness can be enhanced if these intended outcomes are shared and agreed between participants and the facilitator. In this way, participants have some ownership of the outcome, and adventure educators can appropriate feedback so outcomes are more likely to be achieved. Hattie *et al.* (1997: 75) summarise their view of outcome setting as follows: 'a major function of challenging and specific goals is that they direct attention and effort, and thus the participant is more aware and keen for feedback related to attaining these goals.'

Effective adventure education should therefore begin with identifying the needs of the participants. Where possible, this is followed by the development of mutually agreed and desirable learning outcomes that will form the basis of subsequent planning considerations. The recording of these outcomes and careful planning, taking account of research evidence or theory, will increase the chances of the agreed outcomes being met. One example of this is Outward Bound, a world-renowned provider of adventure education, which has increased its range of programmes over time to include those that are more tailored to the specific needs of participants. These include programmes designed to be beneficial for youth at risk, war veterans, grieving teenagers and executive leaders. Each programme contains specific activities that have been thoughtfully designed and planned in accordance with the particular needs of its target group.

Effective adventure education is therefore about meeting the needs of participants. This is done by developing shared goals and then formulating appropriate strategies to allow participants to meet these goals. In this way, whole programmes and specific activities are developed around the needs of individuals. The present challenge facing adventure education researchers is to gather evidence that aids adventure educators in their formulation of appropriate strategies. If we knew more about what parts of an adventure education programme were responsible for bringing about particular outcomes, this would make the task of planning easier and would increase our chances of being effective.

TYPES OF LEARNING OUTCOME

According to Bloom (1956), educational outcomes fall into three broad categories (see Figure 2.4). Cognitive outcomes relate to knowing facts and understanding concepts, whereas psychomotor outcomes relate to physical skills. Affective outcomes making up the remainder cover personal attributes, such as self-esteem, confidence and empathy. An individual activity, or programme of activities, will rarely facilitate only one type of outcome. Climbing, for example, is largely a physical endeavour with a focus on psychomotor skills, but it also requires cognitive effort in order to tie appropriate knots and fit a harness correctly. Spotting a partner during bouldering also elicits affective learning, particularly when participants appreciate the support provided by their peer.

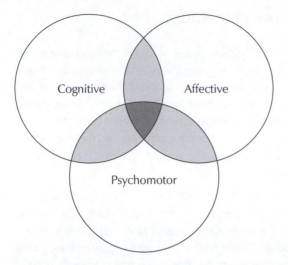

Figure 2.4 Bloom's taxonomy of educational outcomes

The overlapping circles in Figure 2.4 also demonstrate the relationship between the three types of outcome and the possibility of being able to facilitate multiple outcomes from a single learning activity. In truth, it is impossible to separate them because a learning experience engages each domain simultaneously. However, it is useful to consider them in isolation at this point. A canoeing journey would facilitate cognitive and psychomotor outcomes quite naturally. But if greater responsibility is given to participants for planning the journey and recognition of mutual benefit from each paddler, then the educational value can be enhanced by also tapping into affective areas. In many ways, this intentional rather than incidental focus upon affective outcomes is the way in which adventure *education* differs from adventure *recreation*.

DEVELOPING LEARNING OUTCOMES

In creating intended learning outcomes, we are concerned with the behaviours of the learner rather than the educator. Cognitive and psychomotor outcomes are relatively straightforward to plan for, particularly when compared to affective outcomes. An objective planning approach, utilising a clear vocabulary, would set unambiguous, appropriate and achievable outcomes. This vocabulary aids the educator by refining exactly what knowledge, skills and attributes are to be developed, and also makes it easier for all parties concerned to evaluate the extent to which their efforts have been successful.

Typical cognitive outcomes include:

- To *calculate* the distance between two points on a map.
- To *recognise* the symbols on an Ordnance Survey map for contour lines, campsite, river and so on.

- To *identify* the points of sailing on a diagram.
- To *estimate* the time for high tide.

In these examples, the key words are italicised. They pinpoint the necessary composite knowledge and understanding and offer more specific guidance when compared to broader aims, such as '*read* a map' or '*develop* navigation skills'.

Typical psychomotor outcomes include:

- To *belay* correctly, keeping one hand in contact with the dead rope at all times and locking off during transition of hands.
- To *perform* a rescue of a capsized canoe with a partner.
- To *complete* a climb.
- To *demonstrate* effective ruddering in a canoe.

Setting cognitive and psychomotor skills in this way makes it easier to see if the participants are achieving; and, more importantly, competency can be checked prior to individuals departing for more autonomous tasks. As an aid to writing intended learning outcomes, you might choose to include a verb, a context and a quality (Brunel University, 2004).

- *Verb:* Belay correctly.
- *Context:* With a peer on a self-selected climb.
- *Quality:* Keeping one hand in contact with the dead rope at all times, locking off during transition of hands whilst watching and anticipating the climber's movements.

Planning in such an objective manner can be criticised because it could encourage a blinkered view of what is possible for learners to achieve, and it is also somewhat at odds with the constructivist model of learning that is central to the philosophy of many experiential adventure education programmes. Having an objectives-based model for planning lends itself to certain types of learning, but, with reference to affective outcomes in particular, we see how it can be flawed. Affective outcomes are more complex in nature: an improved sense of racial harmony or positive changes in self-esteem are not easily demonstrated and may not even be articulated for some time after the events that stimulated those changes. This is because affective learning is largely implicit and occurs as a result of experiences that resonate with the learner at a more emotional level.

In this case, a learning intention is still a good idea and should still be articulated in your planning procedure. It will direct your attention to the needs of the learners and encourage you to think about which activities are *most likely* to bring about positive changes. Useful words to include when writing learning intentions for intended growth in affective areas include:

- Respect
- Support

- Empathise
- Cooperate
- Volunteer
- Comply
- Participate
- Sensitive
- Consider
- Share

Clarifying the general learning intention will help you select activities that are most likely to encourage particular attributes. For example, kayaking in groups is still largely an individual pursuit for beginners and may not encourage cooperation as much as canoeing in pairs. And a competitive climate in problem-solving may discourage support and respect. Ultimately, activities can be carefully planned and well-executed in terms of organisation and enjoyment. But if the adventure educator does not pay sufficient attention to the learning intentions, there is a chance that the rationale for the creation and selection of the learning activity is not securely grounded, leading to a decline in educational value even when the activity occurs in conjunction with guided reflection. In summary, an over-emphasis on prescriptive outcomes may limit the more organic learning facilitated through complex situations, but we should also be aware that simply letting the experience lead the way might result in missed opportunities and poor learning.

PRACTICAL APPROACHES TO PLANNING

Planning your own sessions, rather than learning sessions by rote from others, sets you apart as a developing professional. The written plan is more than an aide-mémoire to be used during the session. It also encourages greater thought at the stage when it is required most: *before* the session begins. Different types of plan suit different purposes, but here we are concerned with the preparation for a single lesson, session or 'episode' (Mosston and Ashworth, 1986). Mosston and Ashworth draw a useful distinction between planning decisions in relation to a learning episode:

- *Pre-impact decisions* need to be made prior to a learning 'episode' and relate to who, what, when, where and, importantly, how.
- *Impact decisions* are made during the episode. These are mainly adjustments to pre-impact decisions.
- *Post-impact decisions* are made on reflection. These are critical as they inform the planning of the next episode.

There is no ideal format for setting out your planning decisions, but most people tend to develop a format that they prefer based on how easy they find it to use, the type of participant and the nature of activities being planned. Tabular formats are the most common.

42

Matt Berry

Table 2.1 Example of a written plan template

Group details:

Date:

Venue:

Time available:

Resources required:

General aims:

Learning outcomes:

Introduction:	**Activities**	**Learning points**	**Time**
New material:	**Activities**	**Learning points**	**Time**
Application:	**Activities**	**Learning points**	**Time**
Reflections and conclusions:	**Activities**	**Learning points**	**Time**

ACHIEVING OUTCOMES

If outcomes are *what* we would ideally like the learners to know, appreciate, feel or do, then the adventure educator must think about *how* to achieve these aims. One such method is simply to 'tell them'. This may sometimes be a useful strategy, but it is limiting in terms of involvement and should therefore be used sparingly. Remember that adventure education is experiential education, so we should always strive to find ways to meet outcomes that maximise opportunities for involvement for each learner. This is why each section requires input regarding 'activities' rather than 'instructions' to highlight what the learner should be doing as opposed to what to tell them. Always ask if the methods you develop to meet outcomes are not just *likely* to do so but allow the *best* opportunities for the learner to construct their own learning through practical, hands-on experience.

SUMMARY

The research presented at the start of this chapter goes some way to help us provide a stronger rationale for the way that we approach learning in adventure education. In many ways, it is the quest for this rationale that is important, rather than the rationale itself. Even if we do not write the rationale out in explicit detail, there should be due process in this regard. We should also be open to new ideas, or even old ones that might help us develop a stronger rationale for the approaches we use that can be supported through credible sources of evidence, recognised theory or just sensible, critical thinking. In the same way that research alone may not be helpful in practice, we cannot always turn to the field for inspiration, either. For example, classroom studies reveal that whilst teachers recognise the increased learning opportunities of using more experiential approaches, they also admit that they use them infrequently.

Our best chances of success lie with planning activities that are the most likely to allow beneficial outcomes to be reached; questioning practices that we repeat time and again without due reflection; being prepared to question the practice of others in a constructive way; and being hungry for evidence, reading and opportunities to work with others from different fields and organisations. Sharing ideas, debating philosophies and trialling new ideas comprise the lifeblood of adventure education, and we should not shy away from the challenge.

REFERENCES

Bloom, B.S. (1956) *Taxonomy of Educational Objectives*, London: Longman.

Brunel University (2004) *Effective Lesson Planning*, unpublished PGCE Physical Education course material.

Bunyan, P. and Gibbs, C. (1997) The Development of Self-esteem through a Duke of Edinburgh's Award Scheme, *Journal of Adventure Education and Outdoor Leadership*, 14 (2): 3–5.

Carron, A.V. (1990) Group Size in Sport and Physical Activity: Social, Psychological and Performance Consequences, *International Journal of* Psychology, 21 (4): 286–304.

Conrad, D. and Hedin, D. (1981) National Assessment of Experiential Education: Summary and Implications, *Journal of Experiential Education*, 4 (2): 6–20.

Dyson, B.P. (1995) Students' Voices in Two Alternative Elementary Physical Education Programmes, *Journal of Teaching in Physical Education*, 14: 394–407.

Ewert, A. and Sibthorp, J. (2009) Creating Outcomes through Experiential Education: The Challenge of Confounding Variables, *Journal of Experiential Education*, 31 (3): 376–389.

Festinger, L. (1957) *The Theory of Cognitive Dissonance*, Evanston, IL: Row and Peterson.

Goldenberg, M., McAvoy, L. and Klenosky, D.B (2005) Outcomes from the Components of an Outward Bound Experience, *Journal of Experiential Education*, 28 (2): 123–146.

Hattie, J., Marsh, H.W., Neill, J.T. and Richards, G.E. (1997) Adventure Education and Outward Bound: Out-of-Class Experiences That Make a Lasting Difference, *Review of Educational Research*, 67: 43–87.

Kimball, R. O. and Bacon, S. B. (1993) The Wilderness Challenge Model, in Gass, M. A. (ed.) *Adventure Therapy: Therapeutic Applications of Adventure Programming*, IA: Kendall Hunt.

Matt Berry

Kolb, D. (1984) *Experiential Learning: Experience as the Source of Learning and Development*, Englewood Cliffs, NJ: Prentice-Hall.

McKenzie, M. (2000) How Are Adventure Education Outcomes Achieved? A Review of Literature, *Australian Journal of Outdoor Education*, 7 (1): 19–28.

Mosston, M. and Ashworth, S. (1986) *Teaching Physical Education*, Columbus, OH: Merrell.

Nadler, R.S. (1993) Therapeutic Process of Change, in Gass, M.A (ed.) *Adventure Therapy: Therapeutic Applications of Adventure Programming*, Dubuque, IA: Kendall Hunt.

Neill, J.T. (1997) Outdoor Education in the Schools: What Can It Achieve? Paper delivered at the Tenth National Outdoor Education Conference, Sydney, 20–24 January.

Paisley, K., Furman, N., Sibthorp, J. and Gookin, J. (2008) Student Learning in Outdoor Education: A Case Study from the National Outdoor Leadership School, *Journal of Experiential Education*, 30 (3): 201–222.

Piaget, J. (1937 / 1954) *La construction du réel chez l'enfant / The Construction of Reality in the Child*, New York: Basic Books.

Reese, H.W. (1994) *Advances in Child Development and Behavior*, Burlington, MA: Academic Press.

Rheingold, A. (2009) Using Backward Design: A Methodology to Develop Experiential Lessons, in Stremba, B. and Bisson, C.A. (eds) *Teaching Adventure Education Theory: Best Practices*, Champaign, IL: Human Kinetics.

Riggins, R.D. (1986). Effective Leadership in Adventure Based Education: Setting Directions for Future Research, *Journal of Environmental Education*, 18 (1): 1–6.

Rosenburg, M. (1979) *Conceiving the Self*, New York: Basic Books.

Sibthorp, J., Paisley, K., Gookin, J. and Furman, N. (2008) The Pedegogic Value of Student Autonomy in Adventure Education, *Journal of Experiential Education*, 31 (2): 136–151.

Walsh, V. and Golins, G. (1976) *The Exploration of the Outward Bound Process*. Denver, CO: Colorado Outward Bound.

Witman, J.P. (1995) Characteristics of Adventure Programmes Valued by Adolescents in Treatment, *Monograph on Youth in the 1990s*, 4: 127–135.

CHAPTER THREE

RISK MANAGEMENT

PHILOSOPHY AND PRACTICE

Chris Hodgson and Marcus Bailie

INTRODUCTION

Risk management is one of the defining skills of the adventure educator. For those within the sector, this statement will seem almost pointlessly obvious, as we generally pay a huge amount of attention to examination and assessment of safety skills. Likewise, prospective clients or those responsible for arranging adventure education experiences for others often expect that adequate attention has been paid to the safety of a programme and the ability of facilitators to manage the risks as well as providing a high quality of learning that may result from participation. Moreover, many people wrongly assume that all organisations and facilities have been exhaustively audited by independent government agencies.

This chapter will examine the key principles behind risk management in adventure education. We will explore widely accepted concepts, including roles, responsibilities and procedures. Risk is a widely used but often poorly understood term and we aim to arm the reader with a clear insight into the issues surrounding the deliberate and purposeful risk-taking inherent in adventure education. The chapter is based on the principle that risk management is desirable, as opposed to risk elimination. We must, however, be able to justify this with regard to the risk–benefit balance.

THE PROBLEM OF KNOWING

One of the inherent problems with risk management is that it is often very hard to have a really objective system of evaluation of the effectiveness of general or even specific behaviours. Clearly we will want to be pre-emptive and control risks before incidents or accidents occur, and this is at odds with a scientific analysis. It simply is not reasonable to test protocols by waiting for accidents to happen or to test different risk control strategies against each other if we believe that one may not be as effective as the other. Instead, we generally make judgements based on logic rather than hard evidence and the wisdom of best practice handed down from more senior facilitators.

This situation is exacerbated by the fact that, following an incident or an accident, when evidence of its cause can be gathered, we often learn the wrong lessons, and the underlying problem continues. Worse, we think we have solved it, right up to the point when an identical accident occurs.

Direct feedback from our actions is often a poor indicator of the success or otherwise of our behaviours. Often we can do things that are inherently risky and yet come away unscathed, while, at other times, even with the most stringent safety procedures in place, someone may get hurt. This means that we need to be very careful when we attribute a safe return from an activity to the efficacy of our actions and decision-making. Blind luck will often bail us out, even when we find ourselves in quite threatening situations; and clients themselves will often find a way of managing a situation, which will result in the impression that we have managed the activity appropriately. So we do it the same way the next time. This is positive reinforcement of poor practice, and it is very common. 'But we have always done it like that and have never had a problem before' is a frequent response following an accident.

If the odds are already quite heavily stacked in our favour, we tend to trust them even more. And most adventure activity accidents, albeit not all, contain at least some element of bad luck. There is not much evidence of accidents that were foregone conclusions from the start. Most result from an unusual coexistence of seemingly minor issues: the so-called Lemon Theory of Accidents. When all the lemons in a fruit machine line up, you get an accident. Exploring the likelihood of them lining up is often more difficult than investigating each individual lemon.

One of the key tools that the skilled adventure educator will use to evaluate a situation is their own imagination. This, coupled with an accurate understanding of the dynamics of the environment and activity, allows the leader to run through likely and less likely scenarios in the form of a 'thought experiment'. This approach is often referred to as the 'what-if game'. An astute leader will run through scenarios prior to embarking on a course of action and also at appropriate moments during the activity, when new information becomes available or conditions change. In a way, all risk assessment and risk management strategies result from processes like the what-if game. If the game is applied to an activity well in advance of it taking place, this can result in a written risk management plan. This type of formal plan is a popular approach in risk management as it results in a tangible and recorded output. It can be used to reassure stakeholders, clients and statutory inspectors that risks are understood and assessed, and that policies have been created to manage them.

However, the answers from a what-if game need to be put through at least two filters before meaningful information can be extracted and acted upon. The first of these is the 'likelihood–consequences consideration': how likely is a certain mishap to happen, and what will be the likely consequences? The second is the 'risk–benefit consideration': to what extent do the benefits of an activity justify the risks? We will deal with each of these shortly.

The inherent weakness of this proactive approach to risk is that we can start to feel that safety can be arranged through formal policies and written plans. This is at odds with the changing environment in which adventure education often takes place and the human factors inherent in facilitating people through adventurous activities. This realisation leads us to the concept of dynamic risk management and acknowledgement that we must arm leaders with the skills to manage a wide range of potential scenarios.

DYNAMIC RISK MANAGEMENT

Dynamic risk management is the process of playing the what-if game during an activity whilst also managing a client group and applying the two filters of likelihood–consequence and risk–benefit for each individual. This is a high-level skill as the facilitator may well be managing the present situation with their clients whilst also considering multiple future scenarios involving possible environmental changes and human dynamics.

Predicting human behaviour is incredibly difficult even in very simple situations, so an adventure educator needs to monitor the environmental and human factors that contribute to risk. Even then, a perfect solution is almost impossible to find. The best we can do is stack the odds more in our favour. However, we cannot simply ignore the need to anticipate events in order to plan for an acceptable route to a desirable outcome.

Figure 3.1 The field-based Rutschblock snow-stability test: having all the information means that good judgements can often only really be made at the time

48

OBJECTIVE AND SUBJECTIVE RISK

Generally, we think of risk in a particular situation as being a stable thing that impacts on all people in the same way. In many situations, this assumption is true: if we are travelling in a train carriage, then the risk of crashing is the same for everyone onboard. It can also be true in the adventure environment: if a group is standing under a cornice, then the risk of being buried in its collapse is the same for everyone. The leader is exposed to exactly the same risk as the novice participant. This is generally described as *objective* risk, as there is no discrimination between participants.

Subjective risk is a very different beast. It is much more fickle and affects different group members to different extents. If we imagine a scenario where a group of skiers is making a tricky descent down a steep slope, each member of the group will have a different sense of the difficulty . . . and risk. The more technically able skiers in the group may be less worried about falling and twisting a knee, as they are more able to control both skis. The more experienced skiers may be more concerned than the others about the heightened risk of avalanche. A less confident skier might panic because of the difficulty of the descent, and so will be more likely to fall. A fit skier will not become fatigued, and so will be less likely to fall. And so on for each member of the group.

This dual nature of risk is a problem for adventure educators. Generally, during training, we are taught how to look for objective risks, and we find it easy to practise these skills. For example, we will dig snow pits to look for weak bonds between layers of snow that may indicate an unstable slope. Objective risks are generally fairly tangible, so they often find their way into written risk assessments. At the subjective end of the spectrum, risk assessment is much more difficult because we are concerned with the individual with whom we find ourselves working. We need to make assessments based on estimation and judgements about each individual's characteristics and ability. This can be difficult even when working with long-term clients, and even harder when working with new learners. Sadly, with new learners, there is a tendency not even to try, or to adopt a lowest-common-denominator approach based on prior knowledge of work with other groups. In short, we often do not have the tools to do otherwise.

As experienced and professional adventure educators, we really should be able to take individual needs into account during the risk assessment and management process. Here, it is almost inevitable that we will be talking about dynamic risk assessment, and to do this well we will need a huge amount of experience in facilitating a wide range of individuals within the activity in question.

At this point, risk management has definitely become an art rather than a science, notwithstanding the desires of most health and safety officers. However, there is no substitute for the wisdom that comes from a long and varied experience base, as long as the right lessons have been learned from the experiences, especially when things went wrong. One of the problems of accident investigations is that we often do not really understand the true cause, and end up attributing blame incorrectly. There is little useful learning if the true cause of an accident was actually a lack of effective induction and subsequent monitoring, but subsequently written operating procedures were blamed for the fault. We sometimes blame mechanical failure when really the whole procedure was overly complicated. Most commonly, though, what is often called 'management failure' was actually human error due to loss of concentration. These misdirections cause us to try to fix the wrong problems. Here, too, hindsight bias comes into play. Our individual and collective ability accurately to reconstruct what really happened is far from perfect. Various individuals will have seen different things, and their perceptions will differ too, so accounts will always vary. Memories can be distorted both unconsciously and consciously. Reputations are at stake. We jump to conclusions and apply biases.

In the UK, most governing bodies employ a log-book system and set criteria for the minimum amount and breadth of experience that adventure educators must have if they are going to be examined for leadership awards, or even undertake training courses in some cases. The problem here is that it is hard to pin down experience and the learning that will have taken place during it. Activities can be run with easy groups and lots of support in benign conditions, so any experience gained there cannot guarantee that a facilitator will be able to cope in more extreme situations. Nevertheless, in general, more experience will make a good outcome more likely.

There is no shortcut here, which is one of the key problems that managers have when deploying less experienced staff. It is very hard to judge how well an instructor will be able to take individual needs into account and tailor an activity accordingly. When we reach the stage in our career when we appoint and deploy other staff we have to make a two-tiered risk management judgement: we make a judgement on the ability of another person's ability to make a judgement in challenging and dynamic circumstances. For the sake of sanity, we shall leave it at that, rather than consider even more hierarchical management structures!

One sure-fire way of courting disaster is to assume that each member of staff will, in whatever situation, follow what has been written down somewhere in their operating procedures. At best, written operating procedures indicate how *most* staff are *likely* to respond in any envisaged scenario. Assuming anything more, without following it up with scenario-based training and progressive responsibility, leave both management and staff feeling more confident than they should. Accident investigation in adventure activities in recent years has confirmed that overconfidence and inattention cause more accidents than technical incompetence.

SYSTEMATIC APPROACHES

Although there is an art to risk management and it can be seen as a creative and interpretive process, we should not view the process as some kind of spooky sixth sense. The Health

50

Chris Hodgson and Marcus Bailie

and Safety Executive, the statutory organisation in Britain responsible for guidance on and enforcement of health and safety regulations, suggests an approach called 'five steps to risk assessment':

- Step 1 – Identify the hazards.
- Step 2 – Decide who might be harmed and how.
- Step 3 – Evaluate the risks and decide on precautions.
- Step 4 – Record your findings and implement them.
- Step 5 – Review your assessment and update if necessary.

This model highlights something that is often forgotten: not all risks apply to everyone, so we need to consider different groups within our risk management plan. Two groups of people are often ignored in management plans. First, adventure educators are often exposed to additional risks, for example when setting up activities or clearing up afterwards. In a rock climbing top-rope activity, setting up the anchors and de-rigging afterwards are probably the most risky parts of the session, yet adventure educators who have rigorously examined the hazards faced by participants will commonly ignore these aspects of the activity. This omission is borne out by accident investigations, such as that into the sole fatality to have occurred during a supervised single-pitch climbing session in recent years.

The second group of people who are often ignored are bystanders who could be harmed by hazards that we create when working with our group. We once watched in horror as a climbing helmet, discarded by a group member at the top of an abseil, rolled over the edge of the cliff and crashed to the base of the crag, narrowly missing a young mum pushing an infant in a pram. It is also not uncommon to see walkers forced to negotiate around canoes parked across a footpath or tiptoeing over safety ropes tensioned across a path at the top of a crag. In educational settings, members of staff often accompany groups. These people might behave like the rest of the group; or like bystanders; or even like facilitators. We must factor them into our thinking and have a robust plan for them, no matter which role they play.

The 'five steps' work at a very basic level, but as the HSE (2006: 1) itself states: 'This is not the only way to do a risk assessment. There are other methods that work well, particularly for complex risks and circumstances.' Outdoor adventure activities provide examples of more complex risks and circumstances, and likelihood–consequences and/or risk-management analyses may be more appropriate methods.

Likelihood and consequences

A very common approach to risk assessment is to start by separating the likelihood of an incident from the consequences of that incident. In some ways, this reductionist approach can be easily criticised as somewhat simplistic; and, in reality, an experienced adventure educator will often consider both simultaneously during dynamic risk assessment. However, it can help us understand the implications of a course of action to consider them in turn. We therefore consider it a useful tool when trying to improve risk assessment and management skills.

'Likelihood' relates to the chances that an incident will occur following a course of action. This can range from extremely unlikely to almost certain. On the one hand, the more likely that a risk will occur, the more seriously we need to take this risk and the greater the measures we will need to implement in order to maintain an acceptable level of safety. On the other hand, the consequences may be so benign that they can be discounted, or even considered to be beneficial by contributing to the learning process. Falling off a stand-up paddle board is not so much a hazard as a learning opportunity, much like skiing on patches of ice. Likelihood on its own, then, is clearly not a sufficient measure of the level of risk. Some compilers of risk assessments recommend that a number-based risk rating should be used: for example, '1' represents the lowest risk (almost certain success) while '5' is the highest risk (almost certain incident – though I am critical of where this approach often leads).

'Consequences' relates to the severity of an incident. This can range from scrapes and blisters to permanent disability or even death. Again, the idea is that we will need to take more care to manage risks that could result in more serious outcomes. A number-rating approach can be used here, too: '1' represents cuts and scrapes that might require no more than plasters from a first-aid kit; '5' represents a strong risk of fatality.

The numbers from the two categories ('likelihood' and 'consequences') could then be multiplied together and the result called the severity of risk. So, in this case, the numerical risk will range from 1 to 25. If the risk is '1', there is a very low risk of any incident; and even if it were to occur, it would be very minor. If the risk is '25', death is almost certain, so we would be very foolhardy to continue unless we can reduce this through some very effective control measures.

The main problem with this approach is that 1s and 25s are quite rare; generally, the number will be somewhere in between. It also implies that there must be a number that represents an acceptable level of risk. But we have never been able to work out what that number is. Obviously, we would want to avoid 24, and we would be fairly happy with 2. But what about 10, 12, 15, 16 and 18? Also are the various ways in which any given number can occur all equally serious? For instance, is 2 (likelihood) × 5 (consequences) the same as 5 (likelihood) × 2 (consequences)? In basic maths, the answer is 'yes'; but in human risk management terms, it is probably 'no'. A high chance of a minor accident is not the same as a low chance of a serious accident, even though the scores of both may be equal. Even more imponderably, a moderate chance of a serious injury is not the same as a high chance of a moderate injury. (This is comparable to the old legalistic adage that absence of evidence is not the same as evidence of absence.)

This numerical approach is best left as a learning tool, explaining the thinking behind likelihood and consequence. It does not represent a very useful outcome on which to plan. Ultimately, there are only two levels of risk: acceptable and unacceptable.

52

The likelihood–consequences approach is quite useful when it comes to managing risk and planning a response. Some responses are likely to address the likelihood of an incident and others are likely to address the consequences. If we are running a rapid with a group, putting spotters on the bank with throw bags reduces the consequences of a mistake. On the other hand, using round-nosed creek boats rather than sharp-edged low-volume playboats would reduce the likelihood of an incident occurring.

Risk–benefit analysis

'Risk–benefit' is an increasingly common phrase in adventure education, and indeed in any field where the benefits of an activity may offset the risks. In short, we juggle the two components until we like the look of the balance.

We have learned most about risk from sectors where either money or somebody's life is at stake. Predictably, then, the risk–benefit approach was first formalised in the worlds of banking and surgery. However, its origins lie in intuition. We *intuitively* balance risk and benefit, and replan our actions to achieve the optimum balance. The approach is particularly relevant where we have at least some control over the level of risk and decide *not* to go for zero (complete risk aversion).

Adventure education, in particular, has always recognised, endorsed and embraced a risk–benefit approach, but we have only recently had the terminology to articulate it more convincingly. However, sometimes we misjudge the balance, or more likely we suffer the brutal reality of what risk means. (Remember, some risk means just that: there is some risk. It is *never* zero.) We therefore need to ensure that the benefits significantly outweigh the risks, especially when we are exposing other people to the risk. The experience and knowledge that the facilitator holds about the likely benefits of participation are important here. (These issues are addressed in Chapters 2, 6 and 7.) Indeed, being able to demonstrate that you have considered this balance prior to an accident and have decided that the low level of risk was reasonable for the high level of benefits likely to accrue is one of the few justifications, post-accident, for why you did not reduce the risk or eliminate it altogether by not doing the activity. Both the HSE and the courts recognise the benefits to young people of taking part in adventurous activities.

ACTIVE RISK CONTROL

Ultimately, a key job for adventure educators is to manage and control the risk to which participants, instructional staff and bystanders are exposed. It may be that we deem the activity to be sufficiently safe even when an element of risk remains (risk–benefit at work). This is quite common, but the decision will need to take into account the level of risk, the participants involved and the benefits of participation. We also need to consider how safe the activity will be. Even if it is relatively safe, we might still be seen as foolhardy or reckless if we do not include any easy and unobtrusive safety measures that most professionals would employ. (Legally, someone who acts precisely how a body of their professional peers would act in similar circumstances will generally not be found to have been negligent. This is known as the 'Bolam Test'.) When something goes wrong, we will often be judged against the manner in which another professional would approach the same activity. For instance, now that avalanche transceivers are commonplace among off-piste skiing groups, we might be criticised if we did not provide them and were subsequently involved in a fatal shallow-burial incident, even if the avalanche warning was low that day. Conversely, most river leaders will not carry flares on an intermediate river trip because the risks of doing so outweigh the benefits.

SYSTEMATIC FIELD NOTES

A key question is how we can make a reconnaissance trip more systematic. Even experienced facilitators will often conduct their audit in a haphazard way. If we are going to carry out pre-emptive risk assessment, we need to ensure that our notes are comprehensive.

Priority approach

Most adventure educators claim to use this approach. However, it is prone to errors and omissions. It relies on the facilitator identifying hazards without any additional framework or structure. Eye-catching and generic risks that are common within the activity will generally be addressed; but if a risk is less obvious, it may be overlooked unless the facilitator is very experienced and attentive. Even then, there is no guarantee that they will spot it.

Chronological approach

This approach is especially good if the activity is based on a predictable journey or has a set time-line. It uses the time-line to focus hazard identification. The facilitator moves through the activity just as a participant would during a session (either physically or as a thought experiment) and notes down any hazards that will be encountered. The chronological approach can work very well when an activity follows the plan that the facilitator has devised. It can even accommodate detours, alternatives and escape routes. However, it relies on some form of predictable path, which tends to constrain progress through the activity.

It is like packing to go on holiday. At some point, it is helpful to think through a typical day. This often results in previously forgotten items such as alarm clocks and corkscrews being packed and subsequently used extensively.

54

Geographical approach

The geographical approach can be used where a participant's exact movements through terrain cannot be predicted accurately. For instance, in orienteering, the participant is not constrained by the environment to travel in the direction that the facilitator might expect. It therefore makes sense to examine the environment independently of human movement through the planned activity. In mountaineering, highlighting the hazards at certain key points becomes more meaningful than blanket instructions to 'be careful'. 'You might want to be especially careful on this next section of the path because, if you fall off it, you might die' never fails to focus the mind!

PHASES OF RISK CONTROL AND SAFETY MANAGEMENT

As professional adventure educators, we should ensure that we have considered three phases of risk control and management (Dynon and Loynes, 1990).

Primary strategies are taken in advance, with the intention being to prevent incidents occurring. As adventure educators, we are generally very aware of our responsibilities in this area and we normally take it quite seriously. These strategies might be planned a long time in advance or on the hoof, just prior to engaging in the activity.

Secondary strategies help us deal with an incident when it occurs. They involve remedial action to control an incident, such as carrying out a rescue or giving first aid. There is an expectation that adventure educators will have a high level of training that allows them to fulfil this role, and many training and certification schemes concentrate on ensuring that leaders are indeed skilled in this area.

When an incident occurs, we may be in a position to put in place a 'recovery plan'. There may still be an opportunity to prevent a crisis becoming a tragedy or to accept a compromised but still beneficial outcome, rather than continue an activity with a poor chance of complete success. Risk–benefit analysis can really help here. 'Was this component of our plan a crucial benefit of the day, or was it merely icing on the cake?' If the latter, the main benefits may be retained in full. The other name for this situation is 'managed incident', and such incidents are *very* important in optimising an experience.

Tertiary plans deal with the aftermath of an incident. It is important that we know what to do after an incident has occurred, who to contact and how to deal with the remainder of the group. Often this area is neglected, but if an incident does occur then even a very experienced and highly trained adventure educator can feel lost and a concrete plan to help in these circumstances might be a big help. Administrative follow-up, such as talking to the press and recording details for formal reports or inquiries, will often be completely new ground. Now that mobile phones are ubiquitous, ensuring that accurate information is circulated in a non-sensationalist manner can be extremely difficult. For example, even a minor injury that has been dealt with professionally can be blown out of all proportion when a 14-year-old texts one of their friends at home. They might tell a story that bears little resemblance to actual events, with the result that scores of frantically worried teachers and parents will soon be on the phone, trying to establish what has happened.

RISK AND COMPETENCE: COMPETENT PEOPLE, NOT COPIOUS PAPER

As we have already intimated, the most important control measure in adventure education is normally to ensure that an appropriately qualified facilitator is in charge of the activity. By 'qualified' we mean someone with the appropriate competence, training and experience to run the activity in question. This may involve certification, although this is certainly not always essential or even possible. What cannot be in question is that the person responsible measures up against the standards that we, or other professionals, would expect of someone performing that role. In the UK, we have a culture within adventure education of using award schemes to certificate leaders for mainstream adventure activities, and it is often easiest for managers and outdoor- and adventure-based professionals to rely on these as 'proof' of a leader's suitability. However, it is important to remember that there are other indicators of competence. In fact, the Adventure Activity Licensing Regulations (2004) do not require leaders to hold specific awards if their competence can be shown through other records of training and experience.

If the risk is deemed to be sufficiently low simply to proceed, then we would retain that risk as it is. Many activities fit into this bracket, and a well-chosen activity might not need a lot of extra management or training. There will be a degree of risk, but either the risk itself or the consequences will be so low that we can allow things to go wrong. A navigation exercise in a relatively safe and enclosed area might fit into this category. Even if novice participants get lost, they will not come to much harm. Alternatively, the experience level of the group might mean they can cope with the activity as it is, so a flat-water river trip for intermediate and appropriately equipped canoeists poses little chance of harm to the participants.

If the level of risk is considered high, then we need to consider how we might reduce it to an acceptable, or at least tolerable, level. The HSE differentiates between what an individual parent may consider acceptable and what society as a whole might consider tolerable. As long as tragedies are not too numerous, and as long as they do not come too close to home, society is more likely to tolerate them, for the greater good. For instance, as a society, we tend to tolerate quite a large number of fatal road-traffic accidents, rather than insist that every journey should be conducted at no more than twenty miles per hour. But no grieving parent is ever likely to see the risk as acceptable if a member of their family has been killed by a motorist.

Sometimes changing the awareness or improving the knowledge of learners might be enough to control risk. This is commonly referred to as a 'heads up' approach. Merely pointing out a hazard can be sufficient to persuade participants to behave appropriately

Chris Hodgson and Marcus Bailie

around it if the desired behaviour is straightforward and obvious to the group concerned. For example, when we point out that loose stones could be kicked down onto climbers or walkers below, most groups will take more care with their footing. When the appropriate action is less obvious, we might still be able to improve the learner's understanding of the situation and the corresponding good practice that will keep them safe. For instance, we might need to explain the dangers of having climbing gear hanging too low from a harness waist belt, where it can pose a potential trip hazard, especially in descent. Then we could demonstrate how slings and runners can be folded before clipping so that they hang in an appropriately short fashion.

There are limits to this, however, and the next logical step is to 'up-skill' the facilitator. Prudent use of technical advisers is a good way to ensure that adventure educationalists are as technically competent as *necessary* – rather than as technically competent as *possible*, to apply the principle of the Royal Society for the Prevention of Accidents (RoSPA). This, in turn, requires technical advisers to have a good grasp of educational benefits and aims, and to act as an integral part of the team – not independently of it.

The technical adviser is a senior facilitator, either a manager or a consultant, with experience and certification that makes them able to comment on good practice within an organisation. One common role is to deliver 'in-house' training and assessment where it is deemed that facilitators need enhanced training in order to fulfil a role in a particular activity, situation or venue.

The next reduction strategy might be to consider controlling the risk level by employing additional equipment: for instance, using a safety rope on a gorge walk to prevent a slip or wearing crampons to negotiate an icy footpath. Often this might be preferable to avoiding the hazard altogether. After all, purposeful risk-taking is central to adventure education. However, we need to be sure that we are genuinely improving the odds, because adding 'safety' equipment can actually compound rather than solve a problem. For instance, novices tend to trip over more often when they are wearing crampons than when they are not. Similarly, the latest statistics regarding the increasingly common use of helmets for recreational skiing is that other injuries have increased due to the 'invincibility effect' they can generate in the wearer. Conversely, unprotected skiers tend to make good decisions in order to avoid accidents. Again, we should always reflect on the risk–benefit balance and consider whether clients will overstretch themselves because of what they perceive as greater protection.

Extra staffing can be an effective solution in some higher-risk activities, allowing more direct, close supervision and possibly intervention to prevent an accident. In a scrambling session, reducing the number of students per instructor means we can pay more attention to each of them or even employ more sophisticated risk control strategies, such as moving together with roped clients. When sailing, it might be an idea to put a member of staff in each boat, rather than just the lead boat of a flotilla. This will allow much quicker and easier intervention in the event of a problem, but may cause a corresponding loss of student confidence.

Finally, we might need to ask if we should avoid the risk. This does not necessarily mean abandoning the activity entirely, but it might entail changing a small part of it to circumvent a particular hazard. For instance, on a particularly windy day, we might take an alternative path for a section of a walk that normally traverses the top of a cliff. Another example might be to portage around the steepest rapid on a river trip. This small change to the route means that the activity can continue whilst the particular hazard is removed. An alternative solution might be to control the risk in another way that allows participants to enjoy the original activity. Avoiding risk altogether is very popular with industrial health and safety officers, but it is not the most appropriate strategy for adventure educators, who should always try to retain challenge in their activities, and of course challenge inevitably results in at least some sort of risk. Crossing a rickety bridge to get to the toilets has no real place in a factory setting. But crossing a similar bridge, albeit with different aims, may have benefit in outdoor education.

Ultimately, the most extreme avoidance strategy is to avoid an activity altogether by postponing it, cancelling it, or doing something else instead. However, this should be a last resort, as many of the benefits of adventure education are related to overcoming obstacles through a combination of planning, skill and resilience. So if we run away every time we see a hazard, there will not be much of a lesson in the experience. Nevertheless, we must always aim to remain on the right side of the risk–benefit balance.

ESCAPE ROUTE AND PLAN B

Having a plan B, in case of a range of eventualities, may allow you to enter the recovery phase following an incident, rather than moving directly to abandonment or escape. Equally, some escape routes, if taken after a minor mishap, may leave you stranded without transport and support in an unfamiliar location.

However, an escape route and a plan B should both be considered when planning an activity. If we intend to take clients on a potentially hazardous journey, it makes sense to devise a plan for how we might extract ourselves if things become too difficult or dangerous. Of course, an escape route can be tangible – a pre-planned, alternative route that has been mapped out prior to the start of the activity. However, the escape route concept can also be applied to other exit strategies. For example, if a crew member on an ocean-going yacht is struggling in the high-pressure role of winching, you might move him to a less stressful position. This could be considered a plan B for that particular group member, and would allow him to enter the recovery phase.

58

CULTURE OF INDIVIDUAL RESPONSIBILITY

Less experienced adventure educators often feel that they must take responsibility for every aspect of risk management during activities. This is understandable, as there is a comfort in being in control. The leader might also enjoy being seen as the star of the show, with the participants as mere extras. However, there is great danger in adopting this approach. First, it can be a very disempowering experience for participants to be managed through an activity in this way. It can become a little like a theme-park experience, with the adventure done *to* the participants rather than *by* them. Many of the desired benefits of adventure education rely on feelings of mastery that come directly from participants themselves overcoming the inherent challenges that are associated with the activity. If we deny them that opportunity, the activity will lose the very transforming power that provided the impetus for doing it in the first place.

Second, if we adopt this role, we become solely responsible for the safety of our clients. This is at odds with most health and safety guidance and good practice, both of which suggest that participants should always retain at least some responsibility and vigilance for the safety of themselves and those around them. 'The instructor must do everything' gives rise to what the HSE calls 'single point errors' – a single error by one person having a catastrophic effect. For this reason, we challenge the concept of 'instructor infallibility', which some operating procedures seem to demand. Instead, we prefer the principle of 'duality'. Two pairs of eyes and two minds should always be involved in any critical safety decision.

If we embrace these ideas fully, they should allow us to turn around our view of responsibility and control for risk management, and we should ensure that participants take as much responsibility as possible within the constraints of any given situation. An example of this can be teaching students to check each other's climbing harness buckles before anyone leaves the ground. A system where students routinely check buckles and ask a buddy to check their buckles prior to climbing means they are taking responsibility for their own safety. It is a positive behaviour that will maintain their safety within the sport long after the session is over. A climber should also check that the belayers are set up properly, and ready to belay. This is the 'Check? Check!' principle. Scuba divers do this throughout their diving careers and call it the 'buddy system'. If climbers did the same, we would not have nearly as many silly accidents, single point failures that have nothing to do with getting the risk–benefit or the likelihood–consequences balance wrong. The types of accident that are just plain dumb!

> Before we go into the cave system I spend time with the group, asking them about what they see as the main challenges and, more importantly, how they might be able to contribute to their own safety. Initially, the younger ones often come up with silly

ideas because they are a little excited and mostly unused to having to think for themselves. However, by involving the group in some key decisions and allowing them to use their own ideas in consultation with me, I really feel that they not only adhere to their own suggestions but also make more effort to work together and consider if their approach needs adjustment. Creating this sense of responsibility helps to shift some of the emphasis away from me and makes the adventure theirs. I'd really like to think that in some way, by creating a culture of responsibility in caving, the participants can apply the same idea to more aspects of their lives.

Dave Barber, teacher of outdoor and adventure education
at Woodlands Outdoor Education Centre, Glasbury, South Wales

CONSENT

One of the fundamental concepts that adventure educators use to justify the retention of risk within adventure education is that participants (or those acting on their behalf) will accept controlled risks because of the benefits they can generate. In other words, they willingly agree to risks, but only if those risks are properly controlled. However, this argument is fundamentally flawed because, by definition, there are no 'safe' risks. There either is or is not a risk. What is crucial is whether the risk is foreseeable. In 2010, in a landmark case involving the tragic death of a young boy on a caving outing, the jury decided that the risk was unforeseeable, and acquitted the defendant. The Health and Safety at Work Act requires activity organisers to safeguard against *foreseeable* risks, not *all* risks.

However, acceptance of risk needs to be informed. So organisers should make sure that participants (or those acting on their behalf) have a good idea of what they are about to experience, in terms of both benefits *and* risks. Asking participants to acknowledge this in writing is now common, but in no way is this a disclaimer of responsibility. Participants do not lose any of their legal rights to protection by signing such a form. By getting them to do so, we are merely trying to ensure that the wrong person does not inadvertently take part in the wrong activity. If that happens in adventure activities, the consequences might be serious.

Many adventure educators think of consent as a formal process that happens once, normally before an activity starts. This moment of consent is often accompanied by paperwork and the signing of a form that includes a statement about the risks associated with an activity. But this idea that clients accept risk just once – when they agree to go on a trip or a course – is a very narrow view of consent, and there are a number of practical problems with it. First, legally, consent to risk can be given only if a participant is *fully* informed as to what they are accepting. Generally, the point where our clients become fully informed is not in

Chris Hodgson and Marcus Bailie

the office but much later, just prior to engagement in an activity. So it is a good idea to take time to consult your clients at this stage and get some kind of confirmation that they are still willing to engage in the activity. If we are undertaking a journey in an alpine environment, then this point may be as we leave a car park or ski-lift station. This can be even more important if this is effectively a 'point of no return'. For instance, when a group has made even a relatively small amount of off-piste downhill progress on a tour, it may be impossible to abandon the activity, so the group will be committed to continuing at least until an 'escape route' becomes feasible. On a route up a mountain, the point of no return may be much later in the activity, if it exists at all.

Whenever we reach a point of no return, it is good sense to reconfirm that our clients are happy to continue before we commit them, and us, to the activity. If we fail to do this, we could be seen as keeping our clients in the dark, which effectively undermines any argument that they have consented to the activity. Sometimes it will be obvious to the client when this point has been reached and a simple 'Are you OK to continue?' will be sufficient. Other times, we will know we have reached the point of no return but our clients will not. An example might be a river trip that is about to enter rapids in a narrow gorge. In some circumstances, though, verbal reconfirmation of consent might not be necessary. When a client ties herself onto the rope for the third time and starts to climb, there could be no greater statement of confirmation. Her behaviour leaves no doubt about her continuing consent.

Being sure of consent is vital for two reasons. First, legally and morally, we are required to have a client's consent in order to allow them to take even controlled risks. Second, many benefits that clients gain result from their perception of their own competence and autonomy, often called 'challenge-by-choice'. We undermine this aspect if we deny them the opportunity to make their own decisions.

CONCLUSION

The benefits of well-planned adventure education can justify exposure to controlled risk. And, despite the doom and gloom of some commentators, there are still many opportunities to help people enjoy and learn in outdoor and adventurous settings.

They key messages are quite simple. Controlled challenge is a key element in adventure education and we should not seek to eliminate challenge from activities. Were we to do so, we would undermine the experience and the opportunities for learning. We need to be able to justify the resulting risk to which clients are exposed, and we should consider the possible positive and negative outcomes, the risk–benefit balance, who the clients are and what they want from an activity, what is currently viewed as best practice, how we can manage risk and challenge in the specific activity for a specific group, and how our actions would be viewed if something went wrong. We should ensure that clients have every

61

opportunity to understand the risks involved in an activity and that they take as much responsibility as is reasonable for their own safety, rather than abdicating responsibility completely to the facilitator or the facilitator assuming unnecessary levels of control and excluding the clients.

Paperwork is no guarantee of best practice, most of which comes down to having competent facilitators doing the right level of activity with the right client group and the right equipment. It should include some evidence and the opportunity to 'stocktake', and try to ensure that this is happening with the rigour we would expect. It can also allow some information transfer between individuals, which may help in induction and training.

Best practice and knowledge are always evolving, and we need to ensure that we update our practice (and in some cases our paperwork) whenever things change or new information emerges. An adventure education risk management plan is never 'finished'.

REFERENCES

Bailie, M. (2002) Letter to the Editor, *Horizons*, 20: 9.
Ball, D., Gill, T. and Spiegal, B. (2008) *Managing Risk in Play Provision: Implementation Guide*, Nottingham: DCSF Publications.
Dynon, J. and Loynes, C. (1990) Legal Liability and Risk Management in Outdoor Training, *Journal of Adventure Education and Outdoor Leadership*, 7: 9–12.
Gill, T. (2010) *Nothing Ventured: Balancing Risk and Benefits in the Outdoors*, English Outdoor Council. Available online at: http://www.englishoutdoorcouncil.org/publications.
Hallinan, J.T. (2009) *Errornomics*, London: Ebury Press.
Health and Safety Executive (HSE) (2001) *Reducing Risks, Protecting People*, London: HSE Books.
HSE (2006) *Five Steps to Risk Assessment*, London: HSE Books.
HSE (2007) *Guidance from the Licensing Authority on the Adventure Activities Licensing Regulations 2004. The Activity Centres (Young Persons Safety) Act 1995*, London: HSE Books.

Chris Hodgson and Marcus Bailie

CHAPTER FOUR

LEARNING AND TEACHING IN ADVENTURE EDUCATION

Matt Berry

INTRODUCTION

Learning is done by people, not to them.

This is a bit of a cliché in adventure education, but it serves as a constant reminder that participants benefit most through experience, rather than through the mere transmission of facts. This basic philosophy underpins everything that we do in adventure education. No amount of telling, instructing or directing can replace what individuals learn from their own physical acts and cognitive efforts. However, knowing when to give information directly and when to allow learning to develop more organically is a difficult skill to perfect for the developing teacher or facilitator in adventure education. Specifically, how we learn from experience is a tricky process to pin down. But we should be able to examine experiential learning's relationship to adventure education by exploring some of its parameters.

Adventure education is a type of experiential education. Like all experiential education, it is based on the philosophy that individuals learn best through direct experience rather than more passive forms of education, such as classroom-based study. But whilst experiential education as a whole is concerned with anything that can be learned best through experience, such as a child playing 'shops' to develop arithmetic skills, adventure education tends to focus on personal and social outcomes, such as self-esteem development and effective communication skills. These outcomes are typically achieved through the use of compelling adventure activities – caving, rock climbing, independent expeditions and so on – that contain an element of risk and provide real consequences for participants.

Central to all forms of experiential education is the concept of experiential learning. This is commonly accepted as 'learning by doing', but scholars have found it an elusive concept to capture. Debates within education have attempted to set some boundaries for experiential learning and to establish what activities can be construed as 'experiential', with experiential learning being interpreted differently by those attempting to make use of it and with respect to the context in which it is being applied. This has led to experiential learning having loose boundaries. For example, someone teaching practical laboratory skills in a university might view experiential learning in a different way from someone wishing to foster positive attitudes towards immigrants as part of a community education programme.

This chapter will explore some basic strategies and models that are relevant to learning, teaching and facilitation within adventure education. It aims to provide a context and give students and practitioners a stronger rationale for the decisions they make in order to encourage, facilitate and enhance learning.

WHAT IS LEARNING?

In its simplest form, learning can be described as a permanent change in behaviour. If we then think about learning that is experiential in nature, we would say that this change in behaviour comes about through 'doing'. If this is true, is it then possible for someone to learn something by not 'doing'? In order to answer this question, we should first consider what we mean by learning in general. Unfortunately, the products of learning are much easier to observe than the learning itself. School pupils recalling facts correctly during a test indicates that some kind of learning has occurred, but it is impossible to see the changes in the brain that constituted the learning and enabled those facts to be recalled. The process of learning has therefore received much attention from educational psychologists, and the field is rich with various theories, concepts and models.

Ausubel's (1968) treatment of types of learning has mostly been linked to learning in school settings, but it includes a number of important distinctions that are useful at this point. The first is a distinction between reception and discovery learning. In reception learning, you could say that the teacher has done much of the necessary thinking by organising and sequencing material in the most appropriate format for the learner. In language learning, for example, the teacher organises all of the key concepts, starting with what they perceive to be the easiest and the most important – for instance, names and family members. A more relevant example in adventure education might be kayaking. Here, the teacher could map out a lesson structure and then teach the individual skills and strokes that lead to competent performance. By contrast, in discovery learning, the content of what is to be learned has to be discovered by the learners themselves, usually first through some type of problem-solving activity.

The second distinction is between meaningful and rote learning. In meaningful learning, the teacher focuses on drawing links to what the learner already knows. Rote learning, on the other hand, occurs when the learner memorises information in an arbitrary fashion. Here, the teacher does not establish links to what the learner already knows. The information is considered in isolation, not anchored to existing concepts. Consequently, it is more easily forgotten. Memories of my own education are littered with examples of rote learning. The painful experience of memorising the conjugation of French verbs, for

64

Matt Berry

example, was treated as an end-in-itself rather than a means to greater conversational ability.

These two distinctions – reception versus discovery learning; and rote versus meaningful learning – are seen by Ausubel to be independent of each other. In this way, reception learning can be either meaningful or rote, and discovery learning can be either meaningful or rote. This is an important observation for adventure educators because there is a tendency to assume that reception learning can *never* be meaningful and that discovery learning is *always* meaningful. But it is wrong to assume that school-based and classroom learning is always contrived, dull and meaningless. Whilst lessons comprising nothing but note-taking, copying and comprehension exercises do little to encourage meaningful learning, good teachers will always provide the links to prior understanding and conceptual scaffolding that enable better understanding of complicated ideas, even when they operate solely in a classroom. Similarly, discovery learning as part of an adventure education experience may not necessarily result in meaningful learning or indeed in the 'discovery' of anything relevant. John Dewey (1859–1952), whose significant contributions have shaped the field of experiential learning, explained that not all experiences are educative and some are even 'mis-educative'.

The danger lies in oversimplifying either approach, for there are undoubtedly good and bad examples of both. Reception learning can be much more than passive observation, particularly when good practice is delivered by passionate teachers who make particular efforts to consider material in ways that are engaging, enjoyable and relevant. Similarly, an approach to learning that aims to be more experiential should consist of more than simply telling participants, 'Go and work it out for yourselves.'

EXPERIENTIAL LEARNING

Experiential learning results from direct experience. As in reception learning, there is an emphasis on making meaning. In experiential learning, however, the meaning comes from personal reflection upon the experience rather than from a teacher's explicit efforts to link new knowledge to existing knowledge. The main difference, then, is the degree of learner involvement. Whilst reception learning can be made more meaningful by the teacher offering good examples that resonate with the learner's experiences, the risk here is that the learner's role is too passive. In an experiential-oriented approach, the learner, rather than the teacher, is placed at the centre of the experience. In this way the value of the new knowledge, skill or understanding has more obvious and immediate benefits to the learner. This approach aims to increase the level of learner involvement so that learning becomes relevant and meaningful in a way that seems more natural to them.

Dewey, building on the ideas of Jean Piaget (1896–1980), firmly believed that individuals develop understanding through experiences that increase participation and interaction. He was frustrated by his experience of education, which offered little in the way of either participation or interaction. Both of these are essential because they provide opportunities for the learner to test the validity of their own ideas rather than simply receive someone else's interpretation. Dewey believed that we are naturally predisposed to find meaning, but that the learner needs to be given the chance to *construct* their own meaning through experience and reflection. This philosophy is the cornerstone of a constructivist learning ideology.

Dewey skilfully employed a number of experiences to explain his theories. For instance, he would use cooking as a vehicle to contextualise the learning of proportion and weight. The key here is that the learner has an opportunity to make meaning because the relevance of the task is immediately evident. (What could be more motivational than baking a cake?) By contrast, in reception learning, where the learner relies upon so-called 'information assimilation', the relevance and meaning-making would usually be revealed only after the delivery of a theory relating to the concepts of proportion and weight. Furthermore, this meaning-making is facilitated by the teacher rather than the learner, when the former provides suitable examples of when skills relating to proportion and weight are necessary and relevant.

Despite the enduring popularity of experiential learning as both a practical and a theoretical basis upon which to ground professional practice, debate continues about which is the best learning mechanism. Whilst reflection – particularly critical reflection – is a common theme in all theories, only Kolb (1984) has proposed a model of experiential learning (see Figure 4.1). This model has been criticised, particularly because Kolb separates reflection from concrete experience. Some also argue that it is too simplistic, as the various elements may actually occur concurrently. On the whole, though, it has stood the test of time and has been used in many settings where learning from experience is seen as the principal method, including medical practice, corporate training and, indeed, adventure education.

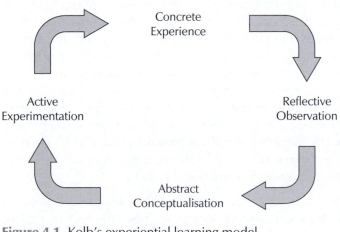

Figure 4.1 Kolb's experiential learning model

Matt Berry

- *Concrete experience* – This part of the model relates to the experience itself. In adventure education, this could be a problem-solving activity, such as building a raft. It could also apply to the end of the first day of an expedition or the successful navigation of a set of rapids in a canoe. In each of these cases, the activity has been engaging and has provided the opportunity for the next phase in the cycle.
- *Reflective observation* – This can occur without prompting and refers to the point when the learner looks back at what has happened in order to begin to develop meaning. In adventure education, we typically encourage this through discussion, although the internal mechanism for reflection is not fully understood. Simply allowing time for individuals to reflect before moving on to the next activity is the best way to encourage it to happen.
- *Abstract conceptualisation* – This is when the learner begins to assimilate their reflective thoughts into general principles. It is an essential precursor if individuals are to succeed in applying new concepts in the next stage. Learning from a number of experiences and situations is organised into a set of principles that may be useful in a specific context but cannot yet be applied elsewhere. For example, facilitators may be able to resolve conflicts in a group on the basis of what they have learned from similar, earlier experiences, but they will not yet have distilled the underlying mechanisms. Hence, they will not be able to explain these mechanisms or apply them in a different context.
- *Active experimentation* – This stage moves beyond bringing together thoughts from similar situations and sees the learner applying their learning to new settings. Participants will use concepts that they have developed in adventure either in other adventure challenges or more widely in the rest of their lives.

Kolb proposes that the cycle can begin at any phase, so we should see the model as a spiral, with each subsequent experience building on the previous one. Longer adventure programmes have the advantage that there are more opportunities for participants to conceptualise and experiment. Interestingly, Hattie *et al.* (1997) demonstrate that the length of a programme correlates positively with all other adventure education outcomes.

As we have seen, experiential learning is a difficult concept to pin down, but it is probably best summarised by Heron (1999: 3), who describes is as: 'learning by encounter, by direct acquaintance, by entering into some state of being. It is manifest through the process of being there, face to face with the person, at the event, in the experience. This is the feeling or resonance level of learning.' This definition enlightens us to the fact that learning encompasses much more than mere retention of facts or our ability to carry out physical tasks. The 'feeling or resonance level of learning' affects us in more profound ways, perhaps by generating a greater sense of fairness, fostering humility or enhancing self-esteem. To this end, adventure education has much to offer by way of experiential learning.

EXPERIENTIAL EDUCATION

Experiential *learning* is an individual act. It does not, inherently, require a teacher, coach or facilitator; it merely describes the way in which we process information and, in turn, learn. Experiential *education*, on the other hand, is the organised and purposeful use of situations that encourage learning through experience, either individually or in groups. Whilst some teachers in schools may encourage experiential learning, experiential education tends to be more about the contexts where the methodology and philosophy of learning from experience can be applied. These contexts may vary, depending on typical goals, and there is usually some overlap in general intention. Organisations that have a bias towards outdoor education with a curriculum-oriented 'outdoor classroom' principle may also deliver some adventure education. Alternatively, centres that focus largely on adventure education may also include some environmental education. Whatever the context or organisation, all of them are underpinned by the philosophy of experiential learning. Put simply, experiential learning is the process, whereas experiential education, whatever the orientation, is the agent of delivery.

There has been sustained growth in the number of contexts where experiential education takes place in both the UK and the rest of the world. Students and practitioners who understand how individuals learn best are valuable commodities in this growing field. After all, those who know more about the nature of learning are more likely to succeed in creating opportunities where it is likely to happen. Many students I have taught have gone on to lead successful careers in schools, having initially studied adventure education. They tend to attribute their success in school teaching to a belief that learning should be about what the pupils do, or experience, in order to learn, rather than what the teachers tell them.

Most of the people who work in educational settings tend to be called 'teachers'; however, in experiential education, the term 'facilitator' is often preferred. The choice of a different title is intended to signal a significant change in role: a facilitator would always aim to devolve more responsibility for learning to the learner. This approach often casts the facilitator as more of a democratic co-learner. However, devolving responsibility to the learner is not always easy. Even some experienced teachers will tend to stay on safe ground, retaining control by sticking to reception methods. This can also be true in adventure education, sometimes with good reason. The obvious risk is to the participants' physical safety (see Chapter 3), but there could also be a risk in terms of meaningful learning. Whilst the intention is always to empower learners by de-emphasising our role, in reality we still occupy privileged positions, perhaps dictated by the organisation we work for, irrespective of the titles we give ourselves. It is important to acknowledge that some situations will always require a greater degree of control, and some decisions will always be beyond the scope of the learner. Experiential educators, and in particular adventure educators, must never forget that responsibility for safety ultimately lies with them, but in that context they should still ensure that learners are free to make genuine decisions with genuine outcomes.

Matt Berry

In truth, teachers can facilitate and facilitators can teach, but the use of the term 'facilitator' to describe the person encouraging learning reminds us that the participant's autonomy within the experience should lead the way whenever possible (Dewey, 1938). A facilitator would also typically be more concerned with aiding participants with their reflection, either at a convenient point during the whole experience or at the end of a day (see Chapter 7). In summary, the most important factor to bear in mind is whether the learning is meaningful. Whether you call yourself a teacher, a facilitator or an instructor, the learning should be meaningful by having immediate and long-term relevance for the learner.

The role of the experiential educator, therefore, is to create the maximum opportunity for meaningful learning to occur. In attempting to do so, however, the budding adventure educator might ask if more learning can be achieved in some experiences rather than others. Although most proponents of experiential education would agree that there is a relationship (of sorts) between more direct experiences and levels of meaningful learning, only Gibbons and Hopkins (1980) have tried to provide a 'scale of experientiality'. At first glance, their principles seem sound because the basis for differentiation within the model centres on the extent to which the participant is directly involved in the activity. The 'receptive mode' end of the spectrum sees the participants involved at a minimum level: watching and listening to presentations, plays and films. Such activities are thought to provide limited roles for the participant. At the opposite end ('psychosocial mode'), participants have much greater involvement by generating new ideas and working with others. This leads to participants having greater responsibility in directing their own activities in order to gain a better understanding of themselves and their relationships with others.

Once again, however, the complexities of experiential learning conspire to challenge this somewhat oversimplified picture. Those who are passionate about literature and film, for example, would contest that these mediums (supposedly of relatively low experiential value) might well allow them to experience the full range of human emotions. Emotional involvement is generally thought to be instrumental in changing attitudes and beliefs, and it is a commonly cited characteristic of more direct experience.

Despite the flaws in their model, at least Gibbons and Hopkins attempted to map the landscape of 'experientiality'. In doing so, they highlighted that learning should be more about direct involvement and creating opportunities for meaningful learning to occur. So, whilst there is little evidence to validate the scale they devised, few would contest that we need to reflect upon what we do and move towards activities that involve the learner more often and at a deeper level.

WHY SHOULD EDUCATION BE EXPERIENTIAL?

You might be surprised to learn that there is little research-based evidence to demonstrate that experiential education is more successful than other forms of education. Once again, the difficulties in defining what constitutes experiential (and indeed non-experiential) education compound the problems of comparison. However, several points are regularly raised to justify experiential approaches to education:

- Due to the problem-solving nature of many experiential education programmes, the learner usually sees the benefit and relevance of the learning straight away.
- Learning is meaningful because links to what the learner already knows are self-evident.
- Coleman (1979) found that whilst reception learning was more time-efficient, clients retained more from the experience-based approach.
- An authentic experience will see that the learners are quickly and actively engaged rather than passive observers.
- There are often real consequences for the learners who, in attempting to influence or control their environment, are more motivated to complete the tasks.
- There are more opportunities for learners to reflect on experience and apply learning straight away. Raising the importance of reflection is the key to more independent learning.
- Experiential approaches require the learner to make choices regularly. There is a strong relationship between choice and learner motivation (Vallerand, 1997).

These points go some way to providing a rationale for experiential education, particularly if we think of learning being about factual knowledge and understanding. A brief revisit to the taxonomy of educational objectives offered by Bloom (1956) reminds us, however, that learning has multiple domains. Factual or cognitive learning relating to intellectual skills such as knowledge, comprehension and analysis, is but one area. We must bear in mind that learning is also about the development of psychomotor (movement) skills and the development of affective traits that relate to such domains as emotions, attitudes and values.

As we know, cognitive learning can be facilitated through reception methods and can be made meaningful through the use of sensible examples. Some would argue that these methods suit the material and the learners because they are time-efficient; and, because the effects of cognitive learning are easier to measure, it is easier to make a claim for their effectiveness. Cramming for exams is an example of this: we work hard for a short period of time in order to pass, but some of the content will be meaningless to us and will subsequently be quickly forgotten. Most teachers would say that, when time and energy permit, their own efforts to use experiential approaches are rewarded by more engaged students learning in a less transient way. When the pressures of assessment loom large for the teacher, however, it is easy to see why they return to reception methods.

Psychomotor learning relates to the development of physical skills. Motor learning is widely accepted as a relatively permanent change in performance resulting from practice or past experience. Whilst this is synonymous with the general definition for 'learning' offered earlier in this chapter, there is a clearer indication that we have to do something physically as well as think about it in order to learn a physical skill. The evidence for this relationship between the mind and body is all around us: we know we cannot improve our climbing

Figure 4.2 Learning from experience can challenge us cognitively, physically and emotionally

or kayaking skills too much merely through reading and observation. Consequently, most psychomotor learning has to be experiential to some extent, even when the teacher retains full control over the learning content and activity.

The clearest area where learning *must* be experiential is the affective domain. Emotions, attitudes and values are less tangible outcomes, and we cannot simply tell people about them and expect to generate positive results. What we are talking about here is changing the very way people think about themselves and their relationships with others. There is no quick fix, and although it may be possible to get people to understand the nature of affective traits through reception methods, the essential mental and physical changes require direct interaction with relevant situations and experiences. Put simply, the ability to *demonstrate* empathy rather than merely *explain* it can come about only through reflection on personal experience. The same is true of many other characteristics that cannot be taught explicitly. For example, self-esteem, as described by Rosenburg (1979), is a complex matrix of attributes that comprises a person's overall judgement of the self. Sub-domains can include such factors as physical competence, physical appearance and social acceptance. These cannot be developed simply through hearing about them from a teacher. First-hand experience is required, enabling individuals to reflect on and make sense of their successes, failures and relationships with others.

Ultimately, education should be experiential because of the inherent opportunities it affords individuals to reflect not just on the experience but on their own thinking. This is called metacognition: the thinking a person does about the way that they think, feel and act. The ability to reflect and evaluate our own cognitive ability is thought to be the key to being a lifelong learner. Metacognition is considered to be the bridge that allows knowledge to be transferred to new contexts, which in some ways helps explain the difference between those who *know* a lot and those who *do* a lot. Most importantly, education needs to be experiential so that we can all live richer, more fulfilling lives and make significant contributions to the wider community.

ADVENTURE EDUCATION AND EXPERIENTIAL EDUCATION

Put simply, adventure education is experiential education, but it is characterised by the planned use of adventurous activities, such as rock climbing and expeditioning, in order to achieve educational goals. This is not a new idea. Learning from adventure has formed the basis of important aspects of education in many cultures for thousands of years. Traditional adventures, including such endeavours as Aboriginal walkabouts and Christian pilgrimages, typically have unknown outcomes. However, modern adventure education owes much to the philosophy of Kurt Hahn (1886–1974), a teacher who extolled the virtues of adventure for developing the whole person – mind, body and soul. Hahn had grave concerns regarding the limited education methods of his time and what he called 'declines in modern youth' in terms of imagination, morality and physical fitness. These concerns led him to create numerous enterprises, the most well known being the Duke of Edinburgh's Award Scheme and Outward Bound, with both programmes becoming recognised around the world. Whilst Outward Bound programmes typically last around three weeks, the Duke of Edinburgh's Award requires a more sustained effort, with participants taking several years to complete all three levels. On the outside, the two schemes appear to have different goals, but Hahn's philosophy of educating mind, body and soul permeates through both of them and remains hugely relevant today.

Adventure education has enormous potential to be good experiential education. Hahn's focus on mind, body and soul and Bloom's (1956) taxonomy of cognitive, affective and psychomotor elements have much in common. Both men insist that a more complete education would address all three areas. Adventure education therefore has great potential to be a more complete form of education. The diversity of activity inherent within it typically draws upon cognitive, psychomotor and affective areas. In planning and preparing for a multi-day kayaking expedition, for example, participants are stimulated cognitively through the development of navigational skills and physically through paddling skills. The expedition itself further stimulates the development of these skills whilst also creating the necessary environment to develop affective skills, because participants need to communicate effectively, share essential tasks and responsibilities and consider the plight of others in order to succeed. Some would argue that the true value of adventure education lies in its ability to resonate with participants at a spiritual level. Those with a particular faith, for example, might feel a greater connection with their God. Meanwhile, those without any religious leanings often insist that the experience has enriched their lives in some way. They might feel a greater connection to nature or even a new-found spiritual connection to something they cannot define.

Clearly, adventure education is a powerful medium for a broad range of learning outcomes. It has received tremendous support from advocates around the world and from a growing body of research evidence. It is wise to exercise some humility as an adventure educator, however. We should not assume that adventure education always has beneficial outcomes for everyone, irrespective of the quality of provision. After all, nothing will hinder someone's education more than contempt for the subject or methods used. It is therefore important that adventure educators constantly reflect on their own practices in order to think critically about their own effectiveness. Being able to select, justify and discount the strategies we use to facilitate learning is the key to being effective. This is one of the key elements of professional development, all of which is explored in more detail in Chapter 13.

TEACHING IN ADVENTURE EDUCATION

The issue of 'teaching' in adventure education is contentious in that the term has historically supported the centrality of the teacher's role compared to that of the learner. The term 'teacher' also usually implies a formally recognised teaching qualification that is not necessarily required in adventure education settings. However, by using the term more broadly – to describe any person who works in an educational setting and is responsible for planning and delivering activities that facilitate learning – we are able to draw upon more models that might aid the developing adventure educator. As was discussed earlier, the ability to evaluate the relative merits of the strategies we employ, irrespective of their original field, is key to improving what we do. This enables us to move from 'what I'm doing' to 'why I'm doing it'.

Whilst adventure education espouses the philosophies of such innovators as Hahn and Dewey, practical application of these philosophies is less straightforward. However, I have found the work of Mosston and Ashworth (1986) very useful in helping us provide a better rationale for the approaches we choose. Their work has two key features that assist the developing adventure educator. The first is the exposition of the idea of a spectrum of teaching styles that relates to the choice of teaching strategies or tactics available. The second is that the spectrum demonstrates two important relationships: one between teacher and learner, and the other between type of learning outcome and types of approach typically used to achieve them. The beauty of Mosston and Ashworth's work is that it is a conceptual framework based on many real-world observations of teaching and learning experiences. This makes it useful as an initial step in exploring the practical relationship between teaching and learning.

THE ESSENCE OF EACH STYLE

Looking at the spectrum (Figure 4.3; Mosston and Ashworth, 1986), the further along it one travels, the more responsibility and decision-making are passed to the learner.

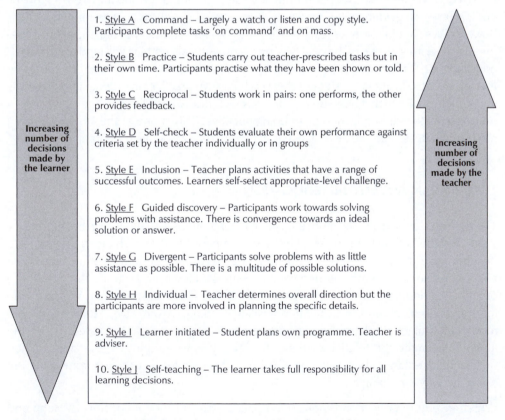

Increasing number of decisions made by the learner

1. <u>Style A</u>   Command – Largely a watch or listen and copy style. Participants complete tasks 'on command' and on mass.

2. <u>Style B</u>   Practice – Students carry out teacher-prescribed tasks but in their own time. Participants practise what they have been shown or told.

3. <u>Style C</u>   Reciprocal – Students work in pairs: one performs, the other provides feedback.

4. <u>Style D</u>   Self-check – Students evaluate their own performance against criteria set by the teacher individually or in groups

5. <u>Style E</u>   Inclusion – Teacher plans activities that have a range of successful outcomes. Learners self-select appropriate-level challenge.

6. <u>Style F</u>   Guided discovery – Participants work towards solving problems with assistance. There is convergence towards an ideal solution or answer.

7. <u>Style G</u>   Divergent – Participants solve problems with as little assistance as possible. There is a multitude of possible solutions.

8. <u>Style H</u>   Individual – Teacher determines overall direction but the participants are more involved in planning the specific details.

9. <u>Style I</u>   Learner initiated – Student plans own programme. Teacher is adviser.

10. <u>Style J</u>   Self-teaching – The learner takes full responsibility for all learning decisions.

Increasing number of decisions made by the teacher

Figure 4.3 Mosston and Ashworth's spectrum of teaching styles

Although the model was originally based on physical education in schools, Mosston and Ashworth, as physical educators themselves, value the idea that we learn much from practical experience. They are also keen to point out that no one teaching style is best all of the time. An effective adventure educator should select appropriate strategies based on the merits of each style and how they relate to the nature of participants and learning outcomes.

Command style

Pure command style is rarely used. It takes no account of individuals' needs or preferences and has minimal intellectual value. Its one advantage is that it is very time-efficient, so it can be of use in high-risk situations when you need participants to respond quickly. We might also use it (for fun) in a 'follow-me'-style activity.

Practice style

Practice style is common in most forms of education, but it is particularly useful in learning motor skills, such as those needed in rock climbing and kayaking. Feedback largely comes from the teacher, but some independence develops in relation to how much practice occurs. If the participants' motivation is low, they might avoid contact or not try too hard. As long as the teacher has good knowledge, feedback is accurate and usually timely. The teacher must be highly attentive, however, because participants who feel they are being ignored will have poor motivation.

Reciprocal style

This is more than just working with a partner. Participants work in pairs or small groups in order to observe and give feedback. The teacher makes many of the task decisions, but having participants observing and offering feedback to each other is useful for affective development, such as communication skills. Learners are involved at a much higher level, but care must be taken to ensure that observers are assisted with content and style of feedback. Learners begin to become more independent.

Self-check style

The participants check their own progress against criteria that the teacher has developed. This is often blended with a reciprocal style. Participants develop greater independence by drawing upon intrinsic feedback from the task. The teacher should offer guidance on

75

Figure 4.4 A reciprocal style entails the participants, rather than the teacher, observing and giving feedback

how to do this, rather than simply telling the learner what the feedback is. In a problem-solving exercise, for example, the group might complete the task, but the success criteria checklist that is given to them would be based on group roles and involvement, rather than just one person knowing the answer.

Matt Berry

Inclusion style

In a broad sense, inclusion is about adapting the learning situation to suit the learner. In adventure education, we often overcome this by offering challenge by choice. There could be multiple versions of the same activity so that there are various ways to be successful at both individual and group levels. Examples include participants selecting the difficulty of a climbing route or planning a journey by selecting paths and overall distance in line with the group's capabilities. The key purpose is that everyone is active and involved at the same time and in the same place. From a cognitive or psychomotor performance perspective, individuals often do better if they are grouped according to ability because there is a tendency for some to under- or over-estimate their own capabilities. The messages developed through inclusive approaches, however, are more beneficial in terms of personal and social development, which is a strong theme in experiential education.

Guided discovery style

This point on the spectrum is often seen as the 'discovery threshold'. The teacher's role is to guide learners to a practicable solution, but he or she incorporates suggestions from the participants. The teacher may appear to have a dual role as teacher and learner if they perform this function well, but in reality their intention is to move the participants towards a common goal. Guided discovery is convergent in nature. It begins with broad questions to generate a variety of responses. All of these responses are valued, but careful subsequent questioning should 'channel' the learners towards a single (desirable) solution. Of course, the teacher knows the 'right' answer, but the learners do not (at least not initially). One could say that this is the point where the ideas within experiential learning and meaningful learning begin to converge. Whilst there is the potential for learning to be more meaningful by using guided discovery, it is more time-consuming and there is a danger that the teacher/facilitator will reveal the answer in order to move on/have lunch/feel important! Guided discovery might be used to develop movement skills in a kayak or in classic problem-solving, such as spider's web, where one solution will be the most effective. Whilst some of the less tangible outcomes in adventure education – such as being a more effective communicator – cannot be taught directly, we can plan activities and provide reflection that guide the participant to discover it.

Divergent style

This is similar to guided discovery in that it is based on problem-solving. This time, however, there are many practicable solutions and participants are encouraged to seek more than one. It is a good method for encouraging creativity and further changes the role of teacher to one of facilitator. Indeed, the teacher may not be able to predict where they will end up. Many believe that education should fundamentally be divergent in nature in that it is through divergent thinking that we make intuitive leaps (members of the Flat Earth Society, pay attention here). Divergent methods celebrate individuality and require the participant to be involved in planning, execution and evaluation of their ideas. They can be used in building shelters and rafts or constructing low-ropes modules, where multiple solutions are feasible. More broadly, whilst we plan activities with general themes, many adventure education activities elicit divergent outcomes because people interpret their experiences in different ways (see Chapter 7).

Individual style

This is where the teacher works in consultation with the participant or group on a project. Goals are individualised but are related to a general theme. The participants are responsible for almost all of the decisions, with only some rough guidelines sketched out in relation to overall aims, time limits or the availability of resources. It offers much in the way of intrinsic motivation and can be a very powerful medium for learning cognitively, physically and affectively. On the downside, it places huge demands on the teacher/facilitator to check the accuracy, relevance and appropriateness of the learning programme developed by the participants. With an individualised expedition, for example, participants can choose the method of travel, duration, departure and return times, group size, terrain and so on. Consequently, individual style might well be impractical, despite its potential benefits.

Learner initiated style

The key difference between individual and learner initiated styles is the role of the teacher/facilitator. In the latter, the learner makes all the decisions in planning and execution. They also develop the criteria for success. The role of the facilitator is simply to 'rubber-stamp' this process.

Self-teaching style

In self-teaching, the individual's cognitive, emotional, ethical and social needs and desires determine the objectives. However, self-teaching never really occurs in formal settings like adventure education because the learner has moved beyond the need for any sort of teacher/facilitator. Nevertheless, some claim that self-teaching takes place in experiential education because participants 'learn by themselves'. In reality, as self-teaching truly occurs only when the learner makes *every* decision independently, a facilitator would never know what the participant had learned, or indeed if they had learned anything at all.

Matt Berry

TEACHING STYLES IN ADVENTURE EDUCATION

A skilled teacher/facilitator will select strategies from the spectrum depending upon the nature of the participants and the nature of the task. In adventure education, we are philosophically wedded to learning from experience, but of course it would be of limited value to allow someone to learn that they had put on their harness or buoyancy aid incorrectly simply by waiting for a nasty accident. Skilled teachers and facilitators blend various strategies into a hybrid that best meets the needs of the learners. Sometimes, there will be a need to retain an element of control and limit participants' decisions; other times, more independence will be appropriate, bringing with it the chance for the development of self-confidence and affective skills. For instance, using a more direct practice style is usually more time-efficient, so that will allow us to devote more time later in the day to tasks that foster more social and emotional outcomes.

There are obvious links here to the Conditional Outdoor Leadership model (COLT). This demonstrates the relationship between leadership style and concerns relating to the environment, group and task. Put simply, when conditions are highly favourable – the group is competent to operate in a specific environment, demonstrates appropriate skill and has sound working relationships – the leader can be more democratic or even abdicratic in style. In situations of low favourability, where the group has poor relationships and the environment is more demanding, it may be appropriate to be more autocratic. In education in general, and specifically in adventure education, it is important to retain a broad experiential learning agenda. Always look for opportunities for genuine problem-solving and participant-centred approaches. Sometimes it is advisable to be more direct, but always ask yourself if better planning might have allowed for more involvement, independence or social interaction.

FACILITATION IN ADVENTURE EDUCATION

Facilitation models are common to most adventure education literature. Facilitation is the cornerstone of adventure education practice and simply refers to the way in which learning is drawn from experience. It builds upon Kolb's Experiential Learning model (1984), where reflection is considered the necessary precursor for conceptualisation and, hence, learning. Facilitation develops through a number of phases or 'generations':

1   *Letting the experience speak for itself.* Participants reflect on the experience themselves with no input from the facilitator at any point.
2   *Speaking for the experience.* The facilitator makes sense of key events and shares them with the participants at a timely opportunity or during a debriefing. The facilitator gives feedback relating to the performance of the group in the task. There is a need to provide feedback that is accurate and true to the events (not as easy as it sounds). Like many

situations in teaching and facilitation, much can be gained from watching others who have done it many times before.

3   *Debriefing or channelling the experience.* In this mode, the participants rather than the facilitator recall and evaluate critical events. Similar to guided discovery, the facilitator's role is to ask open-ended questions, such as: 'In what ways do you think the group was successful?' The aim here is to encourage a wide range of responses and direct, or channel, participants towards beneficial outcomes.

4   *Directly frontloading the experience.* Participants are alerted to a particular focus prior to the activity. Some groups may already have ideas about what they would like to tackle. In addition to the goals of the task itself, this also (and perhaps more importantly) alerts participants to the personal and social aspects.

5   *Framing the experience.* This involves isomorphic framing, which aims to draw links (or isomorphs) between significant events from the activity and the participants' everyday lives through frontloading and reflection. A facilitator may help a young participant to see the links between finally completing a tough climb after numerous attempts and not giving up so easily when they find their maths homework difficult.

6   *Indirectly frontloading the experience.* This could take the form of a story about how a previous group behaved during a task. In the post-activity debrief, attention is drawn to how the current group behaved in comparison. Strong messages can be conveyed through explaining how the current group compared without the need to confront potentially awkward or inflammatory issues directly. For instance, rather than saying, 'This task revealed how selfish you all are,' you can use the experiences and characteristics of the earlier group to guide the current group's thinking.

The debate over whether reflection needs external stimulus from a facilitator is by no means resolved. There is little empirical evidence to support the anecdotally inspired perspective that structured reflection improves learning. It is likely that some individuals need little or no stimulus for experiences to affect them in profound ways, while others may need considerable prompting to recall significant events accurately and interpret them in beneficial ways. However, most participants see the value in reflection, and good facilitators have a range of reflection techniques at their disposal (see Chapter 7). The common view regarding structured reflection is that there is a sound theoretical basis for it and that more therapeutic outcomes depend upon effective reflection techniques. Behaviour modification of offenders and habitual drug users, for example, is considered to be best achieved through the more sophisticated facilitation styles (4, 5 and 6 in the list above), whereas recreational goals tend to be met with less sophisticated styles (1, 2 and 3). Suggestions for further generations involve the specialised use of language and even self-facilitation. However, the large majority of adventure education programmes utilise the more basic models of facilitation (1–3). These methods have certainly been around for longer, consequently seem better understood and are therefore better applied. As facilitation techniques have evolved, so has the need for better materials to assist facilitators with creating more imaginative reflective practices. Greenaway (1993) offers sound practical advice and a suitable rationale to develop your facilitation skills.

Matt Berry

LEARNING STYLE

Recently, in mainstream education, there has been a shift in emphasis away from the 'teacher and teaching' style towards the 'learner and learning' style. To a large extent, this has been prompted by cutting-edge research into how the brain functions. However, whilst educators in all fields have become aware of the significance of individual learning preferences, it is important that our attempts to apply theory to practice in adventure education should take a considered approach.

Cassidy's (2004) overview of twenty-three learning style models demonstrates the diversity of interest and the disparate nature of research in this area. Each of these models has merits and drawbacks, and the diversity alone illustrates why we should exercise caution before consigning individuals to a particular mode of learning. Cassidy points out that we need a much stronger evidence base before we start to employ learning styles in that way.

Of the models used in education, the inventory of learning styles developed by Honey and Mumford (1986) has enjoyed the most application in management training, medical practice and sports coaching as well as adventure education. Taking inspiration from Kolb's Experiential Learning model (1984), Honey and Mumford developed a questionnaire to determine individual learning preferences. Whilst few people adhere to each category exclusively, the questionnaire presents four general types of learning style:

- *Pragmatists* are down-to-earth, practical people. They like to solve problems through trial and error and enjoy challenges. Overall, they are happy as long as things work, but they may be impatient to get on with the task and achieve the result.
- *Activists* enjoy all activity without bias. They are open-minded learners and, like pragmatists, are keen to get on with tasks. Unlike pragmatists, however, they may not bother to see the task completed. Once the initial interest has dissipated, they may look for the next source of excitement.
- *Theorists* like to take abstract ideas and put them into more coherent theories. They enjoy working logically and will work through problems systematically. One of their notable characteristics is that they will ask questions to help them analyse and synthesise information. They generally do not rest easy until they are happy that their ideas fit within a logical framework. They are dedicated to fact and do not like subjective or ambiguous views, which may make them seem unfriendly at times.
- *Reflectors* are cautious. They prefer to collect as much information as possible before starting a task or reaching a conclusion. They enjoy watching and listening to other people before making comments, which may give the impression that they do not like to join in. But in reality they like to see the bigger picture, taking account of other views as well as their own.

WORKING WITH LEARNING STYLES

You can probably see yourself in at least one of these styles, or maybe as a hybrid of all four, depending on the task at hand. No one style represents the ideal learner, so it would be wrong to present such a picture to participants. The experiential nature of adventure education provides regular opportunities to accommodate all learners, whatever their preferences. For example, activists can be stimulated by the variety of practical adventure activities on offer; pragmatists have regular opportunities to see tasks through to the end; theorists can offer logical solutions to logistical issues; and reflectors may play a key role in group evaluation.

Learning styles models are an emergent discipline, and debate is ongoing over whether individuals utilise different styles depending on the task or exhibit one style in all their activities. More research is required, but it is still advisable to bear learning styles in mind. Offering explanations and necessary instructions in a variety of ways will create more opportunities for more participants to understand more key points more quickly. For example, you may need everyone in the group to tie into a harness. Most will need more than one demonstration, some will need to see it again, some will want a different explanation, and some will want to try it themselves repeatedly until they get it right. Seeing things from each learner's perspective will avoid frustration and also go some way to earning their respect. There is no need to allocate each of them to a specific category, but offering variety is simply good professional practice.

SUMMARY

This chapter has introduced some basic ideas about learning, teaching and facilitation. As a practitioner with some experience, you might already be familiar with several of them and use them in your daily practice. But I hope that the chapter has also provided some ideas for how you might develop your teaching style, facilitation style and/or learning style. We should never feel that we have completed our journey in learning. Just as we are dedicated to the learning of others, we should also be dedicated to our own.

REFERENCES

Ausubel, D.P. (1968) *Educational Psychology: A Cognitive View*, New York: Holt, Reinhart and Winston.
Bloom, B.S. (1956) *Taxonomy of Educational Objectives*, London: Longman Group.
Cassidy, S. (2004) Learning Styles: An Overview of Theories, Models and Measures, *Educational Psychology*, 24 (4): 419–444.
Coleman, J.S. (1979) Experiential Learning and Information Assimilation: Toward an Appropriate Mix, *Journal of Experiential Education*, 2: 6–9.
Dewey, J. (1938) *Experience and Education*, New York: Macmillan.

Matt Berry

Gibbons, M. and Hopkins, D. (1980) How Experiential is Your Experiential-Based Program?, *Journal of Experiential Education*, 3 (1): 32–37.

Greenaway, R. (1993) *Playback: A Guide to Reviewing Activities*, Windsor: The Duke of Edinburgh's Award in association with Endeavour Scotland.

Hattie, J., Marsh, H.W., Neill, J.T. and Richards, G.E. (1997) Adventure Education and Outward Bound: Out-of-Class Experiences That Make a Lasting Difference, *Review of Educational Research*, 67: 43–87.

Heron, J. (1999) *The Complete Facilitators' Handbook*, London: Kogan Page.

Honey, P. and Mumford, A. (1986) *Using Your Learning Styles*, Maidenhead: Peter Honey.

Kolb, D. (1984) *Experiential Learning: Experience as the Source of Learning and Development*, Englewood Cliffs, NJ: Prentice-Hall.

Kerr, R. (1982) *Psychomotor Learning*, Philadelphia, PA: Saunders.

Kraft, D. and Sakofs, M.M. (1988) *The Theory of Experiential Education*, Boulder, CO: Association of Experiential Education.

Le Cornu, A. (2005) Building on Jarvis: Towards a Holistic Model of the Processes of Experiential Learning, *Studies in the Education of Adults*, 37: 166–181.

Mosston, M. and Ashworth, S. (1986) *Teaching Physical Education*, Columbus, OH: Merrell.

Rosenburg, M. (1979) *Conceiving the Self*, New York: Basic Books.

Vallerand, R.J. (1997) Toward a Hierarchical Model of Intrinsic and Extrinsic Motivation, in Zanna, M.P. (ed.) *Advances in Experimental Social Psychology*, New York: Academic Press.

CHAPTER FIVE

COACHING IN ADVENTURE EDUCATION

Jane Lomax

A coach should take people where they can't take themselves.

Adventure education is a subset of experiential education. Experiential education has loose boundaries but tends to be 'learning by doing' and 'learning by doing with reflection'. Consequently, adventure education literature, with the focus on the 'experience', has avoided the use of the term 'coaching' due to the perceptions of coaching being about per-formance and winning medals. However, modern perceptions of coaching are somewhat different and this chapter seeks to explore how coaching skills can be applied to adventure education. Whilst adventure educators can learn from coaching research and practice, coaches can also learn from adventure and experiential education because of the focus on the participant and learning from experience. Many recent developments within coach education across a number of sports have put the 'athlete' firmly at the centre of the experience (Kidman, 2005).

Developing affective or behavioural change is difficult to 'coach', but activities within adventure education that are thought to foster 'personal growth' require some elements of coaching. The way we feel about ourselves is linked to what we know we can do and what we think we look like. Performance is part of this complex picture, so an adventure educator who can coach the performance changes that enable the growth in affective domains will make a positive contribution to the participant's developing self-concept.

This chapter focuses on the coaching of motor skills. Many good texts cover this area, but few are considered in light of adventure education settings. Not everything can be facilitated 'experientially'. The development of interpersonal and intrapersonal elements may well be best facilitated rather than coached, but the physical and cognitive skills necessary for participants to complete tasks successfully will rely on skills common in coaching (Sibthorp et al., 2008). Adventure education often prepares participants to undertake independent elements, whether it is learning to read a map prior to orienteering or developing the skill set necessary for an expedition. In order to maximise these opportunities and ensure appropriate levels of competency are developed, particularly with regard to safety, direct coaching of skills is often necessary.

84

DO ADVENTURE EDUCATORS 'COACH'?

When we qualify in the different adventure activity disciplines, we are encouraged to be 'instructors', 'leaders' or 'facilitators'. Often the term 'coach' does not appear until the more experienced stages in professional development, if at all, in adventure education literature. Here, I challenge that perception and suggest that 'coaching' can be applicable within any of these contexts. Whether working within a sport-specific 'instructional' context or providing a broader range of activities as a 'facilitator' within a residential experience, a good practitioner will seek to:

- improve the performance of the group as a whole;
- improve the performance of the individuals within that group;
- develop skills that will be remembered in future sessions;
- develop skills that can be transferred to other situations;
- consider the people in front of them and respond to their needs;
- recognise individual differences, challenge all levels of experience and achieve success;
- provide a positive learning environment with purpose and direction; and
- use a range of communication skills applied appropriately to the group and the situation.

THE COACHING PROCESS

Coaching involves working with people across a range of environments, experiences and ages to enable performance to improve (Wikeley and Bullock, 2006). The coaching skills explored here support the delivery of a single session as well as working with participants over a longer time-frame.

Effective coaching involves a cyclical process of planning a session, conducting or delivering the session and then evaluating and reflecting on the session and its delivery. Good coaches use these reflections to inform the planning and delivery of their next session. Some general principles to consider when coaching in adventure education include:

1 Take into consideration the group you are working with and the context in which the session is to be delivered – i.e. the 'bigger picture'.
2 Identify clear aims for the session.
3 Plan the sequence of activities to enable the participants gradually to progress through a series of tasks that will challenge all those within the session and yet enable success. This builds confidence and motivates learners to continue participation.
4 Deliver the session with effective communication skills and the ability to be flexible to respond to events as they unfold.
5 Plan to cope with the unexpected, whether that relates to changes in individual behaviours or the environment.

6 Organise and manage the equipment, time, participants and environment effectively to ensure the health and safety of all.

7 Bring the session to an appropriate end point that reflects the achievements of the individual(s) within the session and draw a suitable conclusion before the individual(s) depart.

8 Evaluate the session and reflect on the desired aims and context within which the session was delivered. Use those reflections to inform the planning of future sessions. This is a rich learning opportunity for you and discussions with more experienced colleagues are invaluable in the development and refinement of coaching skills.

9 Ensure risk assessments have been conducted and the health and safety of the session has been fully considered.

10 Maintain appropriate risk without exposing participants to unnecessary danger.

This is by no means an exhaustive list. The remainder of this chapter explores skills that will contribute to the effective delivery of these stages.

PLANNING SKILLS

Planning skills are also covered in Chapter 2, but here I shall discuss some of the key points when developing motor skills within an adventure education setting. Prior to the delivery of any session, you need to consider the participants, the task, the environment and yourself (McMorris and Hale, 2006) as well as those of your employers and the package that is 'marketed' to the public. You need to balance these considerations. The format of session plans will vary depending on the activity and the aims of the session, but I will now explore a number of planning and delivery skills.

Giving instructions – why do we need them?

If the focus of adventure education is experiential, you may wonder why we need to use instructions at all. Programmes are often experiential in nature but there are many occasions when instructions are important to outline a task or maintain a duty of care. Sometimes we will also need to make clear any expectations relating to rules or boundaries of acceptable behaviour.

Giving instructions and using demonstrations are the bread and butter of effective coaching, whether the focus of the session is direct teaching or has a more experiential orientation. Instructions are an important aspect of learning, particularly in the early stages, and can be used to prepare participants for the more discovery elements of a programme or for things that might happen in the future, such as what to look out for in a navigational task, or what to look for when choosing a good site for erecting a tent. Instructions tend to be given

Jane Lomax

before or during practice and disclose information as to how to perform the skill. They help engage auditory learners. Instructions are also useful when demonstrations are difficult. For example, when leading a caving trip, you may be in a fixed position and so may only be able to give information verbally to explain what to do during the next section.

Verbal instructions are most effective when:

- They are specific, concise and understandable – use language that the participants understand and avoid jargon so they can easily be related to the learner's previous experiences.
- They are delivered only one or two at a time – particularly important with children, who may have limited concentration spans, though even the most able have limited capacity to remain focused for long!
- The performer has time to listen.
- They are expressed positively – i.e. what you want people to concentrate on doing, rather than what you want them to avoid.
- They are delivered between practices.
- They are supported by sound subject knowledge.
- They can be easily translated into physical action.

Figure 5.1 The coach primes the participant prior to giving a demonstration that will show the other learners what to do in their kayaks. Notice how attention is gained and eye contact established to ensure the instructions are conveyed clearly and heard by the participant

87

Moreover, for instructions to be effective, they need to be heard. So consider where to deliver them and how to gain attention before doing so. It is much easier to give audible instructions on a climbing wall than it is from a safety boat when teaching sailing, so think carefully. Being upwind of your participants helps, but voice projection is often a problem, particularly for females, who need to lower their tone of voice when increasing the volume.

On what should the learner be asked to focus?

Many instructions ask learners to focus on body parts: for example, 'Wrap your hands around the top of your paddle', or 'Place the paddle diagonally across the palm of your hand.' These are *internal* instructions. By contrast, if we encourage focus on the effect a movement has in relation to the environment – 'Use the paddle shaft to angle the paddle towards the target eddy' – this is *external* focus. Research within a number of sports, including teaching eddy turns in kayaking (Banks, 2001), suggests movements learned with an external focus of attention are more successful in both practice and retention, so it is a good idea to use more external than internal instructions.

Do we need to make everything explicit?

Definitely not! Your challenge is to choose from a myriad of possible instructions the key point that needs to be made explicit and can be learned through practice. This is the crux of experiential learning – learning without even realising you have learned something, known as implicit learning (Fairbrother, 2010). In follow-the-leader games, for example, the explicit instructions within a kayaking or sailing activity may relate to the direction or route choice, but the participant will learn steering skills and boat control by completing the task – i.e. implicitly. The skill lies in choosing the practice environment to facilitate implicit learning. If learners do not realise they have learned things, they tend not to meddle with them, so they can be more robust under pressure, perhaps when they are remote from facilitators. Demonstrations can help here.

USING DEMONSTRATIONS

It is widely accepted that learning by watching others and copying is very effective; children are particularly good at this. Demonstrations tap into the learner's capacity to watch behaviour and mimic that behaviour. Watch out, though, as your learners will often copy the things you *least* want them to . . . at any time, too, so you should always illustrate sound practice. Demonstrations engage visual learners and help reduce the length of time spent listening to instructions, so kinaesthetic learners can get moving more quickly. They provide a picture of what the correct movement should look like, enabling the learner to compare

88

Jane Lomax

their efforts at executing the skill in question. Demonstrations are particularly important when the learner has no prior experience of an activity, which is common in adventure education.

Generally, there are four stages to consider when setting up a demonstration:

- *Stage 1: Attentional processes*. Help the learner to pick up on the important elements of the demonstration with verbal cues and key words.
- *Stage 2: Retention*. Help learners remember what has just been seen in the demonstration. Analogies or metaphors are useful. Let the learners try the demonstration without giving them any more information – for example, organisational details – that might disrupt their retention.
- *Stage 3: Reproduction*. Give learners the chance to reproduce the movements they have just seen. It may take a few attempts, so avoid stepping in too quickly to correct their efforts.
- *Stage 4: Motivation*. Provide a demonstration that the learners will want to copy to encourage the necessary motivation to refine and practise the skill.

Setting up a demonstration

There are logistical issues in presenting an appropriate demonstration from a position that all learners can see. Some outdoor environments are more challenging than others, so think through where to position the learners so that they can all see the elements of the demonstration you wish to emphasise, and determine which view will best emphasise the desired learning points.

- When demonstrating tying a knot, I will tend to do so from alongside the participant because they often struggle to reorganise the information if I do it from in front of them.
- When demonstrating any bilateral skill in kayaking, I usually move to give the learners a different view, but sometimes it may be better to move the learners rather than yourself. I position myself so that I, rather than the participants, am facing the wind, rain, snow or sun, so they can watch the demonstration without squinting into the elements.
- To manage a demonstration in climbing or surfing when the movement is taking place, where you cannot stand to observe easily, I prime the learners with cues to know what to look for before I give the demonstration.

Dean (Sid) Sinfield, Plas Y Brenin, National Mountain Centre, Wales

Who should demonstrate?

Decide the level of your demonstration: aim to inspire and challenge the learners but also to be realistic. Demonstrations do not always need to be given by the coach. Choosing the right person to demonstrate is particularly important when your learners are likely to be experiencing anxiety. In this case, using a demonstrator who is similar to the learners themselves can have a powerful impact on their self-confidence (Weiss *et al.*, 1998). The status, age and gender of the demonstrator are therefore important aspects for you to consider. If you are not technically correct in the execution of a skill then you are probably the worst person to demonstrate because your demonstration is likely to set a ceiling on the aspirations of the learners. In these circumstances, a peer model who is learning or coping at a skill would be preferable.

When to demonstrate?

It may be tempting to demonstrate every time for the learner, particularly in a one-on-one coaching situation, but this can seriously detract from any experiential learning and might lead to dependency on the coach. Therefore, your learners should not only be given a few attempts to try to put each demonstration into action but should be allowed a few trials to work things out for themselves before you step in.

Demonstrations are most effective when they are:

- Repeated a number of times by a skilled performer similar to the performers' level. An 'expert' model has its uses but may not always be appropriate.
- Viewed from more than one position, as the view of the skill may be quite different from different angles.
- Positioned away from distractions, such as other groups working nearby.
- Performed at full pace for the learner to gather information about the timings and cadence of the movement. Slow motion helps clarify quick movements, but a full-pace demonstration should be given at some stage.
- Followed by time to absorb the demonstration, remember it and have a number of trials at reproducing it. Avoid filling that post-demonstration time with other organisational details as this reduces the learner's capacity to remember and reproduce the demonstration.

Children often like to have a go before receiving a demonstration (McMorris and Hale, 2006), so factor that into your planning. Demonstrations are very useful where skills have a high cognitive demand (lots of decisions to process): for example, skiing various lines through a mogul field or any kind of 'follow-me' activity in scrambling. Remember, you do not always need to provide a demonstration, so ask yourself whether one is truly necessary!

Jane Lomax

Using a mixture of verbal instructions and demonstrations – getting the balance right

Normally, you will use a mixture of instructions and demonstrations, but finding the right balance between the two is tricky. Get it right and you will tap into different learning pathways. Be mindful of the fact that it is all too easy to explain a task and then show it. This is repetitive and much of the information becomes redundant. Instead, decide which parts of the information to make explicit; use them as cues to direct the attention of the learners to the specific elements of the demonstration that you want them to notice; and allow the rest to be picked up implicitly. For example, when demonstrating the J-stroke, the learner needs to be primed to notice the paddle and hand movement because some of the other necessary information is hidden under water.

MANUAL GUIDANCE

Much of the focus of adventure education is experiential, with learners exploring movements, so manual guidance is not used a great deal. But it can be helpful to give learners support in their efforts to execute a movement. This could include manual guidance from you, such as helping to lock off a belay plate during climbing and moving the learner into the right end point to reinforce the movement. You could also use a mechanical aid where they are available and appropriate. Skiers who are struggling to hold their skis in a snowplough might find an 'Edgy-Wedgy' useful to keep their ski tips in place until they have mastered the technique. This can help kinaesthetic learners, who like to tune in to how a movement feels. But as it is you or the mechanical aid that is moving or supporting the movement, you need to wean the learner off the support as soon as possible. Executing manual guidance involving physical contact also needs to be appropriate and sensitive to the learner's needs.

PRACTICE

Having developed appropriate learning outcomes, consider how much practice learners will need in order to acquire the skill set to achieve that aim. Decide how you will progress the tasks through time to enable success. You will need to extend and challenge the learners, but not overextend them.

Whole or part practice?

You need to choose whether to work on the whole skill at any one time – for example, forward paddling in kayaking – or whether to break that skill down into parts and work on each individually – for example, extending the top arm, releasing the paddle blades or the 'catch–pull–release' sequence. Using part or whole practice will depend on whether the skill is simple or complex in its organisation as well as on the interdependence of the parts. A skill with parts that are fairly independent of each other lends itself to part practice, whereas one with very interdependent parts should probably be practised as a whole.

Whole practice allows the participant to practise in the context in which they will perform, so you can be fairly certain that the learner is developing the appropriate motor programme. In the early stages of learning, the whole skill can be simplified: for example, shorten the distance or reduce the level of decision-making to decrease the demands on the learner, so your role is to shape skill development.

If the learner struggles when trying to practise the whole skill immediately, breaking it down into parts may help. You can practise just one or two parts at a time, or might practise one part and then add others sequentially. If practice starts with the first part of the movement and builds through to the last, this is called 'forward chaining'. 'Backward chaining', on the other hand, allows the coach to start practising the last part of the movement before adding other parts progressively back to the beginning. When learning to coil a rope, for example, forward chaining would start with the pile of rope and build up the coil; backward chaining would start with the coiled rope and uncoil it before redoing it. With a rope anchor system, backward chaining would allow the learner to look at the set-up and take it to pieces, exploring how it had been put together; forward chaining would start at the beginning and work through setting it up. Backward chaining reduces the amount of verbal input required of the coach.

Part practice is helpful in breaking down movements for the learner, but you need to ensure that the motor programme the learner is practising is indeed training the same motor programme as the whole movement requires.

Practising to enable retention and transfer of physical learning

This is essential when preparing learners for independent expeditions. Most adventure activities will involve participants performing in a variety of environments, so the skills you wish to develop are often required to transfer to other situations. There may also be a time lag between developing skills and using them. It is important to choose practice progressions that improve performance within a session to get confidence going, but real learning will have occurred only if the learners can remember the skill at a later date or transfer that skill into other situations. Some practice structures encourage performance development within a single session more than others, and some will result in increased retention and transfer instead. Remember the focus of the session and in what circumstances the learner will perform the skill to help choose the best practice types. Consider the following forms of practice.

92

Specific and variable practice

To structure the practice environment effectively, consider what type of skill you are coaching and the environment in which it is likely to be performed. Where the skill is a closed one, it will be performed within an environment with little variation from one trial to the next. This lends itself to very specific practice conditions so that a consistent approach is mastered. For example, belaying is a relatively closed skill.

In open skills, where the level of cognitive activity and decision-making involved in an activity's execution is higher, the practice environment needs to reflect this. Learners need to practise with different variations of the skill: for example, ferry gliding when kayaking or practising whitewater manoeuvres in different environments. Providing opportunities for varied practice is particularly important for children (McMorris and Hale, 2006). Whether the learner needs to repeat a specific motor skill or adapt the skill to different conditions should be reflected in the progression of planned tasks.

Blocked, serial and/or random practice

Skills can be practised in blocks where the focus is on one skill only and this is repeated a number of times before progressing to another skill. Blocked practice helps when time is short and you are looking for performance improvements within a single session to build confidence or consolidate some basic skills – for example, knot-tying, belaying or forward paddling. However, blocked practice does not engage the learner as much, cognitively, as either serial or random practice, so the amount of retention and the ability to transfer that learning to other situations are limited.

To increase cognitive involvement, you could practise the skill interspersed with other skills, but in a predictable order – called serial practice. This could include working on alternate sides of the body when developing kayak rolling skills, or any other bilateral skill, rather than focusing only on the dominant side. The learner has to work out the skill each time they try it, so their cognitive involvement is increased, which in turn will enhance both retention and transfer.

To reap the maximum benefits of retention and transfer, you could further increase the cognitive element of learning and use a random practice structure. Here, the learner practises the skill being developed but among other skills in an unpredictable order. This is also the most realistic practice environment for many activities within adventure education. Learners benefit from an increased ability to retain the skill and transfer it to other situations – vital when they are being prepared for independent activity. When developing navigational skills, for example, you might practise aiming off, use of the overrun feature (for example, 'If you reach "x", you have gone too far'), and timing/pacing in a random order. Or you might choose a practice area that will teach the learner different skills randomly. Examples are a mogul field for skiers (where they will learn a variety of turns), kayaking through white water, canoe polo and other game-related activities.

You need to realise, though, that it will take longer to see performance improvement in the skill you want to develop when the learner has other skills to consider at the same time, so careful time planning is needed. You should also assess your group and their readiness to cope with a random environment. Make the most of the opportunities your environment offers for random practice and utilise them, rather than overstructuring the activities you plan.

Mental practice: what is it and why is it important?

Mental practice is practising a skill in your head without physically completing the task. It can be a very useful tool in the learning process, but few coaches and even fewer adventure educators seem to utilise it. Admittedly, there is no substitute for physical practice of a skill; but if mental practice is used alongside physical practice, the learner is likely to make more rapid progress than when practising only physically. Learners also develop mental skills that help in performance preparation, problem-solving and coping with emotions.

Mental practice can be used to support physical practice by:

- Thinking through the movement you are about to execute before actually doing it – i.e. mental rehearsal – which helps the concentration and encourages more focused use of the physical trial. Mental rehearsal is a beneficial way to use off-task time, when waiting for a turn.
- Thinking through different aspects of problems and performance, planning 'what-ifs' or even working out and rehearsing the best choice of route. Thinking forward to imagine what the terrain will look like on a walking expedition can prepare learners to pick up on relevant cues within that environment.
- Picturing how a movement feels or what it looks like on completion to enhance the physical execution of the skill. The more vivid the picture, the better!
- Encouraging the learner to relive a good trial in their head, as 'best performance imagery'. This consolidates the learning and helps confidence. Learning to relive good performances is helpful later, when faced with risk, to assist in overcoming the 'I can't do it' feeling and support the development of skills to overcome cognitive dissonance (discussed in Chapter 2).

It is important, though, to check what your learners are mentally practising. People tend to relive only things they have done wrong, so you need to encourage them to keep mental practice positive to get the benefits. Mental practice can help form a direct link to the achievement of the goals of a session for the learner and helps facilitate success and the management of emotions within more risky activities.

94

Jane Lomax

Constraint-led practice

The dynamic systems approach (Davids *et al.*, 2008) to learning opens up more possible practice conditions that are particularly pertinent within adventure education work. Here, controlled and skilful movements are thought to emerge from the interaction between the person, the environment and the task, and learning is supported by becoming better at spotting opportunities within the environment to carry out physical moves.

You need to provide a clear goal and a safe practice environment to allow learners to explore the movements and use self-discovery to help develop the desired behaviours. You also need to manipulate the task, the environment and what you ask the learners to do to mould the learning. This provides a very different practice structure and leadership style from the reliance on instructions and demonstrations discussed earlier in this chapter. Most adventure activities provide a rich variety of environmental constraints to manipulate, and choosing the right environment to practise the skills that the learner is ready to attempt is already an integral part of all adventure coaches' planning. Utilisation of task and organismic constraints in addition is a relatively easy next step. For example:

- *Task constraint:* use of different paddles or poles to explore paddling skills; blindfold/eyes-shut tasks within team-building activities or skill-related work.
- *Organismic constraint:* use of different parts of the hand when bouldering; using only one side of the body at a time.
- *Environmental constraint:* use of a very slow current to develop ferry-gliding skills so the learner explores angling the boat to move across the water to a given point; choice of aspect within skiing to provide opportunities for a variety of turn sizes.

OBSERVATION AND ANALYSIS

Observing the learner's progress and analysing their movements to work out what they can do and where they need help are more 'bread-and-butter' skills for you. Whichever skill you are coaching, have a mental checklist of what the skill should look like when it is executed effectively. This provides a reference of correctness against which to compare what the learner is doing and allows you to assess whether they are competent in the skills they need before you send them away to work independently.

Initially, value judgements should be kept out of your observation of the learner. Look at their attempts a number of times and try to identify any trends. Also observe them from a variety of positions, as different views can provide different information.

Once you have observed the learner, you can analyse their performance, assess improvement and identify which elements match the template and which do not. Then decide what to do with the information. Positively reinforce what the learner is doing correctly and assess how to develop their performance when they are missing the mark. Here you will need to decide how much information to feed back to the learner and what form that feedback will take.

If adopting an athlete-centred approach (Kidman, 2005), you may ask the performers themselves to decide what they are doing well and what they would like to work on next. This allows you to check your own observations but also develops each learner's independence by increasing their self-awareness. If you adopt a more coach-centred style, you may well take the opportunity to give the learner more direct feedback. Coaches could opt to supplement their observations with video analysis to enhance self-awareness, but the dynamic nature of the adventure environment often precludes this. Using your observations and analysis to inform the feedback process is an important step in guiding your learners. Now decide whether you will elicit feedback from the performer or guide them yourself more directly. Learners benefit from quality feedback, particularly in the early stages of learning.

FEEDBACK

Feedback is any information that may be received either during a task or after its completion (McMorris and Hale, 2006). Performers can obtain feedback from two main sources – intrinsic and extrinsic.

Intrinsic feedback is any information relating to their performance that the performer gains from their own senses – feelings, sounds and visual stimuli. Performers can often see what has happened as a result of their efforts: for instance, whether they made the cut-off time during a navigation exercise, or what their tracks in the snow looked like when they were skiing. This provides knowledge of results. Learners can also gain knowledge of performance by recognising where a task went right or wrong. For instance, when assessing why a route was not completed in time, they might look at how much attention they paid during the planning, whether the roles were clearly identified and performed, and where the amount of time needed was underestimated. You can support learners by helping them raise their awareness of intrinsic sources of information. Ask them to consider the sound a ski makes on the snow, the feel of a paddle entering the water, or the crispness of a movement's execution, or to record physical features during a navigational leg (often called 'ticking off features').

Extrinsic feedback is any feedback received from an external source, mostly you, although others sources (such as peers) are available too. You may be able to make any number of points, but you should be selective: prioritise and choose the most important point for the performer at that moment in time.

Extrinsic feedback is most effective when you:

■ Give participants a little time to work out what happened for themselves before giving them feedback. Giving feedback immediately after a task may interfere with the learner's ability to process it.

96

Jane Lomax

Figure 5.2 The coach provides manual support for the participant to help them get in touch with their intrinsic feedback

- Link the feedback directly to what you asked the participant to do.
- Use the matches found in your analysis to give positive reinforcement to the participant about any aspects they are doing well.
- Use the mismatches to highlight no more than one or two points that the participant would benefit most from focusing on during their next few tasks.
- Be specific about your feedback, with enough detail to meet the performer's needs – 'good' is inadequate, because the performer needs to know specifically which aspect was good.
- Give the performer time to digest the feedback before giving more information, such as details of the next task.

How often and when should you give feedback?

It is a challenge to get the right balance between letting participants work through their own mistakes and stepping in to help. In a navigational task, for example, you may be faced with a group that is getting increasingly lost, so you will have to decide how long to allow them to get back on the route themselves, forever mindful of health and safety issues. Perhaps you know that one member of the group forgot their map, so do you tell them to go back for it or let them work through it on their own?

If feedback is given after every attempt, marked improvement should take place during the session. This often occurs in one-on-one sessions. However, giving feedback this frequently tends to prevent learners from developing their own ability to detect errors and work out solutions for themselves, so the end result will be learners who are dependent on you for their feedback. Of course, this is not very helpful if your aim is to prepare them for independent work. Where you give feedback less frequently – i.e. after a number of trials or to summarise a series of practice attempts – learning can be enhanced and coach dependency avoided.

Working out how often to give feedback is difficult, but bandwidth feedback can help here. This allows the participant's performance to determine the frequency of feedback. Set in your mind an acceptable level of error around the target movement – this can be quite precise for advanced performers and relatively broad for the less experienced. Whether you give feedback will then depend on performance: those who fall within the acceptable error band do not receive feedback, which allows you to concentrate on those making significant errors. This can happen quite naturally when working with larger groups, where you find yourself drawn to helping the weaker performers. However, make sure your participants realise what you are doing – otherwise, your better performers may think they are being short-changed.

Communicating feedback

Adventure education normally has a personal and social agenda, and the manner in which you choose to elicit or provide feedback will have powerful messages (both hidden and overt) about whose opinions are important. It is really important to keep feedback positively phrased so that the learner's confidence is gradually increased. It is a mistake to think a coach's job is to tell people what they are doing wrong and then help them to put it right. No matter how well intentioned or technically correct this is, over time such an approach to giving feedback can lead to increased anxiety and decreased confidence. Some texts suggest a 'Big Mac' or a 'sandwich' approach to giving feedback: start with reinforcing the good points (matches from analysis), then give the performer a positively phrased, specific focus to develop performance (derived from the highest-priority mismatch), and finish on a note of encouragement to keep working.

To adopt a more learner-centred approach, use questioning skills to get the participant to identify the strengths of their performance and what they need to work on to improve. This empowers performers to work things out for themselves and develop their own decision-making, which then impacts positively on their self-confidence and perceptions of competence. This is invaluable when preparing participants for independent work and for achieving many adventure education goals beyond the performance-specific ones.

98
Jane Lomax

EVALUATING AND REFLECTING ON THE SESSION

The development of your reflective skills is an important element of coaching and is also the main thrust of the Institute of Outdoor Learning accreditation scheme. Chapters 6 and 7 give detailed insights into the skills of reflection and evaluation, but for coaches it is really important to reflect on each session and utilise those reflections to inform the development of the next coaching session. You need to identify what went well, what you would like to change and how you would like to change it. It helps to keep notes of these reflections so you can refer back to them at a later date. Consider involving others in this process to supplement your own reflections. Perhaps ask the participants themselves or others who have been around your session – for example, parents if working with youngsters, co-coaches or other professionals. It is always interesting to see the correlation between your own reflections and those of others – often a very rich source of ideas.

USING GOAL-SETTING PRINCIPLES WITHIN YOUR COACHING

The use of goal-setting principles is fundamental to providing an effective learning environment. Goal setting underpins so many aspects of adventure education that you will encounter it within several other chapters, too. It provides a focus for the session itself and for each task's progression. Where these goals are agreed with the participant(s), it also helps to engage participants and enhances motivation.

Most of the literature agrees that making the goals specific is crucial to success, with measurable goals infinitely preferable to 'do-your-best' goals (Weinberg and Gould, 2003). Goals should challenge the learners but be achievable in order to build up a bank of successful experiences and hence have a positive impact on self-confidence and self-efficacy. Positively phrased goals help learners know what to focus on and what they need to do to achieve the task. This is much more helpful than goals that ask participants to avoid doing something.

There are 'outcome', 'performance' and 'process' goals. Outcome goals relate to beating others and winning by being fastest, climbing highest or getting down first, for example. They are very useful to develop a competitive environment when this is desirable. However, over-reliance on outcome goals can create problems, such as increasing anxiety and reducing self-confidence, as there will be only one 'winner' and many factors will be out of the participant's control. To get the benefits of outcome goals without these disadvantages, you need to underpin their use with performance and process goals, which are progressively more under the participant's control (Weinberg and Gould, 2003).

Performance goals identify a specific time/distance or frequency of completing task elements for which the participant can aim. They should be underpinned with process goals – what the participant needs to focus on – which could be specific coaching points you have raised, the intensity of work you are after or how well the group is working together. You may want your learners to 'work better as a group', but to achieve this you may need some sub-goals, such as 'be more tolerant' or 'agree our roles before starting the task'. Where the desired goals relate to such affective developments within group processes or social issues, you may need to set some technical goals to break down these affective goals into specific aspects of the task. This has an added benefit of giving more structure to your reflections and evaluations, and it also gives your participants more control.

A session that values and supports the achievement of process and performance goals is likely to encourage the participants to improve their own performance and create a 'mastery climate', whereas a greater focus on outcome goals encourages participants to compare themselves against others and has an ego orientation. A mastery environment should ensure your participants enjoy a more stable development in self-confidence and are more in control of any anxieties than overly emphasised outcome goals. Where time and numbers of participants permit, agreeing goals with your participants, rather than imposing them, improves feelings of self-determination and autonomy. This is particularly helpful when working over a longer time-frame, when short-term goals will need to build into mid- and then long-term ones.

MOTIVATION – UNDERSTANDING THE PEOPLE WITH WHOM YOU ARE WORKING

Adventure educators can enhance their role by recognising the reasons why participants are in front of them and their range of individual needs. To be effective, you need to match the approach you use with the motivations of the participants. Participants may come with myriad reasons for undertaking the course, ranging from 'to have fun' and 'to try something new' through to serious competitors. Meeting the needs of each group and the individuals within it will depend on the coach's ability to set a motivational climate that engages and sustains interest in all of them.

You might meet four broad categories of individuals:

1   Those who want to improve their own skill set and are not interested in how good they are when measured against others – high task, low ego orientation.
2   Those driven by being the best or better than others within the group; the technical aspects of the work are a means to an end rather than an end in itself – high ego, low task orientation. These individuals love competitive activities.
3   Those highly motivated to improve their own performance *and* to outperform others – high task, high ego orientation.
4   Those not really interested in improving their skill set or being better than others. These are the most challenging participants – low task, low ego orientation. Examples include youngsters who are disaffected in school or even children dropped off by parents who are really after a holiday child-minding service.

100

The emphasis you place on the different types of goals influences the motivational climate of your session and will give powerful messages to your learners relating to what you feel is important. Emphasis on outcomes will encourage an ego orientation, whereas emphasis on personal improvement will encourage a task orientation or mastery climate. The former is quite unstable and should be used with caution, but some learners will thrive on it. The latter is more likely to encourage long-term participation with more stable growth of self-confidence and reduction of anxiety as more is under the participant's control. You need to find the right balance for your groups and the individuals within those groups.

OTHER MOTIVATIONAL TOOLS

Understanding the link between intrinsic and extrinsic motivation

To obtain long-term participation, encourage love of an activity – i.e. intrinsic motivation. When this wanes, you can use extrinsic motivators to help top up motivation by providing rewards from a number of sources, either by encouragement from you (prizes, monetary rewards and so on) or, for those within the 'sport' side of adventure activities, by selection to different levels of performance. However, if the extrinsic motivator is used too much, it runs the risk of taking control and undermining the intrinsic motivation it was introduced to support. So you need to balance your use of rewards to keep the focus firmly on intrinsic motivation to maintain your learners' involvement in the activity over a period of time.

Utilising feelings of self-determination and autonomy

This is central to experiential learning. Most motivation literature agrees that learners will be more engaged in their activity and exhibit higher levels of effort and persistence if they are involved in their own learning. This has implications for your choice of coaching and communication styles. An autocratic approach will be helpful at times, but the focus is on you for the learning, whereas other styles give your participant responsibilities and you can question and draw out the learning from them. This will have a more powerful effect on their feelings of self-determination and autonomy. As a result, their attributions for success and failure will be more positive and they will experience higher levels of satisfaction and self-confidence.

Understanding yourself

It is helpful to understand what aspirations you have for your coaching and what brought you to your current work situation. Many coaches have admirable reasons for coaching and do it for the participants' benefit, but others try to achieve their own dreams through their participants' success, which can lead to high levels of frustration for performers and coaches alike. You need to identify your aspirations and then match these to those of the group you are working with; and you must be prepared to make compromises to ensure the match is a positive one.

COMMUNICATING EFFECTIVELY

The ability to communicate effectively underpins all other aspects of facilitation. Sound knowledge and enthusiasm are wasted if you have difficulty communicating with participants. Communication is generally a two-way process, so it is about giving good instructions and demonstrations *and* receiving information effectively. Good listening skills and the ability to use questioning appropriately to draw information from participants are therefore important, and often neglected, parts of the skill set necessary for effective coaching.

Communication skills are tested from the outset of a session, when participants need to be engaged with the activity. An ability to build a rapport with participants is crucial to setting the tone of the session. The coach's passion will be very clearly communicated, and first impressions are often powerful and difficult to recover from when we get them wrong.

Use of verbal and non-verbal communication skills

We have already explored the concept of clarity within the words we use, but tone of voice and behaviour are even more powerful elements in communication. Between 50 and 75 per cent of information is conveyed via non-verbal communication (Weinberg and Gould, 2003), so you need to monitor this to ensure it complements rather than conflicts with your verbal instructions. Otherwise, you might give participants mixed messages. Pay attention to your posture, gestures and how close you stand to people when working with them.

Receiving messages effectively – use of listening skills

The two-way communication necessary for an effective coach–participant relationship means you need to be able to receive information effectively. Listen to your participants and hear what they have to say. This is usually more difficult than it seems, as time constraints often make speaking with each individual participant a challenge.

You need to have big ears, big eyes and a little mouth!

Questioning skills become a natural part of the process when you are genuinely interested in the participants and their development. Asking questions in a manner that requires the participant to think and work things out for themselves in a positive, non-threatening

102

environment is an art and takes practice. Positive engagement can be encouraged by asking 'What?', 'How?', 'How much?' and 'When?', and by the use of 'Tell me about . . .'. Avoid 'Why?' as much as possible, as it regularly comes across as accusatory and participants can often feel they have done something wrong. Some questions are designed to stimulate the participant to do the thinking and the solution-finding for a problem, and you may not always require an answer. Whatever question is asked, you must be ready to listen to the answers and then act upon them.

CONCLUSION: SO, DO ADVENTURE EDUCATORS COACH?

Familiar examples relating to traditional sports and elite athletes have led to the common assumption that the coach always plays the central role in coaching. However, coaching now overlaps with other disciplines, such as teaching, facilitation and counselling. Like many other things, it has evolved, and the coach will now usually give a more central role to the learner whenever it is appropriate to do so.

Having highlighted the use of goal-setting, instructions, demonstrations, feedback, the need to understand appropriate practice environments and the motivation and communication issues faced within adventure education, I think it is clear that knowledge of coaching practices and research relating to coaching will make us all better at what we do in adventure education. However, when utilising coaching-related research, it is important to remember that adventure education is experiential education. As such, it is important to retain a broader educational perspective beyond individual technical performance and knowledge. There is empirical and theoretical support for a link between performance, knowledge and an individual's overall perception of their self. So, whilst knowledge of coaching techniques is significant, it should not be a goal in itself. Instead, think of it as a key means to achieve other, more affective goals.

REFERENCES

Banks, S.D. (2001) The Hard Look, *CoDe*, 97: 10–11.
Davids, K., Button, C. and Bennett, S. (2008) *Dynamics of Skill Acquisition: A Constraint-Led Approach*, Champaign, IL: Human Kinetics.
Fairbrother, J.T. (2010) *Fundamentals of Motor Behaviour*, Champaign, IL: Human Kinetics.
Kidman, L. (ed.) (2005) *Athlete-Centred Coaching: Developing Inspired and Inspiring People*, Christchurch, New Zealand: Innovative Print.
McMorris, T. (2004) *Acquisition and Performance of Sports Skills*, Chichester: Wiley.
McMorris, T. and Hale, T. (2006) *Coaching Science: Theory into Practice*, Chichester: Wiley.
Sibthorp, J., Paisley, K., Gookin, J. and Furman, N. (2008) The Pedagogical Value of Student Autonomy in Adventure Education, *Journal of Experiential Education*, 31 (2): 136–151.
Weinberg, R.S. and Gould, D. (2003) *Foundations of Sport and Exercise Psychology*, Champaign, IL: Human Kinetics.

Weiss, M.R., McCullagh, P., Smith, A.L. and Berlant, A.R. (1998) Observational Learning and the Fearful Child: Influence of Peer Models on Swimming Skill Performance and Psychological Responses, *Research Quarterly for Exercise and Sport*, 69 (4): 380–394.

Wikeley, F. and Bullock, K. (2006) Coaching as an Educational Relationship, in Jones, R.L. (ed.) *The Sports Coach as Educator: Re-conceptualising Sports Coaching*, London: Routledge.

CHAPTER SIX

EVALUATING ADVENTURE EDUCATION EXPERIENCES

THE OUTSIDE VIEW

Malcolm Thorburn and Aaron Marshall

INTRODUCTION

How to convert experiential learning gains into authentic records of student achievement is a far from straightforward matter. Often adding to the difficulty of connecting learning and achievement is the adverse influence of unsupported claims and lack of demonstrable methods. To try to limit this happening in adventure education, we draw upon the advice of Dewey (1938), who highlights how teaching should be informed by a focus on both learning process and learning outcomes. To exemplify these methods in action, we detail how adventure educators could feasibly devise experiential teaching and learning approaches that enable authentic assessments to take place. In developing our arguments, we provide various activity-specific examples of the methods recommended in practice.

We share a similar view on learning as described in Chapter 7, in that we agree on the need to establish practical ways in which adventure educators can place students at the centre of the learning process. However, we also argue that including assessment as part of learning is a necessary feature of sound educational practice. We consider that if outdoor learning experiences are going to play a key role in a student's education, assessment of learning needs to be clear and demonstrable. Through extended references to the work of philosopher of education John Dewey, we outline how the nature of experience and the process of reflection should be measurable as well as meaningful. So, assessment thinking needs to begin when teachers review their aims and begin their planning. It should not be considered as an end-of-course procedure once learning has 'finished'. As such, accurate assessment of learning is a vital component of the education chain that links aims, planning and outcomes with records of achievement. Our task is therefore to explain and exemplify how assessment can become part of this chain in ways that make the most of experiential learning opportunities outdoors.

This is an important matter, as not all educational ideas are necessarily good. Often, educational discussions can be influenced by unsupported beliefs and untested methods. As Matthews (2003: 61) notes, 'in the absence of a verifiable method of data based decision making, teachers and school administrators are left with unsupported beliefs, anecdotal experiences and/or current sociopolitical philosophizing regarding the value of various educational practices'. In schools, there are often discussions about how lowering class sizes will lead to greater student learning gains; about how 'brain gym' exercises might achieve similar improvements; and about how drinking more water is a good idea. However, frequently, when you analyse the details of these claims, you find that there is a lack of research or verifiable method informing teachers' views. Consequently, unsupported arguments are often advanced for, say, reducing class sizes (even by just a few students), even though there are good grounds for being sceptical about whether this will create real opportunities for learning gains (rather than just ameliorate teachers' workload concerns). And so it continues. Time, effort, money and the attentions of politicians and policy-makers are all directed towards something that, in essence, might not be a particularly convincing educational achievement issue in the first place.

We want to avoid such pitfalls in education generally, and specifically in adventure education. We want good ideas and clear thinking to triumph over poor ideas and the perpetuation of educational myths and half truths. However, there is evidence of easy thinking and consensual policy-making in adventure education as well. In Scotland, Thorburn and Allison (2010: 103–104) found that the considerable potential offered for increased outdoor learning in schools (Learning and Teaching Scotland, 2010) has yet to be adequately taken forward due to the limitations of only drawing upon research evidence that is 'not bold or radical enough in making the case for increasing levels of outdoor education'. Instead, there has been a reliance on reporting a 'familiar rhetorical narrative about the potential of outdoor learning', even though this 'fails to offer sustained leadership and curriculum and pedagogical insight about how a change agenda could be enacted' (Thorburn and Allison, 2010: 104). This is a poor situation: invited educationalists and policy-makers ruminating on how outdoor and adventure learning is a good idea at a time when on-the-ground improvements and examples of innovative practice remain difficult to detect.

Furthermore, the quality of students' outdoor learning experiences can be let down by poor decision-making at an individual level. Thus, while it is accepted that adventure educators make extended demands on themselves through volunteering their time for travel, completing arrangements and the like, all of the above counts for little if the context for learning is poor and if the objectives chosen reflect self-interest more than the goals that are most appropriate for students. For example, if a teacher organises an expedition to the English Lake District and then chooses hill-walking objectives that reflect their own 'to-do list', rather than hills that are more suited to the prior experiences and abilities of the students, then the desirable attributes shown in planning the expedition and volunteering the additional time are undermined by poor decision-making at a crucial point in the whole enterprise. Yet, achieving such objective decision-making against criteria should be relatively straightforward. For instance, when selecting ski resorts in the Alps for a school or community group visit, the salient decision-making criteria ought to centre on how many ski runs are available on the right type of terrain for the majority of students' needs and abilities, and how close by the accommodation is (in the event of poor weather and in order

106

to reduce excessive travel time). They should not focus on superfluous criteria about where the leaders would most like to ski.

In order to try to secure more authentic learning gains, in this chapter we offer a method for assessing outcomes that will be helpful in converting outdoor learning experiences into records of student achievement. We consider this to be a matter of particular importance at this time, as many schools demand the articulation of learning with the achievement of national standards of assessment. As often as possible, we link theoretical explanations with adventure education-based activity examples in order to provide 'theory-in-action' connections. Two specific examples are referred to regularly throughout the chapter: a forest walk for primary-age students (5–11 years) and a half-day river kayak journey for secondary-age students (12–18 years). Both examples represent viable experiences for adventure educators to develop in conjunction with class teachers. We feel that they both capture the essence of adventure education in an age-appropriate and feasible manner. Briefly, the forest walk involves students visiting a forest. Once there, they have opportunities to make decisions about route planning, develop their communication skills and share responsibility when working with a partner on other navigation challenges. They also develop a sense of independence through packing their own resources and carrying a small rucksack. Students would remain in the forest for two hours before returning to school. For the kayak journey, completing a river descent comes towards the end of a physical education unit where students have practised basic kayaking skills, paddling techniques and rolls in a pool setting. Some time is also spent discussing the development of kayaking historically and as a sport. More able students are encouraged to assist those who are less experienced kayakers in an atmosphere of camaraderie. The half-day excursion represents a chance for 'real' practice on a moving river with a mix of calm water and low-level rapids. Students are expected to navigate the river and have opportunities to rerun rapids. They share packed lunches at the end of their time on the river, when they discuss their experiences before helping load the equipment and returning to school.

In summary, three main areas are discussed in this chapter:

- The contribution of Dewey in informing how a progressive critique on education can articulate with the achievement of set outcomes.
- The role of adventure educators in developing teaching and learning approaches.
- Measuring progress towards learning outcomes.

Key points include:

- The credibility of educational claims made within adventure education depends on educators taking outcomes seriously.
- Ongoing attention to the learning process will reveal connections between students and outcomes.
- Successful assessment of student achievement is ongoing and situational.

The use of experiences to acquire measurable knowledge has interested philosophers and educationalists for centuries. The contribution of Dewey (1938) has been particularly influential in this debate and is frequently cited in outdoor and adventure education literature. Through the following sections, we consider the impact of Dewey's ideas on adventure education as we seek to balance the need for flexible experiences that engage students with the need to achieve clearly measurable assessment outcomes.

DEWEY AND EQUILIBRIUM

John Dewey was frustrated by entrenched traditional and progressive movements in education at the turn of the twentieth century. Thus, he attempted to navigate a *via media* between them. At the time, the traditional position tended towards transmission approaches to learning, where the educator was responsible for handing over chunks of knowledge to students, who were responsible for memorising it and regurgitating it for exams. Dewey felt that the traditionalists attended more to subject-matter than 'the child's own experience' (Dewey, 1902: 3). Overemphasis on subject-matter limited student interest, engagement and ability to contextualise information. By contrast, progressives advocated curriculum-free learning environments where students drove the experiences and process. Though Dewey applauded progressive interest in child development and self-realisation, he criticised the way their approaches undervalued the role of the educator and the curriculum. Instead, he argued that there was a need to balance curriculum goals with the lives and experiences of students.

Like Dewey, adventure educators can also struggle to locate the balance between engaging students and achieving measurable outcomes. Often the outcomes feel burdensome – a checklist to work through that hinders the meaningful reflection gains that are possible through outdoor learning. Many adventure educators are more comfortable emphasising learning as a process rather than as transmission. On the other hand, some of what adventure educators 'teach' does require, at times, transmission of measured knowledge content – for example, adherence to and compliance with safety procedures, appreciation of risk management and so on. Furthermore, shifts in curriculum development and the availability of finance suggest that outdoor and adventure programmes are likely to face increasing pressure to articulate alignment with more clearly identifiable, measurable curriculum outcomes. For example, under the new Curriculum for Excellence (CfE) guidelines in Scotland (Scottish Government, 2008), it is expected that outdoor learning experiences can feasibly articulate with age and stage national standards in health and wellbeing, literacy and numeracy. Under these arrangements, all teachers of students between three and 18 years have a responsibility to make feasible curriculum connections. As we note more fully later, similar ambitions are planned for England as well.

Within adventure education, students are expected to develop some capacities that are easily measured and some which are not. These are sometimes referred to as 'hard' and

Malcolm Thorburn and Aaron Marshall

'soft' skills. Acquisition of these skills reflects the agendas of both traditional and progressive approaches. For example, hard skills (such as paddling techniques and adjusting a climbing harness) tend to be taught by direct teaching methods, while soft skills (such as increasing self-confidence and working as part of a group) tend to be pursued through more student-centred teaching approaches. Consequently, adventure educators share a keen interest in the equilibrium Dewey sought, given their desire to achieve both sets of aims in meaningful, measurable ways.

Though it can seem an imposition, adventure educators can and should find ways to validate their educational claims as good practice and for curriculum inclusion. Traditionally, assessment in adventure education has focused on the more easily measurable hard skills, whereas soft skills have been somewhat neglected because they are more difficult to assess. Adventure educators recognise that this is a problem, because they know that hard skills and knowledge learning comprise only part of the whole educational picture. Therefore, the outstanding issue is how assessment approaches that capture learning gains might be measured, so that unsupported claims in the soft skills arena are not unnecessarily

Figure 6.1 Assessing technical, 'hard' skills is generally more straightforward than assessing 'soft' skills

advanced. Even though there are good grounds for believing that adventure education develops soft skill capacities, there is a big difference between having a justified belief and being able to prove that you are justified in believing it (Alston, 1976). Showing that curricular goals have been met helps validate programme claims; and this is true for both hard and soft skill claims. In this respect, having clear, measurable outcomes to work towards can be seen as advantageous rather than as a time-consuming bureaucratic burden. Furthermore, undertaking more reliable forms of assessment can inform an ongoing cycle of continued gains in method and pedagogy insight.

DEWEY AND EDUCATIONAL THEORY

Dewey employed two interrelated principles to navigate a middle way: continuity and interaction. The principle of continuity argues that learning is a fluid process. Dewey (1938) observed that, outside of formal education, students naturally integrate past and present experiences. A student's understanding of the world is therefore constantly developing and adjusting. Thus, Dewey recognised the need to connect curriculum to learning that is already under way. His second principle, interaction, points to the interplay between what he called the 'objective' and 'internal' conditions of experience. For Dewey, objective conditions comprise the aims and content of the experience. Within adventure education, these might include such skills as building a campfire and setting up a belay system, recognition of various plant species and understanding the principles of low-impact camping, along with aims relating to personal and social development, such as improved self-confidence and leadership skills. In addition to these objective gains, Dewey was concerned with the student's internal conditions – their unique mental map of the world. Consequently, he aimed to engage students in educational experiences (objective conditions), beginning from their foundation of past experiences and perceptions (internal conditions). By deploying the principles of continuity and interaction, he was able to preserve learning as a process whilst still aiming to achieve predetermined outcomes.

For adventure educators, skill- and knowledge-related outcomes are fairly straightforward. Personal and social development outcomes, however, are often difficult to articulate. Given the explicit claims found within adventure education regarding personal and social development, we think it is important to identify more precisely what adventure educators are aiming at (Allison and Von Wald, 2010). Largely borrowing from Aristotelian categories, personal and social development within adventure education is most often understood as the development of *phronesis*, or practical wisdom/reasoning. Through challenging experiences, students are expected to make meaningful gains in their ability to apply the right skills (*techne*), knowledge (*episteme*) and practical reasoning (*phronesis*) critically, in the right way, at the right times. Experiences that afford significant responsibility and choice encourage students towards active deliberation, discernment and decision-making. Furthermore, students learn through the consequences associated with their decisions, and those consequences lead to new choices. Personal and social development is perhaps

110

most usefully understood, therefore, as the student's increasing ability to apply practical reasoning, individually and in social settings; and making wise personal judgements as well as positively contributing to group deliberation and decision-making (Allison and Wurdinger, 2005; Stonehouse et al., 2009).

It appears to us that adventure educators should be curious about students' prior experiences when teaching skills, knowledge and personal growth. For, like Dewey, adventure educators must embrace both the objective and internal conditions of knowledge in a way that balances process and outcome. Objective conditions give shape to the learning process. As designer and guide, the adventure educator is centrally responsible for developing experiences that meaningfully guide learners towards outcomes. Awareness of these mutually dependent principles – continuity and interaction – challenges the educator to 'survey the capacities and needs of the particular set of individuals' and, simultaneously, to 'arrange the conditions which provide the subject-matter or content for experiences that satisfy these needs and develop these capacities' (Dewey, 1938: 18, 24). Adventure educators therefore need to accept responsibility for creating learning experiences that engage students' internal conditions and can achieve measurable (and often predetermined) objectives.

Table 6.1 Dewey's objective and internal conditions exemplified through a forest walk and kayak journey

Dewey's Principles		Forest Walk	Kayak Journey
Objective Conditions	Development of particular skills	Making decisions about route planning	Paddling techniques; Eskimo roll; stability techniques
	Acquisition of a particular body of knowledge	Assessing different terrains for safe travel; group safety issues when in a forest	Safety considerations; brief historical understanding of kayaking
	Personal and social development	Being responsible in the forest; working as part of a team on group tasks; improving independence on personal tasks	Confidence & self-reliance; cooperative spirit among students; teacher–student relational depth
Internal Conditions	Collection of past experiences, perceptions, and understanding of the world	Unease about being quiet in the forest; concerns about the darkness in the forest; inter-class tensions; out-of-school home issues	Fears of drowning; confidence in water; interpersonal issues with classmates; disinterested participants; students dealing with significant issues at home
	Expectations for the current experiences	Excitement about local travel; link to classwork; a treat	Something different from 'normal' school; social excursion

1 1 1

Consider these Deweyian principles in the forest walk and kayak journey examples. Note the challenge facing adventure educators to encourage students towards meaningful and measurable gains given the diverse sets of internal conditions brought to a given experience.

LEARNING AND ASSESSMENT IN ACTION

Answering Dewey's challenge requires a shift in focus from 'how outcomes can be assessed' to 'how planning and process can aid learning'. When this shift is achieved, the assessment of outcomes becomes more straightforward for students and educators alike, as essentially assessment will have become part of learning. Seaman and Coppens (2006) argue that one way to achieve this shift is to set aside the hard/soft skill distinction and adopt a situational perspective on learning. To some extent, this might initially seem counterproductive as the distinction separates the easily measured elements of experience (hard skills) from those that are more difficult to measure (soft skills). However, Seaman and Coppens found, for instance, that participants involved in learning and practising belaying (hard skill) were also involved in personal considerations, such as emotion management, and social considerations, such as building trust (soft skills). This interconnectedness (typical of many adventure education activities) makes continuing with hard/soft skill distinctions problematic.

Given the natural linkage between hard and soft skills, Seaman and Coppens (2006) argue that assessment in adventure education ought to reflect hard and soft competences. Competences are best measured continually, in view of the capacity of feedback from assessments to inform teaching. Assessment at the end of a block of teaching and learning does not have this advantage. Additionally, ongoing assessment enables the integration of cognitive, physical, emotional and social domains of learning to be assessed. Consider the two examples highlighted in the introduction to this chapter.

On the forest walk, primary students' experience of forests as special places is enhanced by such things as making route-finding decisions alone, with a partner and in groups, and taking individual and group responsibility for packing and carrying equipment. All these experiences are designed to engage students holistically as they connect with cognitive, psychomotor, emotional and social domains of learning. Such an approach recognises that learning is not passive, but rather a complex process that is framed by students' previous related learning experiences, preferred modes of learning, the context for learning and the nature of the tasks involved. As such, assessment is not narrowly limited to teachers' observations of a few aspects of learning. Instead, assessment plans (as we exemplify later) set out to generate a first-person narrative, with tasks set reflecting the breadth and depth of experiential learning in the respective domains of learning.

Therefore, on the kayaking journey, students' ability to respond appropriately to the demands on the river is viewed in conjunction with their prior kayaking experiences, emotional disposition, social engagement and so on. Assessment emphasises holism and authenticity, especially when compared with a hard/soft skill checklist that might test

112

Figure 6.2 Students who respond appropriately when navigating river challenges may well be demonstrating practical reasoning skills as well as technical proficiency

students only in terms of following safety protocols and applying different paddle strokes. The shift to such a perspective considers that a checklist approach is incomplete as it fails to assess the personal and social development characteristics that so many in adventure education claim to value. In both cases, two crucial questions should inform the planning process: what are the anticipated outcomes of the experience and how can the experiences capture students' internal conditions and motivate them towards achieving outcomes? Planning on this basis means that learning and assessment are 'situated' – based on the actual experiences students have had. We discuss each of these questions in the next section.

On the one hand, individual improvement in hard skills and knowledge learning is easily assessed when the adventure educator observes technique proficiency and quizzes orally, or through written exams, with objective or short-answer responses. However, this still fails to offer the robust picture of education desired by a holistic approach to adventure education. Drawing on the philosophical influences of Aristotle and McIntyre, Brinkmann (2007) analyses the merits of a situational approach with a focus on practical reason. Students who develop the ability to detach themselves somewhat from their desires, imagine realistic outcomes and make effective practical judgements exhibit practical reasoning. From an assessment perspective, evaluating a student's capacity for practical reasoning incorporates the objective measures of hard skill and knowledge learning assessment whilst also measuring soft skill gains. Returning to the kayaking journey, students who respond appropriately when navigating river challenges may well be showing more than technical proficiency. Through Brinkmann's grid of practical reasoning, the adventure educator may be able to identify a level of self-detachment in the student's ability to imagine realistic outcomes rationally and make effective practical judgements in spite of such distractions as adrenalin and fear. However, the student's successful navigation of the river does not alone indicate an increase in practical reasoning. All that is clear, at first glance, is the student's technical proficiency. It is not evident that they had any internal dispositions from which to self-detach; nor is it evident that they executed the practical judgement from a variety of other imagined options. Specifically, the situational assessment-based reflections from the student are necessary in order to assess the process by which practical judgements occurred. It falls to the adventure educator to develop experiences with embedded periods of individual and group reflection, so that students can be adequately assessed. Furthermore, as will be more fully discussed later, authentic assessment depends on students' abilities to apply competences appropriately in action and through ongoing reflection. The ability to do this competently reveals an increase in students' practical reasoning.

As we have tried to highlight so far, putting into practice how outcomes can be achieved through adopting a progressive educational critique places considerable planning responsibilities on the educator. Therefore, next we examine these responsibilities and discuss why teachers need to be equipped with a suitable planning vocabulary in order to make sense of curriculum arrangements. Finally, we consider the implications of good planning for teaching and learning, and for the assessment of outcomes.

THE ROLE OF ADVENTURE EDUCATORS IN DEVELOPING TEACHING AND LEARNING APPROACHES

Key points:

- Thoughtful and considered planning (rather than blind faith) is needed in outlining how outdoor education programmes link to outcomes and domains of learning.
- Adventure educators need to accept professional responsibility for designing curriculum experiences.
- Some forms of facilitated learning encourage reflection more than other approaches.

In taking our planning ideas forward, we begin by highlighting how outdoor education programmes could contribute in rich and extended ways to the domains of learning (cognitive, affective and psychomotor) identified by Bloom (1956) in his influential writings on educational objectives. Bloom's taxonomy has been widely referenced and adapted in the years since it was written, as it is considered a helpful and straightforward way to measure and classify types and levels of learning. Our explanations and examples adapt Bloom's original taxonomy of educational objectives by separately defining 'personal' and 'social' objectives within the 'affective' domain. We consider this a good idea for two reasons. First, it is helpful in indicating how the achievement of personal practical wisdom can benefit others in a shared decision-making societal sense. Second, pedagogically, quite how to achieve affective objectives benefits from a finer-grained analysis of the types of situated learning experiences that can most readily articulate with precise personal and social objectives. Additionally, it is worth appreciating that there has been recent unease that some interpretations of progressive and holistic education are emerging around a new, revised code of 'personalisation' in education, but with the driver for personalised learning being contemporary marketing theory rather than education theory (Hartley, 2007).

Note the types of planning issues adventure educators might consider for a forest walk:

- Which local forests are most suitable (situationally) for learning?
- Identifying forest experience (learning processes) that reflect objectives in the different domains of learning.
- Linking objectives with age and stage curriculum requirements.
- Planning for inclusion and differentiation – how can forest navigation experiences engage all students (facilitate learning) but also contain 'headroom' to stretch students of different abilities?

And which they might consider for a kayak journey:

- Which local rivers are most suitable (situationally) for learning (bearing in mind the practical ability and confidence differences within the group)?
- Linking previous pool-based learning with river-based objectives in the different domains of learning.
- Linking wider objectives across the school curriculum and value requirements.
- How can challenge and perseverance be reflected in the river journey, for example through opportunities to rerun rapids?

CURRICULUM CONSTRAINTS AND OPPORTUNITIES

It has to be acknowledged that curriculum arrangements in schools often make planning difficult. A common problem is that there is tension between empowering teachers to make full use of their inspirational teaching abilities while also at fixed points requiring that students can successfully complete specified outcomes covering various age and stage national examination requirements. This, coupled with teachers' planning being subject to quality assurance scrutiny both within school and during external school inspection visits, often adds to the challenge of ensuring that schooling and curriculum constraints do not overtake possible learning opportunities. It is necessary to have adventure educators who are intrigued about how learning can be 'designed' rather than 'delivered', and are prepared to accept a reasonable degree of professional responsibility for creating the best opportunities for learning that apply in their particular employment settings. Those waiting for curriculum support materials to be available for immediate download are underestimating the responsibilities required of a professional educator nowadays.

DEFINING ACHIEVABLE OBJECTIVES

In linking the domains of learning with the achievement of outcomes, securing learning gains is most likely to be dependent upon adventure educators carefully defining achievable objectives. This involves connecting the nature and essence of situated learning experiences with the age and stage of learners' development and the domains of learning. To help exemplify this connection, if you were involved in leading a ski trip with primary-age students (seven years) new to skiing, the situated context for learning would be one where simple *knowledge recall* and willingness to *receive information* were suitable cognitive and affective objectives for their stage of learning. So you might ask students to listen carefully to several mnemonics – 'skis, boots, sticks', 'hat, gloves, goggles', 'money, lift pass, packed lunch' – and try to recall them later. Making simple connections like this can help educators ask students appropriate questions, which in this instance would be based on the knowledge you wish students to receive and recall about the equipment and kit required for skiing, and their responsibility for checking that they have the items in the mnemonic.

A similar matching exercise could take place for the primary-age students (nine years) on their forest walk. For the majority of the students at the 'comprehending' (cognitive domain) and 'responding' (affective domain) stages of learning, asking them to 'distinguish' the feasibility of different route options and 'report' in class presentations on the route-finding decisions they made would be suitably challenging tasks. Adventure educators can check that the assessment task effectively connects the situated learning context with the child

Table 6.2 Appropriate active verbs for stages in the cognitive domain of learning

Evaluation	Appraise, Assess, Conclude, Criticise, Justify
Synthesis	Compose, Construct, Create, Design, Develop, Organise, Plan, Produce, Propose
Analysis	Analyse, Compare, Contrast, Debate, Distinguish, Examine, Research, Separate
Application	Apply, Choose, Discuss, Prepare, Produce, Role-play, Select, Show, Transfer
Comprehension	Distinguish, Explain, Identify, Illustrate, Report, Summarise
Knowledge	Define, Outline, List, Name, Recall, Recite

Table 6.3 Appropriate active verbs for stages in the affective domain of learning

Internalising values	Display, Practise, Question, Revise, Solve, Verify
Organisation	Arrange, Compare, Defend, Modify, Prepare
Valuing	Complete, Demonstrate, Explain, Propose, Report, Share
Responding	Assist, Conform, Present, Report
Receiving	Listen, List, Name, Recall, Reply

116

development stage by selecting an appropriate active verb for the learning stage in the 'pyramid of learning'.

Note, as students progress from the 'knowledge' to 'evaluation' stage in the cognitive domain and from the 'receiving' to the 'internalising values' stage within the affective domain that the active verbs identified as appropriate become more demanding and sophisticated. Thus, selecting suitable active verbs helps ensure that progression is part of planning and that learning and assessment are suitably challenging (yet achievable) for most students. Therefore, by the later stages of secondary schooling, most students should have progressed to becoming involved in 'analysing' (cognitive domain). Thus, continuing with the skiing example, students are likely to have progressed to comparing and contrasting the merits of different ski resorts (and will have moved on from merely remembering the equipment that they need). In completing such tasks, they should be able to resolve any task conflict that exists 'organisationally' (affective domain) and modify plans (where possible) in light of discussion.

Making accurate connections between students' age and stage expectations and the taxonomy of objectives should enable the formal outcomes of a curriculum to be met. In Scotland, the CfE policy emphasis is on achieving 3–18 years curriculum coherence with goals framed by 'four capacities'. The four key capacities are for pupils to become: successful learners, confident individuals, responsible citizens and effective contributors (Scottish Government, 2008). As we indicated earlier, similar classifications of educational intentions are being discussed in England as well, with three of these capacities (successful learners, confident individuals and responsible citizens) being identical with their Scottish equivalents (Department of Children, Schools and Families, 2009).

Table 6.4 summarises how tasks associated with the forest experience could articulate with various domains of learning and with the four capacities specified as curriculum priorities. A key point to appreciate is that while curriculum and assessment aspiration is for tasks and

Table 6.4 Connecting outdoor experiential objectives with national curriculum aims, based on a Scottish example

Task	Age/Stage	Active verb	Learning	CfE capacity
Distinguishing different types of terrain	Comprehending	Distinguish	Cognitive	Successful learner
Recording items needed for forest walk	Responding	Recording	Personal	Confident individual
Summarising responsibilities when route-finding in forest	Comprehending	Summarise	Cognitive	Responsible citizen
Class report on forest walk	Responding	Reporting	Social	Effective contributor

117

outcomes to be presented in an interrelated and holistic way (i.e. from across the different domains of learning and four capacities), if the domains and capacities have to be more individually identified for the curriculum measurement of achievement purposes, then this can be achieved.

TEACHING AND LEARNING

However, as straightforward as making the above connections sounds, there are still some thorny issues in teaching and learning in adventure education that require specific review if a progressive critique of education is going to be used to translate experiential learning gains into meaningful records of achievement. One point of difficulty is when learning environments overemphasise performance and skill development to the detriment of the achievement of a fuller range of outcomes, including personal development. When this occurs, there is often a reduction in the transfer of learning from the experiences in which students take part and an overall undervaluing of the affective attributes many students develop through outdoor learning. For example, when 'assessing' students skiing, surely adventure educators should wish to acknowledge in some way the helpfulness of students who make an effort to step back up the slope and help other skiers who have fallen. Wouldn't you?

Furthermore, Seaman and Coppens (2006) found that some adventure educators unnecessarily overplay the demands of tasks and the risk element involved in order to bolster their own powerful position as leader. When this occurs, not only are learning gains more modest, but there is the perpetuation of an unhelpful stereotype that adventurous activities are primarily the preserve of white, affluent males, with all that this entails for the marginalisation of others who are not white, male or wealthy. Suffice to say, such situations are far from beneficial. This is worth mentioning as Seaman and Coppens note that these concerns are obvious to students but sadly go unnoticed by some educators.

Of more nuanced concern is the precise role of the teacher when facilitating situated learning in outdoor environments. Stan (2009) researched the relative merits of contrasting types of facilitator approach after visiting several residential outdoor centres in England. Some adventure educators adopted a detached approach to facilitation while others took a more controlling approach. Neither was found to be satisfactory. The detached facilitator approach was criticised for its lack of focus on outcomes and for its lack of support and empathy with learners. By contrast, the controlling approach was limited through its lack of flexibility and an overemphasis on achieving outcomes through predetermined methods. The differences between these in-action practices reflect in pragmatic terms the dichotomy Dewey tried to eradicate through his *via media* – where an overemphasis on subject-matter could limit interest and engagement, and where an overemphasis on child self-realisation goals could undervalue the importance of curriculum teaching in meeting defined outcomes.

118

While we recognise that the pressure of assessment could plausibly account for (but not justify) overly controlled facilitation, it seems more surprising that a detached approach to facilitation was ever considered of merit. However, as Watts and Bentley (1991) noted during the infancy of the national curriculum in England and Wales, teachers frequently confused a 'strong' with a 'weak' version of constructivist problem-solving teaching. Strong constructivist teaching contained the capacity for offering students the structural learning support required (without being unduly constraining or lacking flexibility), while weak constructivist teaching was characterised by too much responsibility for learning being placed with learners. This happened through teachers being misguided in their belief that 'taking a step backwards' was required. A similar contrast existed when Rea (2006) researched how leaders facilitated the reflective process with 14–18-year-old students on a foreign mountaineering expedition. Most leaders were inclined towards an approach that was justified on the basis that simply 'being in the mountains' was sufficient to aid reflection. As such, much of the dialogue between leaders and students was on technical mountaineering matters and occasionally, as an add on, whether they were enjoying themselves. Even though some students, who were predisposed to the reflective process, did begin to reflect (often when walking in quiet solitude), there was a sense of wasted opportunity, especially as carefully and purposefully engaging in discourse-with-self is key in informing future planning and behaviour. For example, reviewing and reflecting upon experiences is central within Kolb's (1984) four-stage Experiential Learning model, which is widely advocated in outdoor education (Beard and Wilson, 2002).

The other apparent limitation with Rea's (2006) findings is that more proactive facilitation by leaders might have enabled greater group discussion benefits to occur. Stan (2009: 36) found that a bridge between the detached and the controlling approach was evident when one teacher adopted a 'part-of-the-team' approach to facilitating reflection and learning. In short, the teacher was able to function effectively as a co-learner or co-constructor with the students (Allison and Wurdinger, 2005). This approach was characterised by: prior discussions of tasks with students; providing support when needed (cajoling, reducing conflict, negotiating solutions); encouraging students to express their views; and the teacher identifying herself as part of the team in discussions. Thus, the teacher possessed an informed mix of both considered intentions and the added capacity to act intuitively in often fast-changing and varied situational learning contexts (Thomas, 2008). Jeff Brown provides a further example of such an approach in action.

> We spend a lot of time talking through the principles of navigating down a set of rapids, how to recognise an eddy and where the best line would be. After students have a chance to run the rapids, I paddle a bit with them and reflect on what they saw, how it felt to hit current and what they did to counter its effects. They then walk up to run this section again and implement their findings. This style of running the

119

river and then reflecting on it takes the spotlight off the instructor and allows the student to take ownership of their learning. It is in these moments that they truly begin to understand how to read the river and use the current to their advantage.

Jeff Brown, Director of Outdoor Education,
Valor Christian High School, Denver, CO

Importantly, Brown's type of refined pedagogical expertise appears capable of supporting class/group tasks as well as generating personal experiential learning gains. This matters, for as Dixon (2008) notes, many students may not feel comfortable in the standard class approach of sitting in a circle. Put simply, many of them may feel marginalised, due to a plethora of possible power, gender, culture, race and ethnicity issues. Seaman and Coppens' (2006: 26) sociocultural-informed writings urging adventure educators to enhance their 'repertoires of practice' might provide a helpful theoretical framework for more critical consideration of how personal experiential gains can become of value in a Dewey-informed, society-wide context.

Note how outcomes and the assessment process can be self-checked in the forest walk example:

■ How do outcomes reflect the authenticity of situated learning experiences – i.e. how is assessment true and meaningful for students?
■ How do outcomes include students' age and stage differences in the respective domains of learning – e.g. more creative thinkers; better at working in groups?
■ How does the assessment process capture and value the students' internal conditions (unique mental map) of their forest experiences?
■ How does the assessment process take account of students' past learning experiences in the outdoors?

And in the kayak journey example:

■ How do outcomes reflect pool- and river-based learning in ways that students can easily comprehend?
■ How do outcomes include students' age and stage differences in the respective domains of learning – e.g. more able paddlers, more confident on the river?
■ How does the assessment process capture and value the students' internal conditions of their kayaking experiences?
■ How does the assessment process take account of students' past learning experiences in the outdoors?

120

Malcolm Thorburn and Aaron Marshall

Once planning of objectives has taken place and the fine detail of best approaches for facilitating learning has been considered, what matters next is how outcomes associated with experiential learning can be authentically measured and recorded. Thus, the focus in this chapter now moves on to reviewing how learning outcomes can be feasibly measured.

MEASURING PROGRESS TOWARDS LEARNING OUTCOMES

Key points:

- Assessment should be considered as a natural part of teaching and learning.
- Adopting a first-person perspective on learning contains the methodological basis for integrating experiences, activities and knowledge.

It seems common sense to recognise that teaching, learning and assessment need to be 'in tune' with one another, a necessary part of the 'teaching–learning–assessment' triptych. Yet, we need only look at the widespread use of narrowly drawn rote approaches across education – where passing (by whatever means) is all that is required – to recognise that the imposition of externally set assessment outcomes can distort teaching and learning in counter-productive ways (Thorburn, 2007). Some adventure educators, of course, might argue that assessment is an unnecessary burden that could well be abandoned altogether. As noted earlier, however, we think otherwise and consider that learning gains need to be measurable. In school contexts particularly, being unable to measure learning and to show evidence of how it can contribute to students' overall profile or record of achievement is likely to damage adventure education's credibility to such an extent that it would merit no more than occasional curriculum inclusion. So, how best to proceed in converting experiential learning gains into authentic records of achievement? First, ensuring that assessment reflects a situational, first-person perspective on learning is required. Second (as per our forest walk and kayak journey examples), there is a need for an integrated assessment approach where multiple outcomes can be assessed holistically (and thereafter separated for curriculum outcome measurement purposes, if required).

Reflections on experiences that are generated from the first-person point of view are often referred to as 'phenomenological' in nature. A phenomenological approach is characterised by its intentions, its meaning and its sensations. Phenomenology as a discipline in continental European philosophy dates from the first half of the twentieth century, with Edmund Husserl and Maurice Merleau-Ponty the key figures in its historical development. Phenomenology-based investigations are informed by attempts to describe reality fully and to replace preconceived ideas with analysis of specific learning intentions. Therefore, a phenomenological perspective on learning contains the methodological basis for integrating experiences (thoughts, perceptions, feelings) with associated subject-knowledge meanings to achieve learning outcomes. Consequently, for explanations of experiences, a first-person form of reporting is required initially, with rich narrative description used as the basis for linking together experiences and knowledge in increasingly sophisticated and refined ways. Supported by suitably framed pedagogical approaches, this could effectively enable personal experiences to merge with subject-knowledge imperatives as long as there is recognition from adventure educators and students alike that generating such responses is helpful and necessary. The most immediate challenge, therefore, is to try to resolve pragmatic difficulties about how the essence of personal explorations can be captured, assessed and measured.

For the forest walk, the following points should be considered:

- How will the record of achievement be used in a whole-school context to profile student achievement?
- How will the record of achievement inform the next learning cycle?
- How will the record of achievement help the personal growth of students?
- How could the record of achievement from forest experiences be extended (e.g. through greater links with literacy and numeracy)?

For the kayak journey, the following points should be considered:

- How will the record of achievement be used in a whole-school context to profile student achievement?
- How will the record of achievement inform the next learning cycle?
- How will the record of achievement inform students' future curriculum choices at secondary school level and beyond?
- How can the record of achievement from the kayak journey be extended (e.g. through greater links with literacy, such as man's relationship with the outdoors through reviewing such texts as Jon Krakauer's *Into the Wild*)?

Hughson and Inglis (2002) designed a phenomenological model for exploring the relationship between students, activities and subject knowledge. The main point to appreciate is that differences in one area affect other areas. For example, a more practically able kayaker will develop a greater feeling and sensitivity for water and will consequently understand more about the flow and movements of the water. A less able kayaker will explore the same relationship but in a less sophisticated way. Thus, kayakers of different and contrasting abilities across the different domains of learning can (to a certain extent) be incorporated within the same class and taught effectively, as long as a phenomenological perspective on learning is retained. Encouragingly, we see coherent points of articulation between Brinkmann's (2007) advocacy of increasing practical reasoning in learning and an assessment-of-learning approach that emphasises a certain self-detachment and reshaping of ideas. Such an approach should help students make informed and wise judgements that display evidence of discernment, deliberation and effective decision-making. We also see

122

connections with the theoretical work of Alston (1976), who elaborated on the differences between having justified beliefs and being able to show that your beliefs are justified. Suffice to say that theoretical elaborations about currents in rivers that lack personal experiential insights would be very different to those that include such references.

Scepticism on the part of adventure educators about the merits of this approach might be assuaged by noting that, in the medical community, programmes for the education of doctors blend experiential learning with more theoretical approaches (Claxton, 1997). The intention is that by including reflections in discussions as part of teaching and learning, student doctors can begin to comment on their 'hunches' and 'feelings' about what works best. In these environments, 'the intuitive component of diagnosis either helps to limit the range of possibilities, so that a more manageable analytical approach may be adopted, or it leads to the early generation of hypothesis' (Brawn, 2000: 158). It is argued that such a methodological focus reduces the risk of students generating fabricated or imaginary versions of experiences. This is an important matter as it is to be expected that assessment records can be used for the measurement of continued gains over time. These should be helpful for educators in showing that levels of assessable learning are improving, useful for the personal growth of students and useful for informing the next learning cycle. Note how the effectiveness of records of achievement could be self-checked in the forest walk and kayak journey examples.

CONCLUSION

In this chapter, we have presented methods-based arguments about how experiential learning outdoors can connect with students' generation of authentic records of achievement. We have reviewed the contribution of Dewey, who sought to balance experiential learning processes and the achievement of meaningful and measurable outcomes through applying the principles of continuity and interaction. We have also reviewed (from a curriculum and pedagogical perspective) how adventure education should try to broaden and deepen its connections with each of the domains of learning in order that the educational substance of learning outdoors is emphasised to its fullest extent. From an assessment perspective, we have outlined how a first-person phenomenology-informed approach is viable for generating authentic records of achievement. As far as possible, we have tried to illustrate our ideas for practice in adventure education, particularly through the forest walk and kayak journey examples.

However, contexts for learning often vary widely in schools, private and voluntary organisations. So it would be useful if the possibilities for connecting experiential learning outdoors with students' records of achievement were researched further by adventure educators, with consequent data informing the extent to which our ideas might translate into a verifiable teaching, learning and assessment method. Such research could also address some of the acknowledged limitations of this chapter. We recognise, for example, that if we really wish adventure education to be an all-through (3–18 years) component of schooling, then more widely accessing the methods of assessments possible within Bloom's taxonomy is probably required. For example, with primary-age students, generating written answers may well be problematic. Thus, consideration of other assessment instruments (e.g. measurement of the cognitive domain at the 'comprehend' level by drawing and illustrating answers; and measurement of the affective domain at the 'respond' level by participating actively in group discussion) is a sound educational idea. (Chapter 7 helpfully outlines and advocates a range of possible approaches for learning and reflection.)

We also recognise that assessment through the phenomenology approach views learning in the first instance primarily from a self/emotional perspective, rather than from a group/social perspective. Therefore, a degree of new thinking is required by adventure educationalists in order that the values associated with, for example, group problem-solving can be adequately recognised when using a phenomenological approach as the learning stimulus for assessing experiential learning and measuring achievement.

REFERENCES

Allison, P. and Von Wald, K. (2010) Exploring Values in the Wilderness: PSD on Educational Expeditions, *Pastoral Care in Education*, 28 (3): 219–232.

Allison, P. and Wurdinger, S. (2005) Understanding the Power, Promise and Peril of the Experiential Learning Process, *Teacher Education and Practice*, 18 (4): 386–399.

Alston, W. (1976) Two Types of Foundationalism, *Journal of Philosophy*, 73: 165–185.

Beard, C. and Wilson, J.P. (2002) *The Power of Experiential Learning: A Handbook for Trainers and Educators*, London: Kogan Page.

Bloom, B.S. (ed.) (1956) *Taxonomy of Educational Objectives: The Classification of Educational Goals*, Handbook I: *Cognitive Domain*, New York: McKay.

Brawn, R. (2000) The Formal and Intuitive in Science and Medicine, in Atkinson, T. and Claxton, G. (eds) *The Intuitive Practitioner*, Maidenhead: Open University Press.

Brinkmann, S. (2007) Practical Reason and Positioning, *Journal of Moral Education*, 36 (4): 415–432.

Claxton, G. (1997) Science of the Times: A 20–20 Vision of Education, in Levinson, R. and Thomas, J. (eds) *Science Today: Problem or Crisis?* London: Routledge.

Department of Children, Schools and Families (2009) *Independent Review of the Primary Curriculum: Final Report (The Rose Report)*. Available online at: http://www.publications.teachernet.gov.uk/eOrderingDownload/Primary_curriculum_Report.pdf.

Dewey, J. (1902) *The Child and the Curriculum*, Chicago, IL: University of Chicago Press.

Dewey, J. (1938) *Experience and Education*, New York: Macmillan.

Dixon, T.J. (2008) Reflecting on the Experience, *Journal of Adventure Education and Outdoor Learning*, 8 (1): 21–29.

Hartley, D. (2007) Personalisation: The Emerging 'Revised' Code of Education?, *Oxford Review of Education*, 33 (5): 629–642.

Hughson, J. and Inglis, D. (2002) Accounting for Experience: Phenomenological Argots and Sportive Life-Worlds, *Indo-Pacific Journal of Phenomenology*, 2 (2): 1–10.

Kolb, D. (1984) *Experiential Learning: Turning Experience into Learning*, Englewood Cliffs, NJ: Prentice-Hall.

124

Learning and Teaching Scotland (2010) *Curriculum for Excellence through Outdoor Learning*. Available online at: http://www.ltscotland.org.uk/outdoorlearning/curriculumforexcellence/index.asp.

Matthews, W.J. (2003) Constructivism in the Classroom: Epistemology, History, and Empirical Evidence, *Teaching Education Quarterly*, Summer: 51–64.

Rea, T. (2006) 'It's Not as if We've Been Teaching Them . . .' Reflecting Thinking in the Outdoor Classroom, *Journal of Adventure Education and Outdoor Learning*, 6 (2): 121–134.

Scottish Government (2008) *Building the Curriculum 3: A Framework for Learning and Teaching*, Edinburgh: Scottish Government.

Seaman, J. and Coppens, A.D. (2006) Repertoire of Practice: Reconceptualizing Instructor Competency in Contemporary Adventure Education, *Journal of Adventure Education and Outdoor Learning*, 6 (1): 25–37.

Stan, I. (2009) Recontextualizing the Role of the Facilitator in Group Interaction in the Outdoor Classroom, *Journal of Adventure Education and Outdoor Learning*, 9 (1): 23–43.

Stonehouse, P., Allison, P. and Carr, D. (2009) Aristotle, Plato, and Socrates: Ancient Greek Perspectives on Experiential Learning, in Smith, T. and Knapp, C. (eds) *Beyond Dewey and Hahn: Standing on the Shoulders of Influential Experiential Educators*, Wisconsin: Raccoon Institute Publications.

Thomas, G. (2008) Preparing Facilitators for Experiential Education: The Role of Intentionality and Intuition, *Journal of Adventure Education and Outdoor Learning*, 8 (1): 3–20.

Thorburn, M. (2007) Achieving Conceptual and Curriculum Coherence in High-Stakes School Examinations in Physical Education, *Physical Education and Sport Pedagogy*, 12 (2): 163–184.

Thorburn, M. and Allison, P. (2010) Are We Ready to Go Outdoors Now? The Prospects for Outdoor Education during a Period of Curriculum Renewal in Scotland, *Curriculum Journal*, 21 (1): 97–108.

Watts, M. and Bentley, D. (1991) Constructivism in the Classroom: Can We Close the Gap between the Strong Theoretical Version and the Weak Version of Theory in Practice?, *Curriculum Journal*, 2 (2): 171–182.

CHAPTER SEVEN

EVALUATING ADVENTURE EDUCATION EXPERIENCES

THE INSIDE VIEW

Suzanne Everley

> The act of learning is the result of reflection upon experience.
>
> (King, 1988:4)

One of the questions you will inevitably need to ask of yourself when working in the outdoors is what your starting point is as an adventure education practitioner designing programmes for different groups of clients. Much of your orientation will inevitably be related to the immediate physical and educational context that you are working in, but over time, the reflections of your clients should have a significant impact on the way that you plan. A key question in practice here, is how you evaluate your courses so that you might improve their quality. Is your starting point the programme you want to deliver or the people you are working with?

In this chapter, I will encourage you to think about the ways in which adventure education experiences are evaluated. The chapter will focus on existing forms of reflection and on the extent to which this should inform your ongoing practice.

The role of reflection in adventure education owes much to the work of Greenaway (1996), Luckner and Nadler (1997) and Priest and Gass (1997). Reflection on experience is considered to be the essential precursor for learning. This is evident in Kolb's Experiential Learning model (1984), which has been widely used to explain the learning process in experiential and adventure education.

In this chapter, I wish to explore certain types of reflection process that I believe reflect the construction of experience that takes place during adventure education programmes. I shall seek to establish practical ways in which practitioners who aim to have the learner at the centre of the adventurous experience can further legitimise their position through placing them at the centre of evaluation processes.

I also aim to complement some of the basic models used in reflecting on experience, such as those proposed by Greenaway (1993), who suggests that an individual's ability to reflect can be aided by using a four-stage reviewing sequence:

1   *Experience* – aim to establish what actually happened during the experience.
2   *Express* – aim to identify feelings associated with the experience.
3   *Examine* – aim to draw out meaning from the experience.
4   *Explore* – aim to explore possible futures.

Greenaway's model is widely used in outdoor and adventure education settings and serves as a useful tool for adventure educators setting out to facilitate meaning from experience.

Reflection can be simply introspective – where time is given for individuals to think about the day's events. Most authors would argue, however, that even simple methods, such as discussions, enable more to be gleaned from experience than being left to reflect alone.

This chapter aims to complement these ideas by exploring what might be termed more creative approaches to understanding experience within different environments of adventure activity. It represents a synopsis of different approaches that are explored with adults, young people and children, and highlights key ways in which individuals' rationalisation of their own experiences can be accessed and understood.

The methods that will be discussed here have evolved through the application of incidental occurrences that have resulted in the reflective process with children. For example, much of my initial work began with clients keeping diaries. When children began to draw some of the things they wanted to talk about, it became evident that the incorporation of illustrations (both abstract and literal) could be an effective tool to understand the meanings that individuals were applying to their experiences.

THE CONCEPT OF EXPERIENCE AND REFLECTION IN ADVENTURE ENVIRONMENTS

The concept of learning in the adventure environment is, in common perception, conveyed as extending beyond the immediate context of skill and cognitive development into realms of personal development that involves some kind of transition into lived experiences in different environments. However, there is relatively little evidence to demonstrate that this occurs once participants leave the adventure environment.

Considering ways of reflecting on and evaluating experience is not new in adventure education. Largely, attention has focused on the way in which this can enhance and generalise learning (Luckner and Nadler, 1997). However, the detail and link between construction of experience and the reflective process is still to be developed in the field (Allison and Pomeroy, 2000). In this chapter, I seek to explore some of the theory that can underpin the nature of experience and processes of reflection in adventure education in order to make experience meaningful. My intention is to look very specifically at the way in which processes of reflection can be employed to inform our understanding of experience and our response to it. I shall consider the nature of experience and the way in which this relates to the processes of reflection. My perspective involves the reformation of perception to enhance experience.

WHAT IS REFLECTION AND WHY SHOULD WE USE IT?

It is essential at this point to establish what we mean by reflection and how we should describe the processes that we employ in order to make experiences meaningful and turn them into positive learning for ourselves and our clients.

A number of terms may be used to describe what we may broadly describe as 'the process of making experience meaningful'. Authors variously refer to 'processing' (Luckner and Nadler, 1997), 'reflection' (Moon, 2004) and 'reviewing' (Greenaway, 1996). This can be confusing, but we should bear in mind that it is the commonality between each that is important. The 'procedure' is more than a descriptive account of what has happened: it needs to go a step further to involve analysis and application. Most importantly, it should result in some kind of action.

I prefer the term 'reflection' because it encapsulates a sense of individualism: when we look in the mirror, we see something specific to ourselves and this subsequently affects our self-concept and action. However, it is not semantics but purpose that is important here: the idea of reflection needs to have a sense of consequence for those involved.

Essentially, the concept of reflection has both process and purpose. It involves, in some sense, the reliving of an experience and the identification of meaning within it: what went on, what was the response to it and how is it to inform action? Further to this, it is not sufficient to encourage clients to reflect without utilising their response in your own programmes. Thus, the reflections of others inform your own.

Whilst this chapter focuses on the value of the reflective process for your clients and the way this interacts with the content and nature of the programmes you offer, I hope that you will also be encouraged to reflect on your own experiences and professional development.

My contention is that, in order to be meaningful, reflections need to have purpose for both client and provider; therefore, the intention of reflection is initially to understand and then to facilitate learning and inform practice. This means that much of what is discussed here, although focused on clients in a learning environment, can also be used by you in order to become a reflective practitioner. As a facilitator, you should understand how experience is constructed, and this should inform the way in which you approach reflections with your clients. Indeed, a further intention of the processes you employ – once you have understood that the nature of experience is the relationship between the experiential process and that of reflection – could, as advocated by Moon (2004), actually be to enhance your clients' capacity for reflection.

The means through which we might reflect are discussed later in this chapter, but it is advisable to follow several broad steps, irrespective of the specific methods employed.

128

Suzanne Everley

Reflecting on our experiences is a difficult thing to do, particularly when they may have involved some kind of personal challenge. A good tip here is to remember some of the techniques that journalists use to encourage individuals to talk about difficult events, wherein they take the witnesses through a process of description prior to considering any emotional response. In the reflective process, you should similarly encourage clients to engage in the 'four Ds' of dimensional processing. Start with what may be termed a 'flat' image and extend this into a more complex interaction of perception and meaning:

- *Description:* where the overall experience is retold in some form.
- *Detailing:* where the initial description is revisited and enhanced through additional noticing.
- *Deconstructing:* where the individual identifies meaning that the event had for them.
- *Determining:* where the individual identified how the meaning of the experience is likely to affect future action.

The interaction of these factors incorporates a sense of time, place, cognition and emotion. Of particular significance is the way in which reflection anticipates future experience creating a continued sense of time – hence reflecting in 4-D. These steps will be explored further here with respect to specific approaches to understanding experience that I have found particularly useful.

With respect to actual approaches in practice, measures that are utilised in evaluating adventure experience can often be skill-based, immediate and quantitative: for example, you may include activities such as competing in a rock climb or making it through a particular section of cave. They are therefore limited in terms of their potential to interrogate the depth of an experience for the individual and the genuine implications that it may have. Perhaps that is sufficient, and arguably it is perfectly reasonable to present such material as evidence of success. Nevertheless, if meaningful programmes are to be developed in such a way as to facilitate engagement of clients that extends beyond simple participation for a set period of time, there is a need to engage in a more considered approach to evaluating experience. Through the evaluation of experience, it is anticipated that key features of existing programmes might be identified and key guidance can be given to enhance the engagement of clients with the experiences that are offered.

THE NATURE OF EXPERIENCE

An initial consideration here is inevitably the nature of the concept of 'experience' itself. Essentially, experience is constituted by an individual's perception and meaning. What is perceived in any given situation and what meaning is applied to this? Perceptions may be of the physical or social environment: for example, the height of an activity or working with another individual who has only just been met. Some are noted but do not affect meaning, while others are central to 'experience', depending upon the individual concerned. What

129

I am interested in is how various elements of the physical environment take on meaning and how this determines subjective responses. Will height, as a phenomenon in a climb, be a threatening or a positive challenge? Will the presence of others affect the individual's response to that challenge?

The relationship between meaning and action is highly individualistic, and it is necessary to acknowledge that the programme you offer is subject to several points of interaction that may affect the way in which it is received. Some of these points will be antecedents to the experience that clients have with you and will be out of your control, but they will still form a crucial part of what you offer for the individual. Whatever has happened to the individual within their lives will determine the meaning that is applied to their immediate context. It is therefore important that your review process provides an opportunity to address an individual's past in relation to their present.

Establishing an understanding of perception and meaning requires a willingness to identify new possibilities within the experience that you are offering and the way that this interacts with what clients have 'known' before. Adventure education is a lived experience; by definition, it requires active engagement and an investment by the individual. Very often, when working in the adventure environment, we perceive what we believe to be a clear picture of achievement: we set a task and our clients achieve it. They may initially demonstrate an element of fearfulness and subsequently their success will be evident on completion of the particular activity. They may talk excitedly on return to camp, discussing their achievements for the day. Thus we gain convenient feedback that justifies what we are doing. But there remains a need to assess the exact nature of the experience that the client has engaged in, and aspects of the challenges you have presented to facilitate its realisation.

The need to do this occurs even (or, arguably, more so) when an individual appears not to be engaging with what is on offer. Particularly when participation is a broader requirement of an education or rehabilitation programme, an individual may appear to limit their engagement with what is going on. A typical response (even though we may not articulate it) is to pathologise the individual as lacking the ability to invest in opportunities. But just because an activity is not *meaningful* to individuals, that does not necessarily equate to the experience lacking *meaning*. The individual may be having difficulty because of previous social or physical experiences.

SOCIAL CONCEPT OF 'SELF'

Ordinarily, it may be argued that an individual's concept of who they are, their sense of 'self', is defined in relation to their social environment. But in an adventure education experience it is possible to manipulate social interactions and therefore redefine that perceived self for your client. The potential for adventure experiences to affect the way in which individuals interact with one another, as a result of physical, social or psychological learning, means that,

130

Suzanne Everley

in order to understand what you might be achieving, attending to these realms as presented in the contextualisation of experience can facilitate the improvement of what we might offer. This may mean that in a specific adventure experience, perhaps where an individual is being asked to work with another (such as belaying), we should think in terms of how they deal with the sense of responsibility for that particular person. Their preceding relationship and the likely resulting relationship between the two as the experience continues are important here, rather than simply how well the skill is performed at the time.

Our perspective therefore takes a constructivist approach to reflection, prioritising the social construction of reality as being the most rational underpinning for the understanding of experience.

When considering the phenomenon of experience as an adventure educationalist, there is a heightened need to ensure that you specifically consider the interaction of the physical and social environments in which you are asking clients to work through your review process.

EXPERIENCE AS 'EMBODIED'

There is a need to identify the essentially embodied nature of experience in the adventure environment. The social and psychological phenomena that engage to formulate an experience inevitably rely on the physicality of the activity itself. Adventure education experiences are situations where individuals are always on display; where everyone can see what they are doing and make judgements on what they perceive.

This means that inevitably, for some, an internalised battle takes place between coping with the nature of the activity in a physical sense: for example, through perceived risk and maintaining or developing status within a group or working towards portraying and actually becoming 'the person that they want to be' as a result of the programme. Your clients will be thinking not only about what they are doing, but about what other people are thinking of them as they do it.

PERCEPTION AS HYPOTHETICAL

Essentially, your clients will constantly revise the meanings that they apply to the situations that you design for them. Over a period of time, learning will take place, not simply in terms of skill but in terms of perception: slopes may appear more or less steep; ledges at different heights; and spaces greater or smaller, even though the physical environment remains the same.

The reality that is constructed for the individual is, in itself, a developing phenomenon. An experience, once consigned to history, remains factually as it was in the sense of time and place but evolves as a learning platform as further experience reassigns the meanings that individuals might apply to their recollections. To use an analogy, once snow crystals melt and refreeze, although they consist of the same molecules, their form alters and they provide a different platform for further snowfall. Reality is an 'applied reality', not an objective set of facts. The philosophical standpoint that we are taking, therefore, is phenomenological: the only real way of 'knowing' is through our senses; there is no abstract reality. As individuals, we anticipate experience through theorising about what will happen based on past experiences; thus we take a constructivist epistemology in our approach to evaluating experience.

Consequently, a key concern will be the interpretation of the individual taking part in your programmes and the need to ensure that you evaluate what is 'real' for them – reality being an applied reality, rather than an objective phenomenon.

REASONS AND MOTIVATIONS FOR PARTICIPATION

Some individuals will join programmes of adventure education as singular experiences that they believe will have life-altering consequences; others are already heavily involved in adventure and may be seeking to take on greater challenges. With disaffected populations, adventure experiences are believed to realign the individual with the values of mainstream society, providing remedial action to counteract the deprivation from which they come. Irrespective of the vagaries of the origins of purpose, the intention always is to provide an experience for clients, the profundity of which should remain with them beyond the immediate context.

DIMENSIONAL PROCESSING AND CREATIVE APPROACHES IN REFLECTION

Providing opportunities for reviewing experience has a twofold purpose: giving the client a sense of value (Greenaway, 1992, 1996) and informing the reflective process. When appropriately designed, the review process itself can provide part of the experience by making clients aware of what they have engaged in and, indeed, by drawing attention to elements that may be lost if not consciously addressed.

If seeking to gain an understanding of individual perspectives, the greatest potential is achieved through the devolution of decision-making in the evaluation process to clients themselves. Many approaches that claim to evaluate experiences adopt various forms of 'measurement': experiences are assessed through the preconceived ideas of the facilitator or researcher. However, the use of such processes predefines areas of significance for consideration in the field and thus there is potential for continued reaffirmation of what has gone before; programmes might be continually (re)justified within a relatively narrow field of terms. Whilst this may serve to establish the continuation of adventure experiences

132

Suzanne Everley

within the status quo, if you seek a genuine evaluation of what is being offered and want to open up the possibilities for the introduction of phenomena that have not previously been incorporated, then a new approach that empowers individuals to guide the evaluation process is necessary.

Some of the approaches that I recommend have not been widely employed, largely because they may be time-consuming and demand engagement. Additionally, managers and external bodies, such as funding bodies, demand evidence of the success of programmes that are quantifiable and easily understood. However, if we are really to improve the quality of what is being 'delivered', a more complex approach – perhaps one that is less 'packageable' – is more appropriate.

Clearly, as the facilitator, you will need to define the evaluation framework, but it is crucial to maximise the possibilities for your clients to guide the content that emerges from that framework and the nature of knowledge that is generated as a result. You should therefore aim to give clients themselves the opportunity to identify those elements of the adventure experience that carry most significance both within the immediate environment and beyond it, when they return to their daily lives. Another important point is the extent to which the client's engagement in the evaluation process significantly affects the quality of evidence generated.

Greenaway (1996:14) says that reviewing serves to enrich experience and, if clients know that a review process is coming up, it can 'encourage learners to both more inward and more outward looking – noticing more about themselves, others, and their surroundings'. There is a degree of concern here that an experience may become more about the review process than the experience itself – knowing that you are going to be asked about something might heighten your focus only in relation to what questions you anticipate. So it might detract from spontaneous responses, immediate engagement with the activity itself and even the overall experience.

Therefore, you must take care when deciding when to hold your review process and the point when you make your clients aware of its processes. You will need to decide whether it is of greatest value to engage in the process of evaluation whilst the client engages in the activity, immediately after the completion of a particular experience, or some time later, when the individual has left the immediate context and long-term impact can be considered.

A particular strength of establishing approaches to evaluation is that it may actually also be reflective of the 'process' in which we believe our clients have engaged. Allison and Pomeroy (2000) say that the idea of learning in adventure education may be divided into 'input' (participants and facilitators), 'process' (approaches used to working with groups) and 'outcomes' (the benefits that programmes work towards), and that these exist in a complex network of arrangements. The complexities of the ways in which outcomes can be identified can be reflected in the way in which reviews are organised.

When assessing experience, there 'are times when thorough reviews are appropriate, and there are times when a quick "temperature check" to ensure that you are moving in the direction that you intended is all that is needed' (Greenaway, 1996: 11). Whilst it is inevitable that you will incorporate both into your work, the specific type of review that I am discussing here refers to more substantive reflections that may be integrated into a programme or form its conclusion.

Evaluating an experience as an ongoing process within an adventure environment has several potential advantages over doing so at specific points that follow a particular programme. Embedding reflection into experience itself can facilitate an added awareness for the client of the process in which they are engaged. The experience itself can then be sharpened in its clarity and heightened in its quality. Meanwhile, you, the facilitator, will gain a more dynamic picture of the process that your clients are going through – a continual combination of reflective and ongoing experiences.

Essentially, the review processes that I am recommending here can take place at any stage where you might consider it to be of value to assess progress. It is important to plan these points and link them appropriately to the tools that you choose to employ.

TOOLS FOR REFLECTION

In this section, I shall explore the practical tools that might be employed to facilitate an understanding of experience. In many instances, we need to establish that a programme has 'worked' (often adhering to externally set criteria that are designed to justify what is being done to those outside the immediate adventure environment). But it is to be hoped that we can also explore unforeseen learning experiences to develop complexity within the evaluation process. A vast range of tools might assist in reflection, with some providing simple snapshots of what has happened and others more sustained in their nature (Greenaway, 1996; Priest and Gass, 1997). Here, I shall focus on the two tools that I believe most accurately mirror the experiential process and provide the most comprehensive means through which to understand our own and others' perspectives.

Overall, we should aim to take a hermeneutic approach to reviewing experience: establish 'facts' but also, with the client, explore and interpret the meanings that have been applied to these facts and the perceptions that consequently construct the reality of the client's learning. To achieve this, clients should be free to express themselves, should have the potential to extend reflections in the dimensions of various aspects of learning (physical, psychological, emotional, social and cognitive) and should be allowed to reflect on the way in which these elements of experience interact to create an overarching experience.

There are many ways to achieve this, but here I present specific approaches that provide a practical basis for such investigations. The aim is to understand rather than prove, and to

134

Suzanne Everley

establish a complex characterisation of experience for the individual. In reflections, it is important to get the participants to do most of the talking (Luckner and Nadler, 1997), and the following tools promote this.

Diaries

Keeping diaries and journals (I use the terms interchangeably) encourages active reflection. A key quality of this approach is that you, the facilitator of the experience, can remain largely removed from this process: the client has relative freedom in selecting the time, place and environment for their reflection to take place.

Typically, diaries are written in the first person, and in many instances this is a logical convention to follow: personalising reflections in this way can be a highly effective means of encouraging individuals to consider what they have achieved through an experience. However, particularly where challenging personal issues are present, it may be more appropriate for clients to keep a diary in the third person and essentially adopt the role of the 'other' in their writing. Through this process, the individual will be able to take a step back from the immediate situation and so might be able to identify aspects of their own experience that a more internalised perspective would not allow. It similarly helps clients to identify their projected needs within a programme. It is beneficial to let clients choose their own diary perspective, so that they feel most at ease.

One client wrote:

> When Lucy went forward to have her turn at the abseil she started and then stopped but knew that she had to continue; that there was no choice. She was totally disempowered. She completed it but didn't feel good about it. (Lucy, aged 31)

When this diary entry was discussed with the facilitator, it was possible to establish, with Lucy, how she might have viewed the person who was being described. In fact, that person had a choice: she did not have to continue with the abseil and, indeed, others had already withdrawn. So the pressures being put on Lucy were internalised, and, on reflection, she was able to identify that she had a strength of character with which she had not previously credited herself. She had the capacity to deal with things that she had thought were beyond her.

Keeping diaries lets clients feel that the facilitator (or anyone who reads the text) is able to establish an integral relationship with them:

> The good thing about keeping a journal is that the person reading it can imagine everything that you went through. (Paul, aged 15)

135

Thus, there is a sense of engagement between author and reader that places a sense of value in the client.

Diaries also have the potential to act as a mirror to the evaluator. They will refer to characters in each chapter of experience, and those characters may well include the facilitator or others in the facilitating team. Comments may be integrated into the narrative, or might address you, as the reader, directly:

> And if it hadn't been for [the facilitator] saying she would be with me every step . . . it just wouldn't have happened. She did it so no one even noticed. (Male participant, aged 27)

You might also encourage clients to create a metanarrative commentary on their original diary entries that either expands upon the detail of what has been written or identifies a modification of perceptions at a later date. This could be an annotation to explain how they now feel about their experiences, a 'reflection on reflections' that serves to establish the enduring effect of the programme.

Keeping a diary can be related to the idea that we make sense of our experiences in 'storied' form. We identify key characters and contexts in our experiences and integrate them in meaningful ways. Diaries, if kept regularly, provide a personalised representation of the self. In practice, the way in which individuals manipulate their writing style and include their own annotations – techniques such as capitalisation and underlining, and the addition of a metanarrative around the original text – serve to personalise accounts and establish the client's ownership of the data. However, you should still provide a framework for your clients to follow when they keep diaries. It is tempting simply to invite clients to write anything that comes to mind in order to gain an insight into their personal perspective. However, 'getting started' can be rather difficult, particularly when dealing with groups that find the writing process challenging in itself. A framework will help them overcome this. The following is a typical example (of course, it can be adapted to suit your particular programme):

1   Describe what happened today.
   ■   What were the activities?
   ■   How were they organised?
   ■   Who took part in the activities?
   ■   What were their roles?

2   Identify the emotions that you have experienced today and give examples of where and when you felt them.
   ■   How do these emotions relate to how you feel now?
   ■   How does this affect how you feel about tomorrow?

Journals may be used as evidence in themselves: they are valid records in terms of both content and characterisation, through the means described above. Alternatively, as I have

136

Suzanne Everley

already intimated, they may be used to generate further data for evaluation. On an individual basis, it may be appropriate and helpful for you to explore some of the issues that clients identify in their text or seek clarification of meaning. Individuals may be 'interviewed' to explore the text they have written. Collectively, the themes identified in diaries may be used to form the basis of further exploration of experience, especially in focus groups, wherein you may obtain an understanding of your clients' experiences and hear their recommendations for the development of programmes. In this way, you may enhance your understanding of common themes and prompt clients to discover new meanings that they had not identified originally. They may then reflect on these retrospectively, thus enhancing the value of the programme.

Also of value here, is the way in which you might explore your own use of diaries. One such way could be through collaborative diary-keeping. This could take the form of clients writing diaries together – in pairs or groups – or even you writing alongside your clients. The latter approach reduces the hierarchical nature of the programme and integrates the whole extended experience in terms of personal development. Explore possibilities and find what works best for you.

Obviously, it would be naive to suggest that diary-keeping is always a productive approach to reflection. You and your clients may well even find that they detract from the whole experience of being in an outdoor adventure environment. Another point to consider is that some people simply do not like writing or revealing their feelings on paper. The important thing to consider is how clients relate not only to the experience but to the method that you employ to help them reflect on it.

However, diary-keeping has the key advantage of giving clients the time to reflect alone and without interruption – particularly from you, the facilitator. They also allow a degree of freedom of expression that clients may not feel when more traditional forms of reflection – such as group discussions – are utilised.

Drawings

Sometimes, however, you will need to adopt an approach that is not so reliant upon language. Individuals might have difficulty with language (Priest and Gass, 1997; Moon, 2004) and there will be many instances when writing a diary entry is the last thing a client wants to do (particularly if they have issues with schoolwork and hierarchical academic skills). But there is an even stronger reason for sometimes adopting alternative approaches: they can be more expressive and more closely related to the original experience.

Sometimes, a client might add a drawing to their diary entry to illustrate their meaning. This happens particularly when they feel that words are insufficient to explain what they wish to say or when they have a limited vocabulary. Drawings are very effective means through which individuals express their thoughts and feelings, so they have often been

137

recommended for use in the reflective process (Greenaway, 1993; Luckner and Nadler, 1997; Priest and Gass, 1997).

Utilising drawings as a tool to facilitate review can serve as a means to enter into the mind of a client. They are especially useful when dealing with children, to gain an insight into their reality through a means that is easily accessible to them. Children are used to being asked to draw, so they will readily create images that represent their experiences.

Drawings can also provide a more sophisticated means to understand experience because they are: 'Structures in themselves, yet simultaneously refer to events and objects outside themselves and it is to this dimension of "meaning" that . . . educators should attend' (Arguile, 1990: ii). Historically, art has offered a significant means of communication (Schaverien, 1995: 32), and, as such, drawings can be used by clients to illustrate their reflections on the programme in which they are, or have been, involved. This is a 'natural' means through which to express thought.

Individuals encapsulate meaning for themselves through iconic representation: 'We understand reality only by subsuming it under general class-concepts and general rules, but also by intuiting it in its concrete and individual shape. Such concrete intuiting cannot be attained by language alone' (Cassirer, 1979: 153). In order to make the process of drawing viable as a review and evaluation tool, subjects must feel confident that their images will

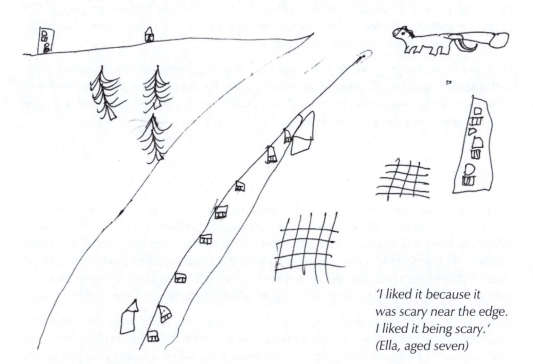

'I liked it because it was scary near the edge. I liked it being scary.'
(Ella, aged seven)

Figure 7.1 A child uses drawing to explain her experience

138

Suzanne Everley

not be evaluated critically, so a degree of preparation will probably be required to help them overcome their inhibitions. They should understand that we are creating a means of communication, not hoping to produce great works of art.

Drawings provide a freedom for expression that individuals may lack when attempting to discuss their experiences verbally. Multiple concepts can be represented simultaneously, and the relative importance of each can be identified through the manipulation of physical relationships. This is a flexible medium, so what is conveyed can go far beyond concrete facts and might readily demonstrate emotion and subjective responses. Size, colour and location can be moulded easily to depict conception.

As with diaries, drawings can be completed away from the facilitator, and the process of their construction is necessarily active, requiring the client to engage consciously with what they are doing. This makes it highly likely that this type of reflection will be a valuable process in itself. Art is an active mode of expression (Cassirer, 1979) – it cannot be created passively and when used in an evaluative context it requires sufficient engagement for sincere identification of the value that existed in the adventurous experience.

Just as individuals might add drawings to their diaries to clarify meaning, they may add words to their drawings for the same purpose. You will find that individuals do this in order to emphasise a particular point or to explain key issues.

One valuable aspect of active reflection through the use of drawing is the engagement that is required of the individual whose experience is being explored: 'every time a figuration is evoked in a drawing, everything about it has been mediated by consciousness' (Berger and Mohr, 1982: 93). Moreover, drawings can be used as a means to initiate engagement between interviewer and interviewee in a way that empowers the latter. Essentially, control of the reflective process is passed to the client and so it becomes a more meaningful process to them. As a result, we move away from the singular question of how successful an experience has been and open up the possibility of unanticipated responses.

Drawings are valuable in themselves (as a 'product'), but this value might well be enhanced through articulation of, or reflections about, what has been represented. As 'pictures can operate on a metaphoric level' (Dubowski, 1999: 8), clients may choose to represent their experiences through symbolic representations (see Figure 7.2).

As with diaries, some cultural perceptions might act as obstacles to your clients readily engaging in drawing. You therefore need to remove the pressure they might feel to be highly artistic and accurate. You could begin by talking to your clients about the approach and why you are using it. Emphasise that they are drawing to express themselves, not to produce a masterpiece, and explain that they will have the opportunity to clarify what they represent in their pictures later. You should remember that:

- The value of a drawing lies in its purpose for the client (not for the art world).
- Drawing is a mid-point rather than a conclusion – it needs to follow reflective thought but it will not be evaluated in itself.

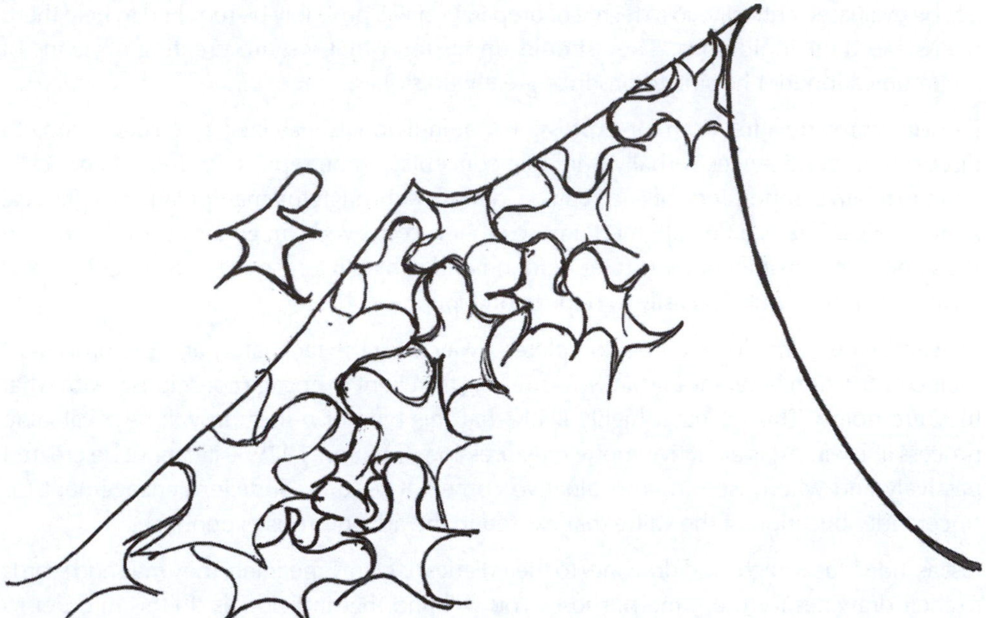

'This is me here – I'm there but a little bit apart from everyone else – we all look the same but everyone else is integrated into the mountain and each other . . . there is an invisible barrier between me and the activity and therefore everyone else that is more to do with what's going on in my head than anything.' (Claire, aged 30)

Figure 7.2 An adult uses drawing to explain her experience

■ Symbolic drawings are often easier to produce yet hold more meaning, especially for adults and young people.

Photography

Whilst many clients will respond positively to expressing their thoughts through drawings (once you have helped them overcome the frequent response: 'But I can't draw!'), for some, the whole idea of drawing will be just too much. However, you can still employ images in your reviews, through photographs. It may even be more appropriate to utilise photography, rather than drawing. Almost all clients will be familiar with using a camera in their everyday lives, and so will be happy to use one in the review process. Also, as photographs can now be manipulated, they afford many possibilities to convey whatever image is desired. This medium therefore has a dual advantage: the technology is easy to use (at least at a basic level), so most clients are not intimidated by it; but the final photograph is still the result of a constructive process. This process occurs both before the image is taken and when it is subsequently altered (should the client choose to do this). The final image might be a symbolic or a literal expression of an experience, or a combination of the two (see Figure 7.3).

'I know that this looks like it's just a picture of where we went and I do love it because it represents the openness and freedom of the environment, but I wanted to use it to represent the whole thing this week . . . the journey that we've been on and the fact that we don't know where it's going to take us. If you look at this picture you can see the footprints but you don't know who they belong to . . . or where they actually end up. It's all a question . . . I know we've been affected this week and I can tell you how I feel now but I think there's more. I think there's still more to find out about how it's going to stay with me. That's why you can't actually see anyone in the photograph . . . it's the unknown.' (James, aged 23)

Figure 7.3 Using photography to explain an experience

Photographs demand singular representations and therefore require the individual to select what is important to them. They act as a means to focus the individual on key reflection before the image is taken:

I liked using photographs because they made you really focus on what was important. (Lisa, aged 13)

Alternatively, a series of images might be utilised to generate a journalistic commentary on an experience as it progresses, or as an overview of reflections:

You can kind of use all the pictures together to make a story – to tell people about what you did – and it helps you remember exactly what you did. (Matthew, aged 15)

As photographic images simplify (Berger and Mohr, 1982), they can highlight significance in a limited context. Photographs can be used to give 'photovoice' for clients to present 'evidence' of their experiences. Further to this, however, if images are manipulated, they can be used metaphorically, in much the same way as drawings. Essentially, you again create the opportunity for your clients to establish what they have gained most from their experiences and how this might translate into their consciousness.

Digital technology enables immediate opportunities for later reflection. Many outdoor and adventure education centres now utilise digital technology, and it is possible to draw much from it. Photography is now an easily malleable form of representation which almost everyone is happy to employ (sometimes in contrast to diary-writing and drawing), yet it offers just as many opportunities for representation of meaning as those other forms of reflection. You should be mindful, however, that some people will find it difficult to use image-manipulation software, and they may even have trouble finding something to represent meaning in a photograph:

Photographs sometimes seem like a good idea to think about what you've experienced, but sometimes what you want to take a picture of just isn't there! (Rosie, aged 15)

Generating interviews from images

The purpose of utilising an image to generate an interview is to focus on the (re)building of an experience. First, pictures should be described, before being deconstructed in order to reconstruct an experience. The interviewer should guide the client through the process of revisiting thoughts and perceptions that were experienced at the time the photograph was taken; have them identify who appears in the image; explain their various roles; and finally describe the relational role that they have with them.

Returning to a particular experience or an aspect of an experience can evoke clear memories of the visceral responses that the client felt at the time. It also helps to establish

142

which elements of the experience were temporary, which have had a more enduring impact on the broader socio-psychological condition of the client, and which are likely to affect the client's future experience in the event that they return to the original context they are describing. Explaining an experience to an external agency can be cathartic for the client and might raise their awareness of what they have gained from an experience. Should they perceive a lack of success, it might also enable them to cope more readily in the future.

Again, actively engaging your client in reflection can help them to be more accurate in their reminiscences. This process inevitably relies the skill of the interviewer and their ability to respond sensitively to the cues that clients give: visceral responses, whilst being useful in identifying the significance of different elements of experiences, need to be intelligently managed. Begin by asking the client to describe the picture as a whole, then move on to more analytical questions.

WHAT TO DO WITH YOUR FINDINGS

This chapter has acknowledged that you, as a facilitator, need to generate evidence of the success of the programmes you offer. However, it should not be forgotten that our ultimate goal is to provide clients with positive learning experiences. Utilising the tools that have been described here extends the benefits that are derived from evaluation to the clients themselves. The evidence that results from the reflective process within adventure education has purpose for both your clients and for you, as facilitator, at different stages. Using the reflective methods described here, the client will benefit from the process itself and from the learning that results from both the initial experience and later reflection. This section considers what you can do with the evidence that they provide in their reflection.

Findings from the activities I have described can be used to create retrospective perceptions (Moon, 2004). A client might be encouraged to reconsider how they felt or feel about a specific situation in order to appreciate their achievements. Additionally, your findings may already have 'done their work' in the sense that the process of reflection will have enabled clients to realise all that they have achieved. They may then carry this knowledge with them into other fields of life.

Essentially, experience in the adventure education environment is highly individualistic, and this is very beneficial. Obviously, though, if you want to integrate your clients' reflections into your planning processes, a more general picture needs to be created. In order to achieve this, you should follow a similar series of steps to those of your clients.

Moon (2004) has written extensively about reflection in professional environments and has identified how reflections can be utilised. She advocates following a process of *association* (relating new data to that which is already known), *integration* (seeking relationships among the data) and *validation* (determining the authenticity of ideas and feelings that have resulted from the reflective process). In short, validating patterns of experience will help you establish what you may wish to retain or develop within a pro-gramme. Ultimately, when 'the reviewing style "fits", learners sense its value, and . . . the whole process of activity and review . . . becomes the adventure' (Greenaway, 1996: 4).

CONCLUDING COMMENTS

At the start of this chapter, I introduced the concept of 'dimensional processing' as a guide for using reflection within an adventure environment. You will have noticed that each of the methods for reflection that has been recommended here addresses these dimensions in a different way and utilises them at a different stage. Additionally, the way in which each of them is used will affect how the essential steps are addressed. In all instances, however, each of the factors is employed to create an overall, 4-D picture of experience. The tool that you decide to use will be highly dependent upon your purpose, your skills and the characteristics of your group.

Experience depends on perception and meaning; we construct our reality and develop perceptions (and therefore meanings) over time. The reflective process is an experience in itself, and can therefore be used to redefine an individual's perceptions more positively (Moon, 2004). Reflection should always be an active, engaging process.

Reflective techniques should be encouraged in the evaluation of adventure programmes in order to facilitate learning for both client and provider. If you are reading this, it is fair to assume that you form a link between theoretical parlance and proactively taking a structured and purposeful approach to turning experience into positive experiential learning, and are thus working towards the implementation of truly informed practice.

Given the centrality of reflection in adventure, it is surprising that more has not been written about it. Have a go at it! It is not dangerous, as long as we do not interpret experience so much that it detracts from the original 'adventure'. We should incorporate reflection as a positive part of the whole experience and help clients (and perhaps ourselves) to develop purposeful skills in it.

REFERENCES

Allison, P. and Pomeroy, E. (2000) How Shall We Know? Epistemological Concerns in Research in Experiential Education, *Journal of Experiential Education*, 23 (2): 91–97.

Arguile, R. (1990) Art Therapy with Children and Adolescents, in Case, C. and Dalley, T. (eds) *Working with Children in Art Therapy*, London, New York: Routledge.

Berger, J. and Mohr, J. (1982) *Another Way of Telling*, New York: Writers and Readers Publishing Cooperative Society.

Cassirer, E. (1979 [1942]) Language and Art I, in Verene, D.P, (ed.) *Symbol, Myth and Culture*, London: Yale University Press.

144

Collier, J. (1967) *Visual Anthropology: Photography as a Research Method*, New York: Holt, Reinhardt and Winston.

Dubowski, J. (1990) Art versus Language, in Case, C. and Dalley, T. (eds) *Working with Children in Art Therapy*, London, New York: Routledge.

Greenaway, R. (1992) Doing Reviewing, *Journal of Adventure Education and Outdoor Leadership*, 9 (1): 15–17.

Greenaway, R. (1993) *Playback: A Guide to Reviewing Activities*, Windsor: The Duke of Edinburgh's Award in association with Endeavour Scotland.

Greenaway, R. (1996) *Reviewing Adventures: Why and How?*, Sheffield: National Association for Outdoor Education.

King, K. (1988) The Role of Adventure in the Experiential Learning Process, *Journal of Experiential Education*, 11 (2): 4–8.

Kolb, D. (1984) *Experiential Learning: Turning Experience into Learning*, Englewood Cliffs, NJ: Prentice-Hall.

Luckner, J.L. and Nadler, R.S. (1997) *Processing the Experience: Strategies to Enhance and Generalize Learning*, 2nd edn, Dubuque, IA: Kendall/Hunt.

Moon, J. (2004) *Reflection in Learning and Professional Development Theory and Practice*, London: RoutledgeFalmer.

Priest, S. and Gass, M.A. (1997) *Effective Leadership in Adventure Programming*, Leeds: Human Kinetics.

Schaverien, J. (1995) The Picture as Transactional Object in the Treatment of Anorexia, in Dokter, D. (ed.) *Arts Therapies and Clients with Eating Disorders*, London: Jessica Kingsley.

CHAPTER EIGHT

ADVENTURE EDUCATION

PHYSICAL EXERCISE AND HEALTH

John Kelly and Julia Potter

ADVENTURE AND HEALTH AND FITNESS

This chapter will outline how participation in adventure-based activity can contribute to improved health. It will consider the current body of knowledge, and explore how this may be used to develop interventions addressing current health-related issues. We will begin by exploring the concepts of health and fitness, then look into the factors leading to ill health in our population. There are practical suggestions for tailoring an adventure programme aimed at adults or children for whom a deficit in nature, activity and interactive exposure to these elements may be leading to poor health.

WHAT ARE THESE THINGS CALLED HEALTH AND FITNESS?

In this modern age we might assume that many of the diseases that have resulted in high levels of child mortality, low life expectancies and persistent diseases have been ameliorated; and, generally, that is correct, at least in First World countries. Many diseases that the Western world once suffered from are now either controlled or have been eradicated through vaccination, pharmacological agents, better sanitary conditions, and an abundance of food and water. Despite this, though, we cannot be considered to be healthy: levels of child, adolescent and adult morbidity are rising, along with chronic health conditions (CHCs), such as obesity, diabetes and cardiovascular disease, resulting in an increased burden on health services and society as well as shortened life-expectancies.

In 1948, the World Health Organisation defined health as: 'a state of complete physical, mental and social well-being and not merely the absence of disease or infirmity' (WHO, 1948: 100). This is a useful starting point from which to explore the dimensions of health, consider our current position and examine how adventurous and outdoor pursuits may be of use in improving the health of participants.

We might ask: 'Why do we care if our population is healthy?' The primary reasons for social concern and investment in this issue are humanistic and altruistic. Biologically, we are driven to protect one another, particularly our children, and society needs a functional population. Healthy children tend to become healthy adults who make a valuable contribution to society, and are therefore 'fit for purpose'; fitness, in the context of health, means little more than this. Those who may be considered unhealthy are unfit because they are more likely to be unemployed, claim benefits, take days off work, and contribute less to the economic and social wellbeing of the country.

It is the decline in both health and skill-related components of fitness that results in a decline in our physical wellness and often concomitantly in elements of mental and social health. The human body is a phenomenal 'machine' and, when treated in the right way, can respond to very many challenges (stressors) over both the short and long terms. The balance between eustress (positive) and distress (negative) is very important for health. Cannon (1993) divided stressors into four types: environment, physical, psychosocial and psycho-logical. The balance between these has shifted dramatically from those in which we evolved, primarily environmental and physical, to a dominance of psychological and psychosocial stress. This leaves us both physically and mentally in a challenged position as we are not receiving sufficient physical eustress in order to maintain healthy bodies but receive too much psychological and psychosocial distress. The physical and social environment in which we live is massively different from the one in which humans evolved and it could be postulated that the further our environment and behaviours move away from our default setting, the more difficult it will be to stay healthy. Many factors have led to the increase in lifestyle-based diseases. There have been dramatic changes in our diet, but the fall in habitual levels of physical activity is even more strongly associated with the rise in chronic health conditions. Therefore, government guidelines and those issued by the World Health Organisation suggest that physical activity should be increased at every possible opportunity.

WHAT FACTORS LEAD TO ILL HEALTH?

Most modern Westerners would have difficulty recognising, let alone prospering in, the environment of our evolutionary past in the Neolithic period (between 20,000 and 50,000 years ago). Our ancestors' lives were characterised by long periods of physical activity with a relatively scarce and fickle food supply. Individuals who were better at storing fuel in the body (carbohydrates and fats) had a greater chance of surviving and passing on their genes. This idea forms the basis of the 'thrifty gene hypothesis', first put forward by J.V. Neel in 1965, which has since underpinned much work in evolutionary genetics. Whilst this theory has strong intuitive appeal, it has only recently been deployed as a research weapon to address the rise in chronic health conditions. The new and rapidly expanding field of 'epigenetics' may yet teach us a great deal more about the interaction of our lifestyle, genes and health, and it has already become apparent that our genes are not as fixed as we once thought.

The changes to the way we live extend to every aspect of our lives, including: food, activity, physical environment and amount of psychosocial stress. To the largest extent, modernisation

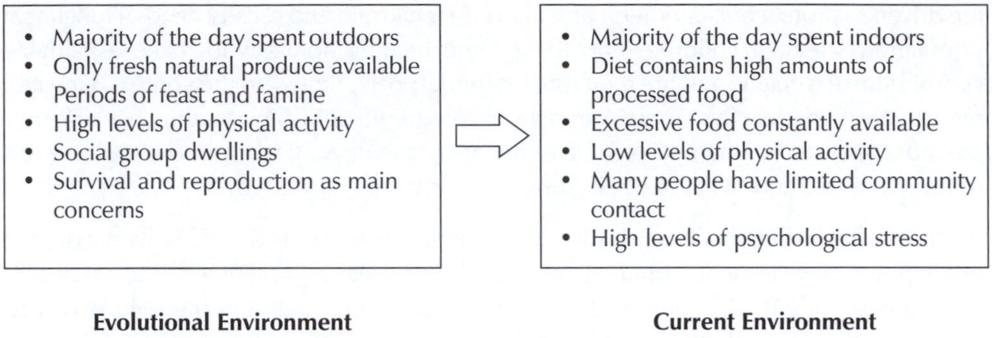

Majority of the day spent outdoors • Only fresh natural produce available • Periods of feast and famine • High levels of physical activity • Social group dwellings • Survival and reproduction as main concerns	• Majority of the day spent indoors • Diet contains high amounts of processed food • Excessive food constantly available • Low levels of physical activity • Many people have limited community contact • High levels of psychological stress
Evolutional Environment	**Current Environment**

Figure 8.1 Contrasts between the environment in which Homo sapiens evolved and that in which we live now

has been very positive for our survival and life expectancy; however, the addition of years to life has not necessarily added life to those years. Morbidity in a number of 'lifestyle diseases' has increased in both children and adults. It is likely that this is occurring because of the shift in the way we use our bodies from an early age and the discrepancy between that usage and our biology.

One of the blessings of the modern age in the developed world is that we can choose the extent to which we dwell in either a more natural or an artificial environment. However, as a population, there has been a shift towards favouring the more artificial, making us (at least to some extent) victims of our own success. As individuals, we are fulfilling our

Table 8.1 Summary of factors including altered behaviours contributing to reduced health and an increase in morbidity

Stressor	Factors presenting a threat to health	
	Increased	*Decreased*
Environment	Roads and cars Technological temptations Wealth	Open spaces Ease of access Freedom to explore
Physical	Fat and sugar in the diet Availability of drugs and alcohol	Nourishment Need to move Playtime
Psychosocial	Media access Value placed on material possessions and celebrity Concern over health and safety Both parents/partners working	Sense of safety and security Sense of community Fathers living in the home Time spent over food
Psychological	Fear	Confidence

148

biological potential by seeking foods that are highly calorific and conserving energy while constructing an environment around us that minimises immediate risks to our survival. Within this construct, adventure education and outdoor pursuits offer the option of exploring the natural environment more fully, pushing the boundaries yet maintaining the right to retreat and an element of safety. However, the importance of this role should not be underestimated if the health of the population is not only to be maintained but improved from its current position.

Whilst adventure theorists often debate what can be classified as 'an adventure', here we assume that any activity that takes the individual into more 'natural' environments where they feel challenged physically, emotionally or cognitively constitutes adventure. For some, this might be no more than a green space inside a city; for others, it might be high mountains or rainforests.

CHILDREN AND ADOLESCENTS

The state of the nation

There has been much media interest over the apparent obesity 'crisis', perhaps because it is one of the more obvious conditions and there is a social fear of fatness in the Western world. But closer examination of child and adolescent health reveals that this is just one representation of broader ill health in our population. Table 8.2 provides a summary of some of the issues affecting the young. (There has been a great deal of research into this problem and the factors behind it, and the References section at the end of the chapter provides details of where some of the more useful data might be found.)

A very revealing report was published in February 2007 by UNICEF's Innocenti Research Centre (UNICEF, 2007). Using data from most of the economically advanced nations of

Table 8.2 Key issues affecting the young and their relationships with the dimensions of health defined by the World Health Organisation

Physical	Social	Mental
Excess body fat	Bullying	Depression
Type II diabetes	Violent crime	Low self-esteem
Early-onset cardiovascular disease	Teenage pregnancy	Addiction to food, drugs, smoking and alcohol
Reduced physical activity	Sexually transmitted infections	Boredom
Metabolic syndrome	Lack of aspiration	Suicide

the world, it provided an overview of the state of childhood in the developed world. Many of the findings were alarming, particularly for Britain, which sits at the bottom of the league table of twenty-one economically successful nations when forty aspects of childhood wellbeing are considered. Interestingly, the report shows that there is no strong correlation between per capita GDP and childhood wellbeing. If this report were to be used as a barometer of our priorities and values, then the outcome would be somewhat embarrassing. We need to make much better use of our wealth to safeguard our children and our future.

What has been done? Health interventions

Initially, interventions aimed at combating childhood obesity were targeted at individuals: they could be summarised as 'eat less and do more'. Not surprisingly, these 'projects' consistently produced success in the short term but there is no evidence of long-term change. Individuals were left feeling as though they had failed, which resulted in maintenance or even exacerbation of low self-esteem and its accompanying psychosocial problems. Unfortunately, this is likely to be the outcome of any short-term health intervention in a static environment. Expecting individuals to behave differently in a physical and social environment that has not been adapted to accommodate new expectations is doomed, particularly in the young, who instinctively react to whatever is around them.

The primary problem with these interventions was that parents had to provide the food and the activity role-modelling. Yet these parents were often not targeted in the intervention, resulting in demands being placed on the children to behave differently in an identical environment – an almost impossible task for anyone. Interventions that include care-givers note a greater level of success in both the short and longer terms, but they are still not universally successful. In addition, they can be resource expensive, in terms of both personnel and time, and are thus limited in their usefulness.

One of the most successful health interventions of modern times has been the anti-smoking campaign. This is not because huge numbers of individuals have decided that they shall not smoke because it might make them ill (although a few might have decided this), but because a many-pronged campaign has made smoking both expensive and socially (and at times physically) uncomfortable. Fewer adults now smoke, so fewer children and teenagers are taking up the habit as it is a much less common part of our culture than it once was.

It is generally accepted that the urban environment in which most of our children and adolescents live contributes to the poor health dimensions that are being observed. But what can be done about it? It would undesirable on many levels to undo technological advances, but a greater access to and greater use of a more natural (less artificial) environment seems essential if we are to achieve balance of the stressors and maximise our health and that of our children.

150

The government has attempted to generate large-scale change through its work with the Food Standards Agency (FSA) and the Department for Children, Schools and Families (DCSF), both of which have roles to play in marketing, local government, social services and schools. As with any government intervention, some believe that they have not gone far enough while others believe that we now live in a 'nanny state'. Regardless of political opinion, there have been large government-led intervention projects and we are beginning to see some subtle shifts in health-related behaviours and outcomes as a result. Physical activity is one of the key targets in the national outcomes of the Every Child Matters: Change for Children programme and the Healthy Schools programme – a joint initiative between the Department of Health and the Department for Education and Skills. Alongside this, town planners are required to consider providing means of active transport – footpaths and cycle ways – and to ensure that outdoor spaces are adequate for the surrounding population. Schools are encouraged to offer only healthy food options and five hours of physical activity each week, as well as a cross-curricular education in all aspects of healthy lifestyles.

In order to improve the health of our children globally, it is imperative that environments and opportunities are provided through which the demands of every dimension of health can be met. This may be difficult to achieve, given the multiple demands upon children's time and limited resources, but the adventure environment does potentially offer a golden opportunity to address issues of the environment, physical activity, and psychosocial and psychological health, while also having the advantage of teaching skills, such as risk management, that can be used in many aspects of life.

Adventure's potential to address child and adolescent health problems

Kurt Hahn formulated his Outward Bound programme in the 1940s in a bid to improve the confidence and self-esteem of young people through mental and physical exertion. However, he also believed that the young people of his era were physically weaker than their ancestors, and felt something needed to be done to address this. There have since been many evolving manifestations of his original model, but his insight remains valid today. Adventurous work can impact on health in all dimensions as a direct result of the multiple areas of engagement (affective, cognitive and physical dimensions) that it entails. Using an environment in an adventurous way creates new opportunities for developing children, in terms of a better understanding of themselves and the world around them, but outcomes that may be particularly key at this time include learning to manage risk, enjoying the opportunity to be spontaneously active, and exploring activities without pre-programmed outcomes.

Escalating fears over individual and especially child safety have resulted in a powerful dread of the unknown and society attempting to 'child-proof' itself. Two factors probably drive this. First, the media has stoked the public's fear of 'stranger danger' in a way that is wholly disproportionate to the risk (which, in fact, has not increased since the 1970s). Second, we now live in a highly litigious culture, which has led to a tremendous wave of concern and policy-making over health and safety. Consequently, we are bombarded by warning signs and disclaimers. These two factors have resulted in parents effectively 'locking down' their children, which seriously impacts on those children's opportunities to learn an important life skill: how to assess and manage risk independently. When using fairly open search terms relating to adventure and children, in both academic and general search engines, we were dismayed to find that the majority of responses emphasised the illness, injury and danger that children were exposed to when making use of the outdoor environment. Researchers have even catalogued when accidents in particular activities are most likely to occur, by activity and month (Loder and Abrams, 2010). Unsurprisingly, snow sports incidents occur more frequently in the winter, and water sports injuries happen most often in the summer! Without wishing undue harm or injury to anyone, we have to ask which approach – the super safe or the one with some risk – is likely to do the most harm. It is possible to cosset both children and adults to the point where the risk of immediate death is minimised but, unfortunately, so is the quality of life, and with that comes a decline in all of our health dimensions. Adventure activities offer a halfway house: the opportunity to perceive and manage risk in a controlled and supported environment. It therefore meets the needs of the developing child while going some way to assuage societal anxiety.

Most of the 'evidence' supporting the use of adventure activities and environments to improve health and wellbeing concentrates on mental, social and (to a lesser extent) spiritual (reflective, philosophical) health. This has been generated because adventure or wilderness therapy is regularly employed to engage and help with depressed and/or disaffected young people and it generally claims improvements in the mental and social health of those involved. Unfortunately, three key factors mean that this data cannot be viewed as entirely rigorous or scientific: the environment; the participants; and the purpose of the experiences. Nevertheless, we and many others feel that the mental and social benefits are undeniable.

As the majority of these programmes are usually aimed at non-physical dimensions of health, there is even less data on their impact on fitness. However, *any* exercise element in adventure activities is likely to have positive physical outcomes. This is explored further in the 'Adults' section below but it can also be applied to the younger population. As has been mentioned, physical weakness and poor physical survival records of young people inspired Hahn's original programme, and perhaps we should now once again use adventure to enhance physical health as well as to promote mental and social wellbeing.

What could adventure contribute to childhood activity and physical health?

Appropriate physical activity is essential for health and wellbeing, and creating a lifestyle pattern of regular physical activity is an important tactic for enhancing the health of children and adolescents as they develop into adulthood. Recent guidance from the National Institute for Clinical Excellence (NICE) recommends that all children should be moderately to vigorously active for sixty to ninety minutes every day in order to maintain their health.

John Kelly and Julia Potter

Physical activity comes in many forms, but it is often interpreted as exercise, sport or training when discussed in a health context. In fact, the only essential element is movement. In young children, this ensures normal growth and development. Inactivity can lead to a range of mental and physical problems; conversely, increasing activity levels can halt the development and continuation of certain issues. For instance, one of the key factors in healthy bone development and maintenance is weight-bearing exercise, such as walking or running. With the most critical periods for skeletal health and development occurring during childhood and adolescence, the importance of appropriate exercise and activity to maximise bone mass through mineral density should not be underestimated. Unfortunately, physical activity is often recognised only for its calorie/fat-burning benefits (particularly in those with weight problems), yet there are psychological and physiological advantages too, for all body types. Increasing physical activity is an essential element in both preventing and treating obesity because it boosts muscle mass, increases mitochondrial volume and improves oxygen delivery as the heart and lungs develop.

Obesity is a condition of excess fat (adipose tissue) and is strongly associated with the onset of other diseases (co-morbidities), although the direct effects of body fat levels are difficult to isolate because inactivity is also a factor in their development. The complex interactions between fat, physical activity and disease are further emphasised by the fact that adipose tissue has direct (and indirect) negative effects on physiological functions (such as blood sugar regulation and immune function), leading to disease states, and the fact that these can be attenuated by activity. There is a great deal of evidence that physical activity improves blood sugar regulation and prevents diabetes and cardiovascular disease in adults. Unfortunately, the same level of evidence is not available for children and adolescents, partly because sufferers are still fairly rare (at present), but also because of a lack of longitudinal studies. Nevertheless, activity's role in disease prevention can be gleaned from the positive effects that it has on insulin sensitivity, reducing stress hormones and improving body composition.

The physical dimensions of adventurous activities offer great opportunities to impact on childhood health and fitness. They can provide a viable alternative to other physical exercise. Children and adults achieve higher work outputs when the physical is not the primary focus – that is, when the accomplishment of some other goal is the stated aim. It has long been established that self-efficacy is a consistent predictor of physical activity levels in adolescents. Allison *et al.* (1999) and Dwyer *et al.* (2006: 85) have stated that promotion of physical activity among adolescents should include interventions designed to increase self-efficacy in physical activity, alongside increasing fun and non-competitive elements – all components that are common in adventure activities. Improvement in psychological states is also key to success in most health interventions, including weight control. Physical activity has been broadly accepted as having positive outcomes on a range of psychological outcomes in children and young people, including self-esteem, self-efficacy and depression. Although much of the evidence is limited to cross-sectional or short-term studies, activity certainly improves blood flow to the brain, increases the release of endorphins, slows the re-uptake of serotonin and has the potential to improve body composition and blood sugar control (mood altering). The challenge lies in getting children to engage in the activity at an intensity and duration that will stimulate these psycho-physiological (enjoyment) responses, which is where some traditional PE/sport activities often fail and adventure may succeed.

The majority of children's natural physical activity tends to be spontaneous, of short duration and sporadic. Consequently, interventions to improve children's activity should take this into account. Often, all that is needed to improve activity levels in pre-teens is to 'take the brakes off'. This might involve little more than providing an environment in which the adults are happy to leave the children to explore, without a great deal of interference, although facilitation of activities and constructs are often well received, too. It might be a good idea to provide adventurous activities that allow these opportunities if we want to increase activity. Young children are frequently reminded to be cautious, and they may be over-protected because of societal fears, but they are still naturally adventurous, exploring their environment and making use of it for their own ends in play. Most likely, they could teach adults something about adventure.

If we want to understand how physically active adventure education approaches might be received by young people, it is worth reflecting on the existing knowledge bases regarding exercise and sports.

Key factors affecting activity levels

School sport and physical education

Examination of children's natural activity may help to explain why some of the more traditional activities, such as team games, used to facilitate activity in children in schools and community settings are not necessarily enjoyable for all. It may also help us understand why the PE and sport available in schools is not achieving sufficient activity levels in enough of the population, despite improvements in staffing and resources. Participation in time-tabled and extracurricular PE and sport declines as children age and develop, with significant drop-off from puberty (especially in girls), and many never recover their childhood activity levels.

Sport and PE in schools often emphasises rules and procedures, frequently set up to establish who are winners and thereby creating losers. Adults who no longer participate in sport often report that they did not like the competitive aspect of it when they were children, or the possibility of letting the team down, and therefore neither perceived nor gained the potential benefits of group activities. Other indentified barriers include: required clothing, group changing and the focus on physicality and physical success. Many children cannot identify this traditional, constructed, competitive and restrictive approach as being on the same spectrum as the inherent joy they feel when moving and playing. Consequently, the

154

John Kelly and Julia Potter

social and environmental limitations are compounded by the education of what physical activity/exercise looks and feels like. In this context, it is not surprising that the 'holy grail' for physical educationalists – 'lifelong activity for all' – remains a distant dream. It is possible that greater use of adventure activities both inside and outside schools could make a significant contribution to children, and concomitantly adults, finding a way to enjoy being active, with the happy by-products of learning new skills and maintaining a healthy body.

The aims, intentions and values of PE have been defined in many places, and well-intentioned attempts have been made to incorporate a range of sports and activities into education, as in 1992's National Curriculum (NC) Outdoor and Adventurous Activities (OAA). However, in many cases, these are limited to occasional residential experiences and orienteering. The 2009 changes to the NC potentially allow the incorporation of more OAA, but the activities and sports undertaken in a school will still largely depend on the specific experiences and skills of the PE teachers, who tend to have more traditional sporting backgrounds. Obviously, this will influence the way in which the NC is interpreted and OAA are employed for their students. For those with a lack of appropriate training, resources or enthusiasm, the inclusion of OAA will be onerous and thus limited.

Family and friends

The primary facilitators for physical activity in children are enjoyment, the encouragement of friends and family, and convenience. While participation in physical activity through enjoyment and improved self-efficacy is likely, the other factors may be less so. The lack of convenience through the requirement of specialist equipment and instruction for some activities and the possibility that friends will not want to or be able to pursue the same activity may present barriers to participation in adventure-based exercise, just as they do in other activities.

Adventure activities may suffer from other barriers to participation, too. Whilst many cultures now accept that girls can participate in sport and physical activity (even when they do not actively encourage it), some parents remain steadfastly opposed to this. Others have an unjustified fear of injury and so discourage their child's participation. It is highly unlikely, at this point, that such parents will encourage their children to take part in adventure or outdoor pursuits outside of the school timetable. So perhaps schools should accept greater responsibility for offering some access to adventurous activities.

ADULTS

Many of the issues for children and adolescents continue on into adulthood; and it is normally adults who develop the chronic health conditions that result from unhealthy lifestyles and need to undertake a health intervention to manage these disease states. Consequently, the majority of the existing research data on health and fitness relates to the adult population. However, very little research has been done into the role of adventure in health maintenance and improvement strategies. This section will present what we do know and what we can infer from other research regarding the potential role of adventure in health and fitness for adults.

Like those among children, adult physical activity levels are at an all-time low, along with population health. This decline in physical activity has been in evidence since the start of the industrial revolution as technological advances have systematically engineered physical activity out of our lives through mechanised transport and a reduction in the manual demands of all work, be it industrial or at home. Mechanisation has 'freed up' more time for leisure and recreation, but most people's recreation now tends to be sedentary. A sedentary lifestyle carries an ominous risk for developing chronic health conditions. The evidence for this, in the adult population at least, is very strong. As discussed earlier, the complex interactions between physical inactivity, adipose tissue and physiological functions mean that inactivity is a primary causative factor in numerous adult health conditions, including obesity, osteoporosis, high blood pressure, type II diabetes, many cancers and cardiovascular disease, all of which increase as we age and are therefore rapidly escalating in prevalence in an ageing, increasingly sedentary population. It is important to note that, given our ageing population, realistically we can aim only to counteract the progressive deterioration that begins around 30 years of age and thereby *maintain* physical capacity and health, rather than *improve* it *per se*.

Potential benefits to adult health from participation in adventure education

There is evidence that just living near a 'green space' reduces stress and improves mental health. Interacting with green spaces has been shown to improve symptoms of depression and anxiety, whilst walking in parks and woodland is recommended by some GPs for those with mental health issues. These issues are highly prevalent in the population and are usually costly and difficult to treat. Adventurous activities provide more opportunities to interact with this sort of environment and have the additional benefits of meeting others, learning new skills and physical activity, all of which can have their own positive effects on mental health.

Physical fitness improvements derived from participation in adventure have received little interest from the research community, even though Kurt Hahn highlighted them back in the 1940s and Alan Ewert suggested that the area demanded further investigation in 1987. However, the *physical* nature of participation in adventure education is regarded as an important aspect by those reflecting on their experiences. Caulkins *et al.* (2006) reported that wilderness experience, with a significant hiking element, impacted on individuals' perceptions of physical health. They attributed the following positive outcomes directly to the backpacking component of the therapeutic process: physical strength, adjustment and growth; competence; enjoying the feeling and scenery; exercise and physical workout;

156

unstructured, distraction-free space and time. Although there is insufficient specific evidence to prove that adventure activities influence physiological systems and health-related components of fitness, it is logical to assume that these activities would produce the same responses and adaptations as other actions of similar duration, intensity and type. Improvements should include blood lipid and cholesterol profiles, glucose metabolism and a transient reduction in blood pressure; and chronic adaptations to repeated bouts of activity (training), such as changes in body composition (more muscle and less fat), enhanced strength and power, and improvements in the cardiorespiratory systems.

Clarification of vocabulary used in exercise and health science

The physical benefits of exercise result from the body's ability to respond and adapt. In order to attain a health benefit from physical activity, it must be of a sufficient quantity and quality to overload the body and provide sufficient stimulus for positive adaptations to occur (eustress). Current guidelines in the UK (and other Western societies) recommend a minimum of thirty minutes of moderate-intensity activity on most days. (These guidelines are very general in order that they can be applied to the general population.)

Exercise to improve general health follows the FITT principle to generate an exercise or training prescription, plan or programme. This stands for *frequency, intensity, time* (duration) and *type* of exercise. Using this principle, the above recommendations would look like this:

Frequency = daily, Intensity = moderate, Time = thirty minutes, Type = aerobic

The frequency and time elements are self-explanatory. But what is a 'moderate intensity' and how can we measure it? This level of activity is recommended because it generates a sufficient cardiovascular stimulus but does not discourage an individual from further participation. Intensity is proportional to dropout and injury rates. However, high-intensity exercise gives a greater stimulus to the body and has been shown to elicit a greater positive impact on physical aspects of health, so it should be encouraged if the individual is keen. When performance is the focus, of course, high-intensity exercise is a necessity.

Quantitatively, moderate-intensity exercise may be expressed as a percentage of an individual's maximum ability to take in and use oxygen for the production of energy. This concept is known as maximal oxygen uptake or $\dot{V}O_{2max}$. This is also the criterion method for assessing aerobic fitness. If we take $\dot{V}O_{2max}$ as our benchmark, then moderate-intensity exercise is somewhere between 40 and 59 per cent of $\dot{V}O_{2max}$. But this does not let people know that they are working at the right level; and, anyway, even measuring it requires sophisticated equipment, skill and expertise.

Heart rate provides a useful way of estimating energy expenditure, and the intensity of exercise can be expressed as a percentage of maximal heart rate. Maximal heart rate can be estimated by subtracting the individual's age from 220, to give beats per minute ($b \cdot min^{-1}$). As an example, 55 per cent of $\dot{V}O_{2max}$ is approximately 50 per cent of maximal heart rate. Whilst this method is much cheaper, it still requires some equipment, and it is not perfect.

Although the assessment of $\dot{V}O_{2max}$ and heart rate are excellent measures of exercise intensity, they have limited use for adventure educators working in a field environment. A much more simple, cost-effective and well-evidenced method is individual perception of those exercising (internal rating of perceived exertion) or the person leading the exercise (external rating of perceived exertion). The Swedish exercise physiologist Gunnar Borg (1998) has devoted a lifetime to quantifying people's perception of effort. On the 'Borg Scale', moderately hard work is represented by the numbers 11 to 13. With a little practice, people can provide a number that best represents their perception of workload, and this may then be used to moderate the activity. Without a scale, something similar can be achieved simply by asking, 'How hard do you think the exercise is?' This will provide a qualitative response: 'easy', 'hard', 'very difficult', or some other adjective. Adventure activities are likely to have an advantage here over traditional gym-based activity as they tend to have a reduced perception of effort and concurrently a greater adherence and participation. Some interesting research could be done into perception of effort in adventurous and 'traditional' activities, but anecdotally it appears that perception is much lower for both children and adults in adventurous activities, which certainly provides opportunities for longer durations at health-benefiting intensities.

In the adult population, the greatest health gains are likely to be achieved by activities that impact on body composition and cardiovascular endurance. These are two key health-related components of fitness that have concomitant effects on a range of physiological functions and disease states. Adventure education has the potential to improve both, with associated improvements in factors relating to health.

Cardiovascular endurance

Cardiovascular endurance has a primary influence on being able to sustain activity and it is synonymous with fitness. Highly fit individuals can carry out physical activity over a considerable period of time – many hours or even days. The most 'fit' people tend to have the best cardiovascular endurance. Cardiovascular endurance (fitness) shows the strongest correlation to health out of all possible measures.

The simplest way to improve this dimension is to engage in prolonged (more than thirty minutes) sub-maximal (moderate-intensity) exercise. So prolonged-duration, moderate-intensity adventure activities – such as kayaking, mountain-biking and hill-walking – provide the necessary stimulus to increase fitness. Although a substantial amount of literature has investigated the high-performance aspects of these activities, there is surprisingly little on

158

potential health benefits. Studies investigating the recreational aspects of these sports provide a more useful insight for adventure educators, but they are few and far between.

Kayaking provides a good example of the potential of these sports for improving fitness, and it is commonly used in many adventure education programmes. It fits the criteria for an exercise likely to improve fitness: it is usually of a prolonged nature (time), predominantly uses the large muscles of the upper body (type) and may be undertaken at a moderate pace (intensity). Data from our laboratories, and field research by Baldock (2008), have shown that twenty minutes of recreational-paced kayaking elicits an energy cost of approximately 160 kcal when measured using a portable gas analyser. This equates to 68 per cent of maximal heart rate and a perception of effort between 10 and 12. Hoffman et al. (2006) studied a short kayak trip (twenty–thirty minutes) and found similar data: heart rates were approximately 40 per cent of heart-rate reserve (about 64 per cent of maximal heart rate) at around 119 b·min^{-1}. They then calculated an approximate value of nearly 300 kcal for a thirty-minute paddle. Pederson and Samuelson (2005) studied a two-hour kayak trip and found that it was close to sufficient stimulus for health benefits. These data, although limited in their scope, suggest that kayaking at a self-paced moderate intensity will elicit a physiological response that is similar to traditional forms of exercise, such as walking and cycling. And, if continued on a regular basis, it will have a positive influence on health.

Body composition and weight control

In 1992, Dr Mike Stroud and Sir Ranulph Fiennes skied across Antarctica, hauling (skiing) a sled of supplies (which initially weighed 222 kilos) for 10 hours a day for 95 days. They had estimated that they would need to consume 5600 kcal per day. In fact, this level of energy intake was rarely achieved, and they consumed an average of just 5100 kcal. Energy expenditure was higher, averaging 6700 kcal per day and sometimes reaching 11,500 kcal. Given this mismatch between energy intake and energy expenditure, both (initially normal-weight) men lost 25 per cent of their body mass (Stroud, 1995). This was not a healthy endeavour and would be physically, financially and practically inaccessible to the general population. So what about less extreme activities? All activities that 'use' calories can elicit a weight loss.

Hill-walking probably represents the most effective adventure activity for the promotion of health through good exposure to 'green spaces', high levels of energy expenditure, and associated cardiorespiratory stimulus. So it is somewhat surprising that it has been little explored. In 1999, we observed the effects of five days of hill-walking totalling 105 miles (Tour du Mont Blanc) on moderately fit undergraduates. All reported weight loss and considerable improvements in cardiovascular fitness and leg strength. Ainslie et al. (2002) investigated the metabolic effects of hill-walking in the Scottish Highlands. The participants completed a 12-kilometre hill-walk in times that varied between 48 minutes and 5 hours; the elevation varied between 100 and 900 metres above sea level – typical of a mountain

159

environment. Body mass dropped an average of two kilos in the group as a consequence of considerable calorie deficit. Further analysis of this data suggested that exercise at this intensity and probably for this duration results not only in an energy deficit but in a preferential use of fat as an energy source. This is a positive result not only for weight loss but for other aspects of health, such as cholesterol and fat transport in the body.

These examples indicate that participating in low-intensity, prolonged-duration adventurous sports will elicit physiological responses sufficient to provide individual health benefits, such as improvements in cardiovascular endurance and body composition through increased fat burning and stimuli to increase muscle mass. It is highly likely that adventurous activities and sports can offer sufficient stimulus to maintain and improve all components of fitness, but lack of activity-specific evidence means that these assumptions must currently be based on 'like-for-like' comparisons with activities of similar intensity and duration that engage similar volumes and types of muscle mass.

Lifelong participation in physical activity

As the benefits of any physical activity are only transitory, the primary goal of any exercise intervention is to promote patterns of habitual physical activity over the life course. Yet we know the majority of UK people are sedentary and do not do adequate physical activity, hence the rise in chronic health conditions. Many of us will make short-lived attempts to 'get fit', so why is it that we struggle to adopt long-term physical activity and maintain it?

Our genes, which were selected thousands of years ago, allow us to complete great feats of physical strength and endurance, and they also govern our motivation to engage in these activities. It is unlikely that during our evolution there would have been any advantage in participating in voluntary exercise that did not have a utilitarian goal, such as 'going for a run'. Our activity patterns were forged out of necessity. We would move to find food or to avoid becoming a predator's dinner. Other than that, we would rest, refuel and conserve our strength. It is highly unlikely that men would return from a three-day hunt and women from gathering food over many square miles only to decide that they then needed to go for a jog. Humans are probably hard-wired to *avoid* physical activity whenever they can. This makes us fairly resistant to performing unnecessary physical activity.

This behaviour can be observed throughout daily life. Most people will opt to expend the least amount of energy possible: taking the lift rather than using the stairs; going through an automatic rather than a manual door; and driving to the shops rather than walking all reflect a preference for physical activity avoidance rather than any inherent motivation to exercise. Given this background, professionals working in health promotion and physical activity face a gargantuan task. In order for adventure educators to influence long-term patterns of physical activity, they must be aware of behaviour-change strategies and factors that are likely to improve adherence, and try to work against those thrifty genes.

John Kelly and Julia Potter

Attempts to model individuals who can change health-related behaviours have led to a range of theories. Behavioural-change theories that have the most to offer are those that acknowledge the dynamic relationships that exist between an individual's attributes and resources, the physical and social environment, and the behaviour targeted for change. These theories provide a framework through which interventions can be individually tailored.

The broadly applied Prochaska and DiClemete (1982) Stages of Change model describes individuals as moving through a series of stages when changing a behaviour. These (not always discrete) stages are: pre-contemplation, contemplation, preparation, action, maintenance and relapse. Prochaska *et al.* (1992) demonstrated that success in behaviour change is directly related to an individual's stage before the intervention, allowing the professional to tailor the approach or strategy to the stage. People who are in the *action* stage are clearly more likely to change their behaviour than those in the *pre-contemplation* stage. A successful outcome (adoption of lifelong activity) is unlikely if we force someone who resides in the pre-contemplation stage (never thought about activity and have no intention of doing so) through an aggressive and punishing week-long expedition. This model is a simple-to-use tool; and if used before an intervention begins, it allows us to tailor activities. It may also be used as an evaluation tool, to measure progress.

Many factors influence the adoption of physical activity and exercise adherence, all of which interact with each other. The American College of Sports Medicine (2000) identifies the following as influencing adoption and adherence: personal and behavioural factors, environ-mental factors and programme-related factors. Manipulation of these factors can improve adoption and adherence. We will now consider some of the most common adoption and adherence issues (a fuller review of these factors can be found in Dishman, 1994).

Personal and behavioural factors

Previous experience of physical activity and exercise

Every adult will have had some experience of activity and sport through school PE lessons. Unfortunately, for some, this may have been a negative experience, and may have led to exercise avoidance. Reassurance should be given that exercise does not have to be difficult or painful; and that moderate-intensity exercise is sufficient for health benefits, with no requirement to 'bust a gut'. Confirm the benefits of moderate-intensity exercise to your clients, dispel myths and make activity more accessible.

Relevance of the programme and goal-setting

Programmes (interventions) need to be personally relevant. Both the client's goals and the activities that are used should meet the expectations of the client. For example, weight loss is a common goal for individuals who take up physical activity, but some may be happy not to gain any more weight whilst others will anticipate considerable losses.

Environmental and programme-related factors

The most cited reasons for failure to adopt physical activity or to drop out from programmes are time, cost and convenience.

- *Time.* You should consider how the client might continue to exercise when they leave your programme, given their time constraints, and suggest ways in which the activity might be incorporated into their daily life.
- *Cost.* Some adventure activities are very costly. On the other hand, others are relatively cheap: for instance, bouldering and surfing require an initial outlay, but then all they demand is the right environment. Walking is perhaps the cheapest activity of all, yet offers many physical and mental health benefits.
- *Convenience.* The greater the effort to prepare for physical activity, the greater the drop out. Therefore, try promoting activities that involve small amounts of travel and equipment (at least initially) to encourage engagement. Walking, cycling and local exploring each offers a good route into adventurous activities.

Increasing the adoption of and adherence to physical activity

The first and perhaps greatest challenge to promoting physical activity is getting individuals to adopt and then adhere to a new exercise and programme of activities. While many individuals enjoy going to the gym, a larger proportion do not. Adventure activities may have the advantage here in being more enticing, stimulating, varied and therefore enjoyable than more traditional exercise programmes. Few people report experiencing pleasure *while* exercising, but many experience a sense of pleasure, competency and mastery *after* exercise. This is because exercise stimulates the release of endorphins (opiate-like substances) that generate feelings of happiness and pleasure. However, for enjoyment to be achieved on this physiological level, the activity must be of sufficient intensity and duration. This can be particularly difficult to achieve in previously sedentary individuals, resulting in low levels of satisfaction and therefore a lack of engagement in the exercise activity. However, this can be overcome by adventure activities, because they have something else to offer.

Besides the physical benefits of exercise, adventure activities allow participants to experience new environments, socialise with new people and master new skills. These benefits might be most appreciated by the participant upon reflection of the activity and their achievements, which means that adventure activities have another advantage, because reflection is an essential part of most adventure education experiences. This period of reflection draws out good and bad experiences and attempts to reinforce the good, thus increasing enjoyment during subsequent activities, and concurrently increasing the possibility of adherence. Such reflection rarely happens outside of adventure education or

John Kelly and Julia Potter

a formal coaching session. As an adventure educator, you are an advocate of physical activity and exercise, and should show enthusiasm for the activity, highlighting the fun and enjoyable aspects of the activity. It is therefore worth asking your clients which activity they enjoyed most, and even to rate their level of enjoyment on a scale of 1 to 10.

Guidelines for physical activity in adventure education

Tailoring an adventure programme for physical activity

Some adventurous programmes are more physically demanding than others. If you wish to use adventure as an intervention to improve health, it is worth considering the following points:

- The PAR-Q (Physical Activity Readiness Questionnaire) might help establish a current level of fitness and allow you to adapt the exercise intensity. It will also provide important information on health issues, such as heart disease and diabetes.
- Prochaska and DiClemente's (1982) Stage of Change model may help you determine which activity is most suitable.
- Find out which activities the client is most looking forward to and have them rate how much they think they will enjoy it.
- Use an exercise modality (activity) that best meets the needs of your client. Hill-walking might be the best activity for cost and convenience, and the intensity level will be relatively easy to adjust, but it is essential that your client wishes to do it.
- You must be flexible during the programme. You should be prepared to adapt an activity or even change to a different activity.
- Provide positive feedback where appropriate.

When trying to improve long-term adherence to physical activity:

- Identify which activities clients enjoyed most and discuss a plan for the long term with them.
- Provide clients with information on their local clubs, contacts and facilities that would facilitate social support.
- Discuss with your client how they might involve their family and friends in the activity.
- If possible, provide some simple follow-up via telephone or email.
- Familiarise yourself with basic training techniques and be prepared to give advice on training.

SUMMARY

The physical and social environment in which we live is massively different from the one in which we evolved; and, to some extent, the further our environment and behaviours move away from our default setting, the more difficult it is to stay healthy. Therefore, any activity that helps an individual to increase physical activity should be encouraged. It is unlikely that adventure activities will have a significant impact on chronic health conditions on a global level, but for the individual who is not inspired by traditional forms of leisure activity – such as organised games, frequenting the gym or running – providing non-traditional or adventurous activities may be of considerable benefit and could provide information for other positive changes.

Adventure activities comprise three elements that almost invariably have a positive impact on health and wellbeing: adventure, physical activity and the outdoors. Each of these improves the dimensions of health, but in combination they can act as a tour de force in counteracting the West's ever-growing problem of lifestyle diseases. Unfortunately, as yet, there has been little scientific research of the type that is routinely employed for other health-intervention strategies to determine the true benefits of adventure education. Therefore, we would encourage all adventure educators to take an active role in evaluating their programmes and contribute to a data-gathering process that will provide an evidence base for adventure education. By collecting simple data and getting the results into the public domain, we will increase understanding of and support for adventure interventions as part of a physical health agenda.

REFERENCES

Ainslie, P.N., Campbell, I.T., Frayn, K.N., Humphreys, S.M., Maclaren, D.P.M. and Riley, T. (2002) Physiological and metabolic responses to a hill walk, *Journal of Applied Physiology*, 92: 179–187.

Allison, K.R., Dwyer, J.J. and Makin, S. (1999) Self-efficacy and participation in vigorous physical activity in high school students, *Health Education Behavior*, 26: 12–24.

American College of Sports Medicine (2000) *Guidelines for Exercise Testing and Prescription*, 6th edn, Philadelphia, PA: Lippincott, Williams & Wilkins.

Baldock, L. (2008) The energetic of paddling kayaks of different hull shapes, unpublished undergraduate dissertation, University of Chichester.

Booth, F.W., Chakravarthy, M.V., Gordon, S.E. and Spangenburg, E.E. (2002) Waging war on physical inactivity: using modern molecular ammunition against an ancient enemy, *Journal of Applied Physiology*, 93: 3–30.

Borg, G. (1998) *Borg's Perceived Exertion and Pain Scales*, Champaign, IL: Human Kinetics.

Caulkins, M.C., White, D.D. and Russell, K.C. (2006) The role of physical exercise in wilderness therapy for troubled adolescent women, *Journal of Experiential Education*, 29: 18–37.

Cannon, J.A.G. (1993) Exercise and resistance to infection, *Journal of Applied Physiology*, 74: 973–981.

Dishman, R.K. (1994) *Advances in Exercise Adherence*, Champaign, IL: Human Kinetics.

Dwyer, J., Allison, K.R., Goldenberg, E.R., Fein, A.J., Yoshida, K.K. and Boutilier M.A. (2006) Adolescent girls' perceived barriers to participation in physical activity, *Adolescence*, 41: 75–89.

164

Ewert, A. (1987) Research in outdoor adventure: overview and analysis, *The Bradford Papers Annual*, 2: 15–28.

Hoffman, A., Garner, K., Krings, M., Ottney, D. and Becker, R. (2006) Energy expenditure of recreational kayaking, *Journal of Undergraduate Kinesiology Research*, 2: 26–31.

Loder, R.T. and Abrams, S. (2010) Temporal variation in childhood injury from common recreational activities, *Injury*, 41: 886–899.

Pederson, H. and Samuelson, M. (2005) The physiological effects of recreational kayaking, *Journal of Undergraduate Kinesiology Research*, 1: 30–38.

Prochaska, J.O. and DiClemente, C.C. (1982) Trans-theoretical therapy: toward a more integrative model of change, *Psychotherapy: Theory, Research and Practice*, 19: 276–288.

Prochaska, J.O., DiClemente, C.C. and Norcross, J.C. (1992) In search of how people change, *American Psychologist*, 47: 1102–1114.

Stroud, M.A. (1995) The biochemical and physiological effects of 95 days' endurance exercise in negative energy balance, paper presented to the Research and Technology Organisation's 'Effect of Prolonged Military Activities in Man' workshop, Oslo, April.

UNICEF (2007) *Child Poverty in Perspective: An Overview of Child Well-being in Rich Countries*, Innocenti Report Card No. 7, Florence: Innocenti Research Centre.

World Health Organisation (WHO) (1948) *Preamble to the Constitution of the World Health Organisation*, Geneva: WHO.

CHAPTER NINE

ADVENTURE EDUCATION AND DISAFFECTED YOUTH

Ed Christian

If you believe that outdoor and adventurous experiences can be so powerful that they have the potential to transform the way we feel about the world and everything in it, and if you have an interest in working with young people to aid their social development and improve their wellbeing, then this chapter is for you. Read on!

INTRODUCTION

There is a long-standing and commonly held belief amongst the adventure education community that adventurous experiences offer particular advantages for promoting personal development and pro-social behaviour. Much of the philosophy surrounding this belief originates in the teachings of the German educationalist Dr Kurt Hahn. Much of Hahn's philosophy stemmed from his observations of what he termed the 'decline of modern youth' in Germany during the 1920s. These observations, coupled with the view that young people's development should centre on education for active citizenship, formed the basis of Hahnism, which essentially promotes the use of adventure and challenge as a medium for learning and survival.

Hahn's legacy continues to this day, primarily through the ongoing success of the Outward Bound movement and Gordonstoun School. Furthermore, Hahn's philosophy has guided the enduring belief of adventure educators that outdoor and adventurous experiences, when facilitated appropriately and effectively, can provide a catalyst so powerful that it may elicit positive behavioural change amongst disaffected populations. Many of us working in adventure education will reflect on experiences in the outdoors that have been so significant that they have literally changed the way we think and behave. This philosophy is the bedrock of adventure education as an intervention for disaffected populations, with the central tenet being positive behavioural change.

The aim of this chapter is to draw on some of the literature that has formed the contemporary approach to dealing with disaffection. I will draw upon related disciplines such as clinical psychology, mentorship and counselling and consider the idea that it is the responsibility of the educator to move towards a philosophy of accountability. We live in a culture where securing funding and encouraging investment in dealing with disaffection is ever more challenging. This presents us with the demand to provide evidence that our undertakings in working with disaffected populations is actually doing what we say it is doing. This need to validate practices could be seen in a negative light by many, with the idea of accountability seen as a threat to operations that we might have been doing well for years. We might 'just know' that adventure education can change people's perceptions, attitudes and behaviour and that our anecdotes and experiences are sufficient to justify this. Many practitioners have great stories of the 'bad kid turned good' as a result of personal growth and social development; and we know that adventure education is particularly effective at promoting such growth. As history has shown, however, it is often politicians and the economic climate that dictate the availability of funding for programmes in social care and public services. With this in mind, there is a growing sentiment that adventure educators should aim to provide empirical evidence that beneficial behavioural change is facilitated by the effective use of adventure education.

So, how should we go about providing this evidence? One approach that I shall look at in some depth centres on becoming *mechanistic* rather than *descriptive* in the way we look at dealing with the problem of disaffection. By doing this, we will consider the mechanisms behind how behaviour change occurs and how we can drive, facilitate and ultimately account for this. In an age driven by evidence-based practice, understanding these mechanisms and having specific tools to deal with disaffected populations will be vital to the practitioner. The intention of this chapter is to move towards an understanding of the complex picture of dealing with disaffection and promoting positive behaviour change. Furthermore, the chapter intends to raise awareness of how we might use particular techniques and tools to foster development and pro-social behaviour.

WHAT IS DISAFFECTION?

This is a tough question because 'disaffection' is often used as an umbrella term to describe all behaviours that are not socially desirable. Given that different people have different ways of defining the term, it is necessary to look at how the literature goes about classifying people as disaffected. Williamson and Middlemiss (1999: 13) say that disaffected populations might include anyone who is 'temporarily sidetracked, essentially confused or deeply alienated'. This is a pretty loose definition and could refer to a wide range of people, from those who temporarily disengage from school all the way to those who repeatedly commit criminal acts and are removed from society. Already, then, it is obvious that we are talking about a group of people who are not easily identifiable. Disaffected populations, like all populations, consist of individuals and they are therefore intangible and hard to categorise. Newburn and Shiner (2005) refer to disaffected people as those who are excluded from mainstream society in some way and are therefore at risk of being socially polarised. The idea of social exclusion is a common theme throughout the literature and paints a picture of a significant proportion of society that is, for whatever reason, 'on the outside looking in'. Another common feature is that being labelled 'disaffected' has negative connotations, with the danger that we create something of an 'underclass' (Murray, 1990). This, however, is a somewhat destructive view and one that will further alienate the majority from the minority.

Perhaps a better way of understanding disaffection is to divide populations into sub-groups. The first group Newburn and Shiner describe are those who are of compulsory school age and are absent from education either because of truancy or exclusion, and those who remain in education but are significantly underachieving or displaying antisocial behaviour. The second group comprises those who are of post-compulsory education age, have not continued in education or training, and have not entered the workforce. These individuals are usually labelled NEETs (not in education, employment or training) in the UK, and similar classifications exist worldwide.

Newburn and Shiner's classification is a useful way for adventure educators to subdivide disaffected populations as it gives us a platform to classify a given group and to begin to understand their needs. As mentioned in Chapter 2, understanding the group you are working with and facilitating experiences to meet their needs are fundamental skills for the adventure practitioner. We cannot assume that groups that look similar have exactly the same needs, and we should always plan for the most relevant individual outcomes. So what do disaffected populations look like to the adventure educator?

> In my experience of working with youth groups deemed to be 'disaffected', the key to a successful programme is to understand quickly and accurately who we are delivering to so we can approach them in the right way. Although we get information prior to a group arriving at the centre, it is still important for us to make out own judgement of the individuals we are working with. I've worked with young people from a real mix of backgrounds, from inner-city kids all the way to some of the most extreme young offenders, and I can honestly say that the key to successful delivery is quickly to establish realistic outcomes with group leaders and gain as much information as possible about the individuals in the group. This helps me set clear goals and also to recognise when it's time to push them hard and, more importantly, when to back off.
>
> Simon Luck, development tutor, Skern Lodge, Devon

Before we look at where disaffection has come from and why it is a growing problem, it would be useful to consider if adventure education can play a role in dealing with it. In adventure education, we will need to answer questions from the wider community, such as:

- Who cares?
- Why should we do anything about it?
- Why not just lock them up and throw away the key?
- Why should naughty kids get fun activities and holidays?

Although these questions might seem harsh, we hear them often, so we should be able to answer them. Society demands that we are accountable for our practices and have a solid argument for justifying the role of adventure education (which is seen by many as a fringe activity or even a 'treat'). Even private sector organisations, in the form of residential care homes, will bid for government funding, so it is important for the sector as a whole to have a solid basis for the justification of its practices.

With respect to who cares and whether we should we do anything about it, let us first examine some statistics. According to the Prince's Trust, in 2007 an estimated 1.2 million young people were not in work, education or training in the UK (Prince's Trust, 2007b). You might feel that this means there are a lot of young people with no direction, perhaps with low self-esteem and lacking confidence, and that this in itself is reason enough to tackle the problem of disaffection. But another perspective is that there are over a million young people who are able to work but are not part of the workforce, do not pay taxes and do not contribute to society. As we will see in greater detail later, the Prince's Trust report (2007b) estimates the cost to the economy of disaffected young people to be around £10 million a day. Consequently, we could argue that there are 10 million good reasons to meet the challenge of disaffection every day.

Let us look at the extreme end of the disaffected youth problem. There is an obvious link between disaffected young people and crime, and a small minority of those we refer to as disaffected will certainly spend some time in prison. The annual cost of keeping a prisoner in jail in 2010 was estimated to be somewhere in the region of £30,000 to £40,000 – a figure that is comparable to Eton College's school fees. But how many young people are we talking about here? According to the Prison Service (2010) and the Prison Reform Trust (2010), at the time of writing there were between 14,000 and 15,000 people aged between 15 and 20 serving custodial sentences in the UK. Clearly, then, the cost of locking up disaffected youngsters who have turned to crime is significant.

All of this means there are two costs involved with disaffection. First, there are the actual costs of keeping the most extreme cases in prison and supporting those who are not in education, employment or training. Second, there is the cost to the economy of not having young people in the workforce and contributing financially to society. We often switch on the news to hear headlines about overcrowding in prisons or the latest pressure on the economy, and with this we hear judges and politicians calling for alternatives to custodial sentences in order to alleviate the burden of disaffection on society. So, with respect to the question 'Who cares?', we all should! If there were less pressure on the public purse and more people in the workforce, we would all benefit from economic stability and growth. Put simply, education is cheaper than incarceration.

The notion of providing offenders with adventure interventions is regularly challenged, but let us consider what makes disaffected people reintegrate with the rest of society. Or, to put it another way, what cures disaffection? The Prince's Trust (2007a) interviewed ex-young offenders and asked them why they had not re-offended. These young people highlighted some key reasons:

- Advice and support from a mentor.
- Access to courses and qualifications.
- Incentives and rewards.
- Engaging with activities and programmes.
- Something positive to do and interesting places to go.
- A consistent worker or mentor who makes sure appointments are kept.
- Being around other young people you can trust.
- Taking on responsibility.
- Increasing confidence and motivation.

Adventure education is well placed to provide much of this: trust, support, reward, positive activities, consistency, responsibility, confidence and motivation. Research has repeatedly demonstrated that participation in adventure education initiatives results in significant improvements in all of these areas for many participants. So, if you are ever asked, 'Why should bad kids get fun activities and holidays?', perhaps you might answer that there is more to it than meets the eye. The activities themselves are secondary to the development of the life skills that they foster and develop.

WHAT ARE THE ORIGINS OF DISAFFECTED POPULATIONS?

We live in a changing world. Huge changes have affected young people in Britain over the last three decades. These have included transformations in the education and labour markets towards the end of the last century and into this one. For example, Newburn and Shiner (2005) state that in the 1970s over two-thirds of young people left school at the compulsory age of 15 and immediately entered the workforce. By the early 1990s, this proportion had dropped to less than one-fifth. Central to this change was the contraction of the youth labour market in the 1980s and the subsequent rise of youth unemployment to a number in excess of one million. This changing dynamic contributed to a growing national crisis at the time and gave rise to riots in 1981 and 1985, predominantly in areas of high youth unemployment.

In an attempt to resolve the crisis, Margaret Thatcher's government introduced a series of strategies aimed at increasing skills and qualifications among young people. Most notably the Youth Training Scheme (YTS) and the Youth Opportunity Programme (YOP) were introduced in a bid to cut the number of unemployed young people. Successive governments have continued to build on the management of youth unemployment by introducing various new initiatives, training schemes and expansions and diversifications of further education.

Consequently, the transition from school to the workforce, which was once straightforward, has become considerably more complex. Today, there are myriad options and potential pathways that young people must navigate between to find the transition that is best for them. Fundamentally, for many young people, the length of time needed to make a successful transition has been significantly extended.

In addition to increasingly difficult school–work transitions, Coles (1995) outlines further problems compounding young people's development. In particular, he focuses on the transition from the parental home to independent living and the domestic challenges that this represents. Perhaps you can relate to this by reflecting on the trials and tribulations of moving out of home to 'fend for yourself' for the first time.

When we consider today's school–work transitions alongside these domestic challenges, we begin to get a sense of the increasingly complicated choices facing young people that generally did not exist a generation ago. At best, the diversification of options facing young people may be perceived as a challenge that will lead to greater self-determination and ultimately independence. At worst, it could be seen as a risk with daunting consequences if you make the wrong choice.

Not every young person is equally at risk of disaffection. Evidence suggests that both school and youth disaffection are rooted in particular circumstances that result from the changing society in which we live and more specific and situational social contexts. In 2000, the UK government launched its National Strategy for Neighbourhood Renewal. With respect to disaffected young people, its report stated:

> The odds are heavily stacked against those who have experienced multiple disadvantages:
>
> - Family life characterised by disrupted relationships, poverty and worklessness;
> - Education that fails to meet their needs or motivate them;
> - Peer pressures that encourage sexual activity, drug taking or crime;
> - Low expectations and the absence of adult role models;
> - Victimisation and bullying; and
> - An inadequate response from public services.
>
> (UK Government, 2000)

THE COST OF EXCLUSION

To comprehend the extent to which young people are exposed to disadvantage (and to gain an appreciation of the financial implications of disaffection), we can look at the findings of the Prince's Trust's (2007b) investigation into the subject: *The Cost of Exclusion*. This study focuses almost exclusively on the financial implications of disaffection in the UK.

171

The report stated that there were 1.24 million 16- to 24-year-old NEETs in the UK in 2006, representing a 15 per cent increase on 1997's figure of 1.08 million. In other words, almost one in five young people of post-school age in the UK were not in education, employment or training. The report then details the cost of youth unemployment, youth crime and educational underachievement. The statistics are alarming:

- The productivity loss to the economy as a result of youth unemployment is estimated at £10 million every day.
- Youth unemployment and inactivity cost the economy £20 million a week in job seeker's allowance.
- These two points combined represent a cost of £70 million a week.
- The total cost of youth crime in Great Britain in 2004 was estimated to be in excess of £1 billion.
- In 2005 the percentage of young people with no formal qualifications stood at 12.6 per cent, 12 per cent, 8.3 per cent, 8.3 per cent and 19.9 per cent in England, Wales, Scotland and Northern Ireland, respectively.
- The UK has between 15 and 25 per cent lower output per hour than France, Germany and the US, much of which is attributed to poorer levels of employee skills.

(Prince's Trust, 2007b)

Clearly, the Prince's Trust's findings demand action. From an adventure education point of view, the study provides a good rationale for using adventure interventions. With the cost of one person's incarceration standing at between £30,000 and £40,000 per year, not to mention strong evidence that imprisonment does little to modify behaviour, there are clearly grounds for investment in educational interventions that *do* support behavioural change, such as adventure education.

THE ROLE OF ADVENTURE EDUCATION: RESEARCH AND PRACTICE

Youth disaffection is clearly a problem for society from various perspectives, such as educational, criminal and cost to the tax payer. However, this fails to take into account the emotional aspect of the young people themselves, who may suffer from low self-esteem and confidence as well as other issues. A major problem with disaffection is that it is often a cycle that is difficult to break. Antisocial behaviour leads to alienation and polarisation from the majority, which pushes young people ever further away, leading to even more antisocial behaviour. The concept of society not caring and being antagonistic towards young people results in a mentality of resentment that is destructive for everyone. In order to break this cycle, it is vital that young people have positive alternatives and a means of re-engagement with society. In this section, I shall explore the role of adventure education in promoting behavioural change and developing more pro-social behaviour.

Ed Christian

The study of adventure education programmes' work with disaffected populations is by no means new. As far back as the late 1960s, adventure education practitioners sought to provide empirical evidence of the behavioural change resulting from the experiences they offered. Kelly and Baer (1968) studied 120 juvenile offenders aged between 15 and 17. Their aim was to assess participant levels of recidivism (re-offending) in the aftermath of a US-based Outward Bound adventure education programme that consisted of a high degree of physical activity followed by periods of quiet reflection. The study showed that the programme produced fewer than half the number of recidivists (20 per cent) than a control group (42 per cent). Interestingly, though, Kelly and Baer's study also showed that, after the first year of the programme, recidivist rates of those in the programme started to increase. Unfortunately, this trend continued over the next five years until, finally, the recidivism rate of the programme group equalled that of the control group.

These findings tally with other research into the impact of adventure education programmes: the short-term effects tend to be good, but these benefits often erode or are lost completely over time, especially when the participant is reintegrated into their habitual environment. Kelly and Baer also suggested that several key variables were related to recidivism, including the type of offence, age and parenting issues. Moreover, one issue raised by Kelly and Baer's research resonates through much of the subsequent literature: the importance of individual differences.

It is something of a paradox that adventure educators and researchers have tended to rely heavily on *group*-based research in order to assess the impact of adventure education programmes on *individuals*. It is worth briefly reflecting on researchers' over-reliance on the 'average' in group-based research designs. In this approach, variables such as school attendance or violent outbursts are grouped together and averaged out in order to establish a mean, which then becomes an indication of the effectiveness of the independent variable (often an adventure education intervention). The problem here is that an individual's data (attendance, number of violent outbursts and so on) are lost among (or, at best, masked by) the tendency of the group, so we are left with little or no idea of the effectiveness of a programme on that individual. To overcome this problem, we must pay close attention to the needs and development of individual participants *during* the programme, as well as afterwards.

Contemporary research has tended to focus on particular aspects of social functioning, such as peer relations, group cohesion and self-esteem, with promising results often arising from such studies. It is worth considering some of the potential mechanisms that underpin modern experimentation in our field. Although we cannot expect to find a one-size-fits-all approach to dealing with disaffection, we can try to provide an academic underpinning upon which to base our programming. To illustrate this, it is useful to borrow a concept from clinical psychology.

THE BIOPSYCHOSOCIAL MODEL OF HEALTH

In 1977, the American psychiatrist George Engel introduced the Biopsychosocial model of health (Figure 9.1), which was originally adopted by the medical profession to diagnose and treat illness and disease. The model focuses on the interconnection of the psychological and sociological aspects of a patient's life, rather than just considering the biological component of their health. It is holistic and proposes that overall health will emerge from achieving the balance of all three components. An example might be a patient suffering from a migraine. Of course, a doctor might do no more than prescribe painkillers – address the biological component of the problem by trying to reduce the physical pain with a drug. However, using the Biopsychosocial model, the doctor might also undertake an analysis of the social (work or family pressures) and psychological (stress or fear) components of the patient's life and seek to remedy these, too. The idea is that social and psychological pressures often lead to ill health, so treatment should consider addressing these (the causes), rather than just the condition itself (the effect). For example, students frequently fall ill around exam time, due to stress, lack of sleep, anxiety and peer pressure. Doctors using the Biopsychosocial model would attempt to tackle these problems at their source. For example, they might advise development of a strong social base with friends and tutors (the sociological aspect) and could deal with the anxiety by recommending relaxation exercises (the psychological aspect).

The Biopsychosocial model has been applied to a variety of areas in health and wellbeing, but not specifically to adventure education. Fox and Avramidis (2003) use it as a basis for considering dealing with young people with emotional and behavioural difficulties, but

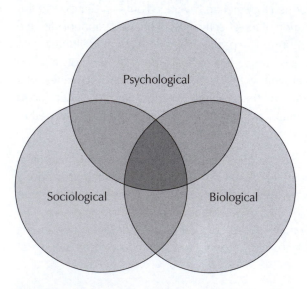

Figure 9.1 The biopsychosocial model of health

174

they fall short of testing its propositions. So how might we, as adventure education practitioners, use the Biopsychosocial model when dealing with disaffected young people? From an adventure education perspective, we might consider 'health' from the perspective of emotional and social wellbeing, rather than simply physical condition. Emotional and social wellbeing promote reintegration of disaffected young people into mainstream society, and the sociological and psychological components are best developed through adventure education interventions.

Fairbridge is an organisation that specialises in such interventions by supporting inner-city youth in the most disadvantaged areas of the UK. It works with young people to develop self-belief, confidence and other essential life skills by operating community centres and residential experiences with a strong emphasis on adventure activities. An integral part of its operations is to facilitate a social environment that is positive and supportive. Whilst we must accept that much of a young person's environment is determined by factors outside of our control, organisations such as Fairbridge offer a consistent support structure where young people are encouraged to express themselves in a variety of contexts, such as art, media production and outdoor sports. When young people engage with such an organisation, they know that they are entering a safer and more supportive environment than they generally experience in the rest of their lives. They also have the benefit of interacting with professional tutors. Consistency in social structure and interpersonal relationships promote pro-social attitudes, and these two factors can often reduce antisocial behaviour. Fairbridge is an excellent example of an organisation that contributes meaningfully to the sociological component of the Biopsychosocial model.

When thinking of the psychological component, we might well focus on negative personality constructs. In the case of disaffected young people, such issues as low self-esteem, high anxiety and low confidence might come to mind. Here, we are seeking to diagnose the problem. Once we have established the most pressing issue, we need to think about prescribing an experience or activity that might address it. No one expects a young person to change their behaviour after a single day of an adventure intervention, but continual reinforcement of positive behaviour over time might well reap rewards. The following case study is an example of such an approach.

TOM'S STORY

Tom was a student in a pupil referral unit and was reluctant to engage in any task, be it academic or physical. He had developed a defence mechanism of refusing to participate in any kind of activity simply because he was afraid of failing at it. Our unit placed particular emphasis on adventure education, with young people taking part in some sort of activity every day. In Tom's case, it was essential for us to plan and facilitate activities that would ensure some degree of success on his part, usually through setting and working towards goals. These goals might be pre-planned or based on impulse. For example, with

175

a problem-solving task, such as a river crossing, a pre-planned goal might be to work out a solution and present it to the group. Initially, this might be done with a member of staff prompting and helping. Then, over time, that help would be phased out. Often the staff would have various members of the group working on several different goals simultaneously. It can be a bit like spinning plates!

An impulse goal might be a reaction to the day's events. If, for example, tensions had been high between Tom and another participant, we might suggest completing the activity without using any negative language towards that person and offering rewards if this was achieved. With Tom, lots of support was given initially, but this was then reduced as his confidence and skills improved. Over time, with small increments in effort, Tom started to realise that he could contribute and achieve. With this self-belief came increased confidence and growth in self-perception that transferred into physical and academic activity and even entered his home life.

Tom's story is a happy one as he successfully reintegrated into mainstream education after his time with us. However, with others it has felt like one step forward and two steps back. We must be mindful of this and maintain our commitment to the young people we work alongside. Being flexible and creative in your approach is paramount. If something is not working, you must be prepared to go back to the drawing board.

Tom's experience highlights how we can affect cognitions and behaviour through adventure education and manipulate a person's psychology in relation to the Biopsychosocial model. It also provides an example of the kind of support that disaffected young people need in terms of their sociological environment. If we think about the psychological and sociological components of the model together, we can start to think about the ways in which we might provide support, positive experiences and social interactions that promote pro-social attitudes and behaviour.

THE STAGES OF CHANGE MODEL

Although the Biopsychosocial model offers an intuitive and insightful approach to influencing young people's behaviour through providing support and promoting positive behaviour, it does not really give a mechanistic approach for how people might change their behaviour.

The Stages of Change model (Figure 9.2) was developed by Prochaska and DiClemente in the late 1970s and became widely known a few years later (Prochaska and DiClemente, 1983). It has traditionally been utilised by cognitive behavioural therapists in the treatment of undesirable addictions, such as smoking and alcohol abuse. Before we look at the model and how we might apply it to dealing with disaffection through adventure education, it is worth pointing out some of the underlying principles of behavioural change and how the model accommodates these.

176

Ed Christian

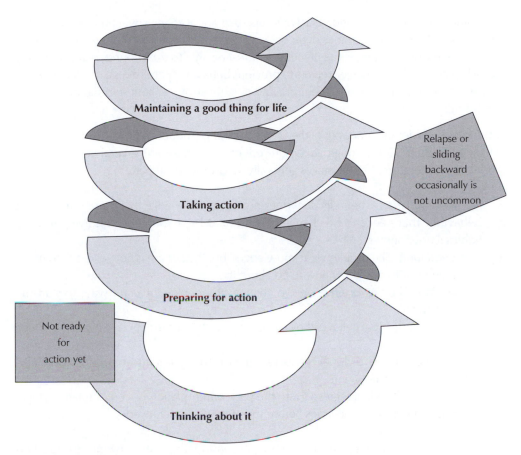

Figure 9.2 The stages of change model

First, the model assumes that change is a highly individual process: what works for one person might not work for another. The fact that the model allows us to look at individuals in detail is one of its major advantages when using it in adventure education. Another assumption is that change occurs in stages, and often over a considerable amount of time. This is an important point as we often (naively) expect change to occur almost immediately, as the result of a particularly influential experience, for example a weekend hiking expedition. Rather than seeing such an experience as an instant fix, the model assumes that it will form an integral part of a much bigger picture – an element in a progression through stages to a point of behaviour change.

Another significant feature of the model is that it accepts that progression through the stages is not straightforward or wholly linear. More often than not, individuals will relapse and regress to a previous stage. Again, this is a particularly pertinent factor when dealing with disaffected young people, as relapse into old behaviour is very common when they re-engage with their habitual surroundings.

The points discussed so far – individual differences, gradual change over time and potential relapse – highlight the importance of the role of the practitioner in mentoring young people through behavioural change. The practitioner must be able to treat young people as highly individual cases who might well regress to previous behaviour patterns as a result of internal or external influences. Clearly, then, practitioners must be resilient and flexible in their mentoring.

Let us now consider the processes of the Stages of Change model and relate them to dealing with youth disaffection through adventure education. There are several variants of the model in the literature, but the stages generally follow the same pattern:

- *Pre-contemplation*. The individual does not yet acknowledge that there is a problem behaviour that needs to be changed. This could be a young person living in their habitual environment.
- *Contemplation*. The problem is acknowledged but the person is not yet ready to make a change or does not know how to go about it.
- *Preparation*. The first positive step to change: the person looks for ways to start the change process.
- *Action*. The individual believes they can change and they are actively engaged in doing so.
- *Maintenance*. The individual resists temptation to regress into old behaviours and maintains positive new ones.
- *Relapse*. The individual regresses into the pre-contemplation or contemplation stage. This might happen several times before maintenance is achieved.

Let us now look at these stages in more depth and consider the role of adventure education in each.

Pre-contemplation

In pre-contemplation, the individual is not thinking about any kind of change as there is no awareness that their current behaviour requires attention or modification, so they are not interested in any form of help. An example of this might be young people who are failing at school or becoming known to the police for minor offences. People in this stage tend to defend their current behaviour patterns and do not see them as a problem. It is relatively easy to identify individuals in pre-contemplation as they are likely to treat any confrontation with hostility and attempt to avoid the subject or blame others for their behaviour.

In order for adventure educators to mentor young people through this stage, they need to create awareness of the negative effects of existing behaviour. Several well-documented facilitation techniques appear in the adventure education literature – such as reviewing, framing and metaphoric transfer – and all of these might prove useful in this stage. It is

178

Figure 9.3 Adventure education activities promote behavioural change by challenging negative behaviour

essential, when challenging young people's behaviour patterns, that the practitioner offers acceptable alternatives for new behaviour that the individual considers desirable. This permits the development of goal-setting and looking towards the future. Empathy and unconditional support are essential here. The use of such phrases as 'I'm not challenging you; I'm challenging your behaviour' is a direct but non-confrontational way to engage with young people.

Contemplation

In the contemplation stage, individuals are more aware of the consequences of their current behaviour and spend a lot of time thinking about them. Introspection is pivotal in forming a commitment to change and it needs to be well supported. At this stage, the individual is able to contemplate the *idea* of change but still tends to be ambivalent about it. The push and pull of emotions can often result in mood swings and instability.

Some people may progress through this stage in a matter of days, whilst others never get any further – always failing to turn contemplation into action. Again, close mentorship and effective programming are crucial to help individuals reach the next stage. Practitioners should reinforce the advantages of adopting new behaviour patterns and offer encouragement. In terms of adventure education, extended periods of residential activity or expedition may be particularly beneficial in this stage, as they have the potential to provide the kind of sustained exposure to positive behaviour that confirms the decision to commit to change. Adventure education experiences should also offer participants the opportunity for reflection. If we deliberately set aside time for self-reflection and review, this will aid the contemplation process.

Preparation/determination

This stage represents making the decision to change and signifies a commitment to adopt new behaviours. Entrance into it should be celebrated, as it is the first concrete step towards action. Preparation is characterised by individuals making such comments as: 'I have to do something about this. What can I do?'

Trust is essential here and is a key component of the relationship because the individual will be taking new steps towards behaviour cessation that are potentially uncomfortable. Part of the mentoring process at this stage might be well served by the facilitation of activities and experiences where the participant is able to confirm their trust in the practitioner so that trust can be transferred in turn from the adventure environment to everyday life. This makes it really important for us to conduct activities where trust can be earned. High-ropes activities are commonly used in this context because trust is required even though there is little objective danger.

Once an individual has recognised the need to change, they will search for alternative behaviours that are in line with their expectations. Some authors refer to this simply as 'information gathering'. This places a huge responsibility on mentors to provide alternatives and information that support the young person's thinking. Goal-setting in the preparation phase has been shown to be an effective method of organising information and starting to translate it into action. Adventure educators might use a progressive goal-setting process, using such goals as:

- Maintaining attendance in a ten-week adventure education programme.
- Learning how to read a map.
- Achieving an award in sailing.
- Making new friends.
- Applying for a college course.

Goal-setting is a really good way to prepare for action. However, it is essential to remember some of the key components of good goal-setting. These include making sure that the individual is part of the process and comes up with or at least agrees to all the goals that are set.

180

Action/willpower

This is the stage where people believe they have the ability to change and actively engage in doing something about it. With disaffected young people, this might involve a variety of actions. Participation in adventurous activities, days out or weekend residentials should form the basis for positive action. Many organisations use residential programmes as opportunities to practise new behaviour. This might involve taking part in new activities, such as gorge walking, canoeing or climbing, but we must not dismiss other, less obvious aspects of the residential experience. Working with others to erect tents or cleaning the minibus at the end of the day are examples of times when good work that has been achieved throughout the day can be lost in seconds by a little disagreement with a peer that escalates. It is paramount that facilitators remember this and take steps to manage even the most trivial daily tasks, because if these are unsupervised they might prove to be tinderboxes for problems. In other words, when we are engaged with disaffected young people, our working day is never really over.

Action and willpower extend beyond the organised activities. Positive changes can be lost when individuals return to their habitual environment, so action must be taken to counteract this. For instance, adventure education practitioners might look to forge links with other mentors. Schoolteachers, youth workers and social services might all provide support to ensure continued positive action. Short-term rewards are a good way to top up motivation, so you might use increased independence or added responsibility ('Can you check all the boats are tied tightly on the trailer?') to reward positive actions and reflect your growing trust in the young person.

Maintenance

With respect to disaffected young people, 'maintenance' means successfully resisting the temptation to return to previous negative behaviour. The goal in this stage is to maintain the status quo. Evidence from clinical applications of the Stages of Change model (especially in cases of smoking cessation) shows that this stage requires the most support. Oscar Wilde once famously said, 'I can resist everything but temptation', and the same might be said of many disaffected young people today: much good work can easily be undone by the slightest temptation.

Several years ago, I worked with a young person called Dan. He was well known to the police because of his persistent joyriding and he spent five months in a unit set up by the youth service. It was through this that he undertook an adventure education programme. Dan made encouraging progress throughout the programme, especially in terms of forming relationships with adults, whom he had previously viewed as 'the enemy'. However, one Monday morning, towards the end of the programme, he entered the centre followed by two policemen, who promptly arrested him for stealing a car the previous Friday night. This is an example of a young person taking positive action to improve his life, only to have all his hard work ruined by one moment of weakness. (In Dan's case, this was giving in to peer pressure to steal the car.) Such relapses will always occur, but close support and mentorship will at least reduce their frequency.

Maintenance is the stage that is most commonly associated with relapse. Individuals in this stage need to be constantly reminded of what they are doing and why. Ticking off goals as they are achieved and rewarding progress are both vital. Acceptance that things might not always go according to plan is also a valuable quality for the practitioner to possess, as it is highly likely that the people with whom you work will relapse at some point.

Relapse

So relapse happens, but it is important to remember that it does not, in itself, represent failure. The path towards permanent cessation or stable reduction of negative behaviour is a rocky one. We should think of the Stages of Change model as circular, and it might be that a young person has to go around several times in order to reach their end point. Obviously, if an individual relapses, it is better for them to go back just to determination, action or maintenance, rather than all the way back to contemplation (or even pre-contemplation). Good facilitation skills, patience and empathy can help here. We need to remind young people what they are capable of and help them reflect on their previous

Figure 9.4 The end of a long journey: empowering young people increases motivation, develops positive self-perception and helps them avoid relapse

Ed Christian

successes. Empowering people is a good way to increase motivation, develop positive self-perception and limit relapse.

I have used the Stages of Change model to show how behaviour change might be fostered in disaffected young people. But you, as practitioners, will have to make it work for you in your own way.

MENTORSHIP

One of the key themes in this chapter has been mentoring. But what exactly is this and what role does it play in adventure education? As adventure facilitators, whether we work with individuals on a one-off basis or as part of a longer-term programme, we are invariably seen to be in a position of responsibility. Young (2005) explains that mentorship is an act of guardianship and guidance that occurs in a wide range of settings and circumstances. As adventure practitioners, our core role is to provide guidance and guardianship in the outdoors. If we failed to fulfil this role, we would not bring back many of our clients at the end of the day! As adventure education has evolved, it has become more professionalised, and guidance and guardianship entail more than simply facilitating activities safely. Now, we are expected to mentor young people in terms of their developmental life skills.

The provision for accommodating disaffected young people has grown exponentially in recent history. A vast array of organisations in both the public and private sectors now deals exclusively with disaffected young people. This work relies heavily on frontline staff who often have experience in activity delivery but may not have professional qualifications in such areas as mentoring and counselling. However, these skills are central to the work of the adventure educator who works with disaffected young people and enables them to facilitate their clients' behaviour change successfully. Therefore, there needs to be development of counselling skills in adventure education.

The first steps in this development should not be too difficult to achieve, particularly if we follow the practices of such successful programmes as Big Brothers, Big Sisters of America (BBBSA). In this programme, disaffected young people from single-parent homes are matched with a 'big brother or sister' whom they meet between two and four times each month for a year. BBBSA is aimed at developing the whole individual in terms of social wellbeing and life skills, and it is one of the few mentoring programmes that has been subjected to rigorous evaluation.

According to Young (2005), extensive research on BBBSA has shown significant reductions in drug and alcohol abuse, physical abuse, and truancy, all indicating the effectiveness of the programme. (Incidentally, Young (2005: 4) calls the evaluation of mentoring in the UK 'small scale, qualitative and largely atheoretical' when comparing it with the US research.)

If we reflect on the models described earlier (Biopsychosocial, Stages of Change), we might argue that adventure educators, in our various guises, are uniquely placed to offer disaffected young people mentorship that helps facilitate behavioural change. For example, nearly every model of mentorship described in the literature involves some form of residential adventure activity to establish relationships and improve cooperation with others. This is usually followed by a goal-setting process and an ongoing relationship between a mentor and a young person who have been specifically matched.

In the early stages of my career I was fortunate enough to have the opportunity to work in both mainstream and adventure education settings, and with 'looked-after children'. From early in my career, it became apparent to me that outdoor adventurous activities could provide an effective vehicle for mental, physical and emotional growth in young people who were not attending mainstream education, as long as they had ownership of the process, rather than the process being thrust upon them. The humanistic philosophy that I developed in my adventure education work contributed in part to my setting up a service in Scotland providing young people (usually caught up in the legal system and considered to be at risk of re-offending), with a programme of residential adventure activities. This programme aimed to disrupt the cycle of offending behaviour in the home environment and focus the individual's energies in a more constructive direction, with the support of a mentor.

We provided breathing space for both young people and their families/carers. Offered in an intensive support setting (a staff-to-student ratio of at least one-to-one), it afforded the young person the opportunity to shape their own programme and choose a mentor to provide guidance and support. The key to the success of our service was the mentorship of the staff team, and the skills and experience that they brought with them. They were selected as a result of their experience and training in a variety of behaviour interventions, including counselling and hypnotherapy. However, these skills were never used explicitly in the contrived manner that many of the young people had experienced before; being sent to a counsellor or therapist 'to be fixed' will often prompt resistance. Our mentors were able to take a much more subtle approach. Reassuring each young person that they were 'good enough' helped resistance melt away, allowing the staff to use gentle, rapport-building strategies. Through these, the staff were able to build a rhythm with the young person that enabled the mentor to draw upon the naturally occurring learning experiences within the programme and make suggestions on how situations could be managed differently.

I do not subscribe to the belief that adventure education is a 'cure-all pill'. Rather, with the right people, our service provided an opportunity for individuals to choose and engage in activities that they found interesting and challenging, and that provided sufficient excitement and satisfaction to maintain motivation levels.

Ed Christian

The value of the service was highlighted to me when a young man – Mark – was referred to our team. Until he entered our service, he had represented a one-man crime wave to Glasgow Police. Not surprisingly, Mark's home and social environment was traumatic – filled with violence, crime and abuse. The residential phase of our programme saw Mark experience, perhaps for the first time, a period of calm and unconditional positive regard, where boundaries were set in a firm yet non-threatening and blame-free manner. This fostered trust and a sense of safety between Mark and his team, and we quickly saw a significant change in the way he presented himself. He began to take an interest in all aspects of the programme, including domestic responsibilities (unheard of prior to this point) and an appreciation of his environment as well as the more 'physical, exciting' stuff that he had planned with his mentor.

My overriding memory of Mark is of him, his mentor and myself sitting on top of a crag next to the Solway Firth in August, watching the Perseid meteor shower in a moonless night sky and enjoying a mature conversation. Having had the luxury of an external perspective on the mentor's relationship with Mark, there is no doubt in my mind that it was the time and energy that went into building a relationship based on mutual respect and nurturing his development with activities he found engaging that contributed to his growth and development as a mature young man. Examples such as Mark's reinforce, for me, how worthwhile and beneficial adventure education can be when used appropriately.

Chris Heaney, former managing director, Life Gateway

CONCLUSION

The emergence and rise of disaffected young people is problematic for both the young people themselves and the society in which they live. It is clear that the cost of dealing with extreme cases of disaffection is far greater than that of either preventative or intervention-based education. This chapter has focused on the use of adventure-based interventions that serve as catalysts to achieve desired outcomes. This area is ripe for a type of development that would see adventure educators increasingly embracing social work and counselling skills.

So what is the future of adventure education and disaffected populations? Numerous organisations worldwide are currently working with young people in meaningful ways, and they are doing fantastic work in turning around many lives. But an increasing number of adventure education professionals and graduates could and should be working towards evidence-based practice and the professionalisation of this area. As with all areas of behaviour-based interventions, there is a need for high-quality, rigorous research that supports the use of adventure education interventions. With the increase of adventure education programmes in higher education, it would seem that the time is now ripe for this.

In terms of practice, we need to follow the central rules of adventure education: identify the needs of the individual and plan suitable experiences that are based on them. In this chapter, I have looked at supporting the individual and have considered the change process that is fundamental to dealing with disaffection. We should also remain mindful that change is difficult, and behaviour can often deteriorate before it improves. Adventure education interventions are not a cheap or a quick fix, so we must be realistic about the time, effort and investment that are required to train professionals and provide effective interventions. But if that is done, we may be able to make a considerable contribution to overcoming disaffection in the young.

REFERENCES

Coles, B. (1995) *Youth and Social Policy*, London: UCL Press.

Engel, G.L. (1977) The need for a new medical model: a challenge for biomedicine, *Science*, 196 (4286): 129–136.

Fox, P. and Avramidis, E. (2003) An evaluation of an outdoor education programme for students with emotional and behavioural difficulties, *Emotional and Behavioural Difficulties*, 8(4): 267–283.

HM Prison Service (2010) Website. Available online at: http://www.hmprisonservice.gov.uk/advice andsupport/prison_life/juvenileoffenders/.

Kelly, F.J. and Baer, D.J. (1968) *Outward Bound Schools as an Alternative to Institutionalization for Adolescent Delinquent Boys*, Boston, MA: Outward Bound.

Murray, C. (1990) *The Emerging British Underclass*, London: Institute of Economic Affairs.

Newburn, T. and Shiner, M. (eds) (2005) *Dealing with Disaffection: Young People, Mentoring and Social Inclusion*, Devon: Willan Publishing.

Prince's Trust (2007a) *Breaking the Cycle of Offending: Making the Views of Young People Count*, London: Prince's Trust.

Prince's Trust (2007b) *The Cost of Exclusion: Counting the Cost of Youth Disadvantage in the UK*, London: Prince's Trust.

Prison Reform Trust (2010) Website. Available online at: http://www.prisonreformtrust.org.uk.

Prochaska, J.O. and DiClemente, C.C. (1983) Stages and processes of self-change of smoking: toward an integrative model of change, *Journal of Consulting and Clinical Psychology*, 51 (3): 390–395.

UK Government (2000) *National Strategy for Neighbourhood Renewal: Report of Policy Action Team 12: Young People*. Available online at: http://www.cabinetoffice.gov.uk/media/cabinetoffice/social_ exclusion_task_force/assets/publications_1997_to_2006/pat_report_12.pdf.

Williamson, H. and Middlemiss, R. (1999) The emperor has no new clothes: cycles of delusion in community initiatives with 'disaffected' young men, *Youth and Policy*, Spring: 13–25.

Young, T. (2005) Young people and mentoring, in Newburn, T. & Shiner, M. (eds) *Dealing with Disaffection: Young People, Mentoring and Social Inclusion*, Devon: Willan Publishing.

CHAPTER TEN

OVERSEAS YOUTH EXPEDITIONS

Pete Allison, Tim Stott, Johannes Felter and Simon Beames

INTRODUCTION

Travel and overseas experiences, particularly those involving some form of outdoor education, are regarded by many young people, parents, university admissions departments and employers as beneficial to a young person's development. Expeditions have been used in the UK as an educational tool since 1932, when the Public Schools Exploring Society ran its first expedition to Finland.

While gap years and expeditions are slightly different (as the former often incorporate the latter, but not vice versa), no specific statistics are available on the number of people engaged in expeditions from the UK each year. Jones (2004), however, estimated that 250,000–350,000 Britons between 16 and 25 years of age were taking a gap year annually. Four years later, Rowe (2008: 47) reported that 'the gap year market is valued at £2.2 billion in the UK and globally at £5 billion. It's one of the fastest growing travel sectors of the 21st century, and the prediction is for the global gap year market to grow to £11 billion by 2010.'

Expedition experiences happen at crucial times in life (the teen years), when metaphysical (rather than empirical) questions dominate. In other words, people are primarily interested in thinking about who they are, what they want to do with their lives, what is important to them and how they interact with society in different ways.

The development of British Standard 8848 (specification for the provision of visits, field-work, expeditions and adventurous activities outside the UK) in concert with the Learning Outside the Classroom (LOtC) quality badge scheme (underpinned by the Expedition Providers Association) are further indications that significant numbers of people are travelling overseas on expeditions and gap years. At the time of writing, the UK government was considering proposals for a National Citizen Service (NCS), a non-military national service comprising a two-month summer programme for sixteen-year-olds and including both residential and at-home components. It would be delivered by independent charities, social enterprises and private businesses. Whether there will be a role for overseas residential experience, perhaps through expeditions, in this scheme remains to be seen.

In order to understand expeditions, it is helpful to consider their historical development in the UK.

THE ORIGINS OF OVERSEAS EXPEDITIONS

Expeditions in the UK have a long history that can be traced back to exploration for geographical purposes. These expeditions can be linked to such pioneers as Scott, Shackleton, Watkins and Herbert in the polar regions, and Younghusband and Mallory in the Himalaya. As an example, we shall briefly consider Scott's Antarctic expeditions.

Robert Falcon Scott (1868–1912) was a British Royal Navy officer and explorer who led two expeditions to the Antarctic: the Discovery Expedition of 1901–4, and the ill-fated Terra Nova Expedition of 1910–13. Scott enjoyed the company of scientists, and his ship was the best-equipped vessel for scientific purposes in the polar regions. The scientific crew included meteorologists, hydrologists, zoologists, glaciologists, biologists and geologists. During their second venture, Scott led a party of five to the South Pole on 17 January 1912, only to find that they had been preceded by Roald Amundsen's Norwegian party in an unsought 'race for the Pole'. During their return journey, Scott and his four comrades all perished through a combination of exhaustion, hunger and extreme cold. The bodies of Scott, Wilson and Bowers were discovered the following spring in their tent, some twelve miles from One Ton Depot. Surgeon E.L. Atkinson RN, of the recovery party, reported:

> We recovered all their gear and dug out the sledge with their belongings on it. Amongst these were 35 lb. of very important geological specimens which had been collected on the moraines of the Beardmore Glacier; at Doctor Wilson's request they had stuck to these up to the very end, even when disaster stared them in the face and they knew that the specimens were so much weight added to what they had to pull.
>
> (Quoted in Evans, 2006: 108)

A total of 1919 rock specimens from the expedition are housed at the Natural History Museum today.

On board the *Terra Nova* en route to Antarctica, Scott assessed the calibre of his party in his diary. He was particularly dismissive of George Murray Levick's ability, except as a medic. Little did he know what was to come. Levick was a member of the 'eastern' party, which, after a brief meeting with Amundsen, became the 'northern' party and occupied Evans Coves in order to conduct summer fieldwork. As a result of impenetrable ice, they were not picked up by boat and were forced to overwinter. After their tents were ravaged by blizzards, their only hope was to dig a cave in the largest snow patch they could find. They ate seal meat throughout the winter, and took a photo of themselves (Figure 10.1) when spring finally arrived. Their clothing and hair were thick with grease because all of their cooking had been conducted over a seal-blubber stove.

188

Figure 10.1 The northern party of Captain Scott's last expedition, stand outside the entrance to the snow hole in which they have just spent the 1911–1912 Antarctic Winter in darkness. The low spring sun allows the zoologist and photographer of the party, Surgeon George Murray Levick RN (2nd from right), to take this picture

Source: Scott Polar Research Institute, University of Cambridge, UK

After returning from Antarctica, Levick served in the Royal Navy in the First World War and then worked as a doctor in London. He also spent some time training disabled (mainly blind) people in useful occupations.

At the time, expeditions were leaving the UK on a regular basis. The most notable set out from the universities, such as those led by the undergraduate Gino Watkins, of Cambridge, to Greenland between 1930 and 1932. But there were no opportunities for young people who were still at school to obtain adventure experiences abroad. Reflecting on his own experiences, Levick saw a need for tough, demanding challenges for schoolchildren, so in 1932 he took eight boys to Finland with basic equipment at a cost of thirty pounds per boy (see Figure 10.2). The following year, he founded the Public Schools Exploring Society (PSES) and continued to lead expeditions that grew in size each year.

The aims of the society were described by Levick himself (c. 1939: 5–7):

> The expeditions are not pleasure trips, designed to occupy a boy's summer holiday . . . we give the boys a real experience of the conditions under which an explorer or pioneer carries on. And for these reasons.
>
> Our country has contributed many fine chapters to the world history of exploration, and ought to go on doing so.
>
> Further, the British Empire still has its undeveloped regions and its outposts in the wilds, and it is of paramount importance that the flow of youth, ready and willing to pioneer beyond the confines of our super-civilization, shall go on undiminished.
>
> 'Safety first', which leads boys to banks and office desks, is a terribly dangerous doctrine for a world-wide Empire, aching for settlers, and demanding men of action,

Figure 10.2 Leaving King's Cross Station, 27 July 1932

Source: British Schools Exploring Society archive, Royal Geographical Society

initiative and enterprise for its far-flung frontiers. Boys are being brought up with the idea that their first duty is to secure a safe job. If our forefathers had been brought up with that idea, there would not have been any British Empire. Unless we foster a spirit of adventure and the taste for manly life we stand a good chance of losing it.

Many of us believe that we have a mission to fulfil overseas, and must, if we are not to fail in it, maintain the pioneering, exploring spirit.

I know that it exists in boys – often latent, awaiting the opportunity to be brought out, to be tested by practical experience. Seven years' work for the society, among the boys who have joined, has proved that beyond question.

Reading this takes us back to a time when boys and girls were treated very differently and the British Empire was of great importance. Of course, times have changed, but some issues remain the same – most notably what Levick had to say about 'safety first'. He went on to describe the expeditions he led (Levick *c.* 1939: 10–11):

First, then, of the realities. We go out into wild and trackless country . . . They learn to march by compass. They have to carry their own food and their own equipment.

Pete Allison et al.

We have no guides and no porters. Their food is that which any explorer would take, but it is scientifically correct and ample.

When the cooking is done, the boys do for themselves. At every turn they have to fend for themselves. There is nothing which can in any way be described as a luxury.

The most physically fit boys undertake the longer marches day by day through forests or across trackless wilds – but always with an object. They come back healthier and fitter than they were when they started.

Now, as to the serious purpose of our expeditions. We have this object: to teach the boys that exploration has always a scientific end; that it is not all rough adventure; that an explorer must be more than physically fit. So, on our expeditions, we survey, and we map. We can say, as a result, that we have usefully increased the geographical knowledge of the areas which we have explored.

The PSES continued to grow, and in the late 1930s concepts that might now be called 'inclusivity' or 'social justice' were developed (inspired by the summer camps set up by the Duke of York – later King George VI). Levick started to take boys from grammar schools, with one of the first, in 1938, being Terry Lewin (later Admiral of the Fleet Lord Lewin – commander of all forces in the Falklands War). Levick also served in the Second World War, when, for obvious reasons, the PSES did not run any expeditions. In 1947 the society changed its name to the British Schools Exploring Society (BSES), and in 1980 it started to take girls on its expeditions. The society continues to thrive and run expeditions to many exciting destinations.

In this section, we have offered a short history of the first youth expedition organisation in the UK. Interestingly, it was not until 1978 that a second organisation was formed with similar aims: Operation Drake. Then, in 1984, Operation Raleigh (known as Raleigh International since 1991) was founded. Thereafter, the 1980s and 1990s saw the appearance of many similar organisations. These expedition providers operate in the commercial and charitable sectors and have a wide range of aims and objectives. Most of them offer some combination of adventurous activities, science work and community projects for time periods that vary between three weeks and twelve months. Some work directly with individuals while others operate through schools, education authorities and youth organisations. The expeditions are staffed by a wide range of qualified personnel, including professional outdoor leaders, scientists and researchers, educators and outdoor enthusiasts. These may be paid staff, volunteers or a combination of both. In addition, expeditions increasingly offer awards from such organisations as the Duke of Edinburgh Award Scheme and the John Muir Award.

CONDUCTING EXPEDITION RESEARCH

Research can be undertaken on expeditions in two broad categories: research into the environment that is being visited (e.g. geology or tourism); and study of participants and leaders in order to establish the influences and processes that occur during and after an expedition. Expeditions to remote regions have given scientists numerous opportunities to conduct research far from communications networks. (We have undertaken science expeditions to Greenland, Svalbard, Kenya and the Indian Himalaya, amongst other places.) In these cases, the expedition is used as a means of accessing a particular environment or problem. The research is usually carried out by researchers working for universities, government research councils or research institutes, but they will often require a supporting team to help with logistics. This provides opportunities for young people to work alongside experienced scientists in a supportive or assistant role and allows them to learn some valuable field skills. Investigations in remote regions can be, and sometimes are, conducted by anyone who is comfortable operating in the expedition environment. Graduates and undergraduates frequently undertake research on expeditions, often to meet the requirements of their degree programmes. Younger students may undertake school projects for GCSE or A level, and a few youth expedition providers, such as the BSES, include science as part of their itinerary.

Scientific research on expeditions may be subject-based: for example, investigations into a region's geology, meteorology, glaciology, geomorphology, hydrology, zoology or botany. Over the past few decades, questions about climate change, in particular global warming and its impact, have driven a great deal of research effort, and they continue to do so. For example, an expedition to the Tasermiut Fjord in south-west Greenland in 2009 studied the impact of climate change on the glaciers of the region.

Biggs (2009) examined the retreat of the Sermitsiaq and Itillersuaq glaciers, which feed into the fjord. Coordinates along the snout of each glacier were recorded using GPS. The data collated were then mapped in a geographic information system (GIS) (see Figure 10.3). Current glacial extents were compared to those of archived remotely sensed images (aerial photographs) and maps. Glacial change was also investigated using archived data on the Sermeq Glacier. The main aim of the project was to determine the distance and pace of glacial system change in the region. It was discovered that Sermitsiaq has retreated by an average of 27.7 metres per year since 1987 (see Figure 10.4), while Itillersuaq has retreated by 13.6 metres per year. Sermeq has also retreated.

In a second study (Nuttall, 2009), conducted during the same expedition, a group monitored glacier melt rates, microclimate and stream waters. Melt rates were higher during the day than at night, and higher in the first part of the study, when warm Föhn winds were blowing down from the ice sheet. In a third study (Stott, 2009), a group monitored the hydrology and microclimate of a river flowing into the fjord. Figure 10.5 compares the glacial melt rates with the river discharge, showing the response to the onset of cloudy weather in the second half of the study.

Pete Allison et al.

Figure 10.3 Taking GPS measurements along the snout of Sermitsiaq

Source: Allison and Stott, 2009

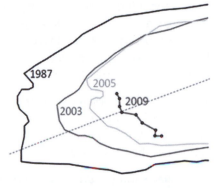

Figure 10.4 Sermitsiaq Glacier snout positions

Source: Biggs, 2009

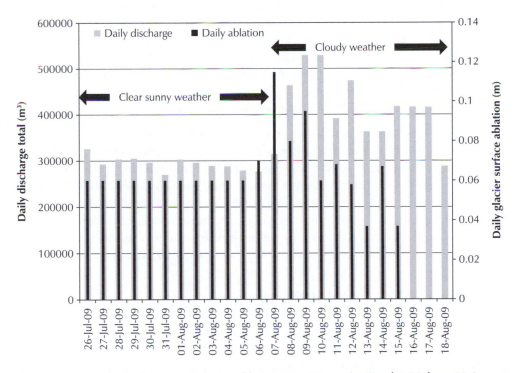

Figure 10.5 Daily discharge and glacier ablation rate, Tasermiut Fjord, 26 July to 18 August 2009

Source: Stott, 2009

The fact that the glaciers melted faster and the streams carried more water during cloudy weather was unexpected. One hypothesis suggests higher evaporation rates in Arctic regions for a future warmer planet. This could lead to more moisture in the atmosphere, condensing to form clouds. Extrapolating the findings of this study, increased cloudiness could result in increased melting of glaciers (for a time at least).

This relatively simple study, carried out by university scientists with the help of young people on an expedition, shows the value of a systematic approach to data collection in a remote location where field studies could not have been conducted without the logistical support of the expedition.

As we have shown, Britain has a heritage of more than seventy-five years of organised youth exploration, which has largely aimed to provide adventure and challenges for young people. But most youth expeditions have also carried out a significant amount of fieldwork. Much of this has involved surveying and mapping glaciers, mountains and lakes in 'trackless country', very much in the tradition of geographical exploration. Today's scientific expeditions do even more, exploring climate change, the functioning and conservation of fragile ecosystems, and human impact on diminishing resources.

The second aspect of research during expeditions involves study of the participants and leaders themselves, in order to gain an understanding of the influences and learning processes that are taking place. Undertaking empirical research on expeditions can present challenges beyond those that are associated with studying people in their home environment. It is relatively straightforward to collect data *after* the experience – through questionnaires and interviews, for example. But there are pros and cons to conducting research on one's fellow expedition members *during* an expedition.

First, it is inevitable that a researcher on an expedition will influence people's interactions and behaviour. So the degree to which one participates in expedition life and the openness of one's data-collection methods both need careful consideration. For example, if a researcher does not participate fully in expedition life (which is difficult, in itself) but sits near by, taking copious notes and asking people to complete questionnaires at regular intervals, this process can impact on individuals in numerous ways. Participants may alter their behaviour because they know they are being watched (the 'Hawthorne Effect') and may attempt to present themselves in a positive light in the questionnaires (social desirability bias).

By contrast, a researcher who participates fully in expedition life and is never seen conducting a formal interview or taking notes may gain a deeper understanding of what people really think and do. Nevertheless, there are potential problems with this approach, too: the researcher becomes such a part of the team that they exert an influence on the others; and they lose their objectivity towards the group and their role within it (sometimes called 'going native'). Subjectivity in a research process can sometimes be seen as a strength, but if the study is to remain an investigation into individuals and the group (*not* including the researcher), then some distance needs to be maintained.

194

Collecting data on expeditions is also influenced by the meteorological conditions. For example, pouring rain and a howling gale at the campsite may not be the most suitable conditions for conducting a recorded interview with a participant, as he or she may not be fully focused on the discussion. Certainly, with a nod to Maslow (1968), it is worth considering the degree to which one's primary needs (food, shelter and warmth) are taken care of, and how this may affect the state of the interviewee. A researcher who is hoping to capture a deeper sense of 'the moment' may choose to put microphones in front of participants during stressful or uncomfortable occasions. However, some parts of an expedition may be so stressful that it would simply be unfeasible to pursue any kind of data collection: for example, while descending a mountain ridge during a blizzard, or while attempting to take down a sail during a storm at sea. This raises further issues regarding researchers' assumptions of when people may be more or less stressed. For some, descending a mountain ridge might be extremely stressful; but others might find making a meal at camp much more challenging. Thus, the timing of any approaches to research will inevitably be better for some participants than others.

In these scenarios, it may be more useful to make field notes. This might involve pulling out a small notebook once on our hypothetical ridge, and trying to record a particularly meaningful item that was discussed or observed. Informal conversations may also serve as rich data. After the storm at sea has passed, insightful comments might be offered by participants over a cup of tea in the galley. The point of these examples has been to emphasise that, whatever the decisions of the researcher, they need to be considered on both logistical and ethical grounds. Research of this nature is rarely straightforward and invariably involves some compromises.

It is worth noting four final points. First, while scientific research on expeditions through fieldwork has traditionally been a key focus (e.g. Scott's 1910–13 expeditions), the expense of it, perhaps combined with a decline in its teaching in schools, has seen it decline in modern overseas expeditions, particularly among young people. Second, the little research that has been conducted into the impact of expeditions on the leaders and participants has been primarily empirical. So there are still extensive opportunities for *philosophical* exploration of educational expeditions. Third, little, if any, research has focused on certain individuals' learning during an expedition (such as leaders, assistant leaders, members of local communities visited and organisations). Rather, the research has focused on the learning of young people or participants. Fourth, there is growing pressure for outcome-focused research to 'prove' the value of expeditions empirically. However, this is methodologically challenging and thus far has met with little success (Allison and Pomeroy, 2000; Thomas and Pring, 2004).

CURRENT ISSUES

This section addresses five areas of practice within the expeditions sector that are contentious and therefore worthy of examination: volunteer work; cultural sensitivity and environmental responsibility; psychological considerations; regulating practice; and accessibility.

Volunteer work

A contentious issue in the current expedition climate concerns expedition organisations sending young people to developing nations as untrained labourers. Participants might teach in primary schools, help with zoological surveys, or work on conservation projects in national parks. Many of these projects do not fall under the strict definition of 'an expedition', as they do not involve a journey. The participant might well be based in the same place for several weeks – although this place might well be remote and the participant will need to be self-sufficient.

Critics suggest that Western young people who travel to developing nations to work in this way may be considered agents of neo-colonialism (Simpson, 2004), because there is an imbalance of power in favour of the participants and the expedition provider. For example, the UK would not tolerate an 18-year-old Ghanaian boy coming to the south-west of England to teach in a primary school for six weeks; yet a British volunteer, often without appropriate qualifications or experience, might take on quite a prominent role in the formal education system of a developing nation. While of the latter altruism may be laudable, it is worth considering that this practice is possible only because of the wide gulf between the resources of the visitor and the host community. The practice of going overseas to learn through volunteering is sometimes known as 'service learning'.

A number of papers have described this increasingly widespread branch of experiential education (Jacoby, 1996; Jakubowski, 2003; Warren and Loeffler, 2000). Jacoby (1996: 5) defines service learning as 'activities that address human and community needs with structured opportunities intentionally designed to promote student learning and development'. Typically, service-learning programmes involve living and working in a host community on projects that have been deemed important by the members of that community (Jacoby, 1996; Kendall, 1990).

Another feature of service learning is reciprocity: all parties 'are learners and help determine what is to be learned. Both the server and those served teach, and both learn' (Kendall, 1990: 22). Furthermore, it is imperative that the members of the host community identify the service tasks and then control the service that is provided (Jacoby, 1996).

Clearly, expedition providers who use service as part of their programme can draw on the literature to guide their own practice. Crucially, volunteer work on expeditions to facilitate learning needs to be thoroughly considered and not added in some tokenistic manner.

196

Pete Allison et al.

However, well-conceptualised and well-implemented projects have considerable potential for learning.

Cultural sensitivity and environmental responsibility

Along with the issues of health and safety that proliferated in the 1990s, expeditions in the twenty-first century have faced yet more new areas of concern. Critics have identified several potentially problematic aspects of some current youth expedition practices, including cultural sensitivity, the use of drugs, and the environmental costs associated with young people travelling outside of their home country (Allison and Higgins, 2002). First, they were particularly critical of expedition groups that did not show appropriate cultural sensitivity when travelling in developing nations (Allison and Higgins, 2002). Participants wearing shorts and sleeveless tops in Muslim nations are obvious examples.

Second, critics have questioned whether the benefits of an expedition outweigh the cost of flying, say, fifty people halfway around the world (Allison and Higgins, 2002). In a time when air travel is widely accepted as being a significant contributor to global climate change, it might seem surprising that so many operators and participants remain convinced that they *must* visit distant lands, even when they know little of their homeland. The Young Explorers Trust (YET) – an independent educational charity – has responded to this criticism by arguing that the benefits do indeed outweigh the costs (Smith, 2008: 5). Individuals and organ-isations involved in expeditions need to consider this debate carefully, especially as global-warming-based objections and the 'market' for gap-year travel both seem certain to grow in the future. Any decision about personal involvement in an expedition will be complex, as Macklin (1991: 40) indicates: 'A wheel mark in the desert lasts for decades. A footprint in the Arctic takes years to fade. Yet the expeditions which make these marks may further our knowledge of the world in which we live, helping us to conserve it.'

Most schools and universities still recognise the value of fieldwork in their ecology, geography, earth and environmental science curricula (Andrews *et al.*, 2003; Lonergan and Andersen, 1998; Warburton *et al.*, 1997) as a means of gaining first-hand interaction with the real world, learning field techniques used by researchers, and providing students with opportunities to conduct their own field-based investigations. Some argue that expeditions provide an ideal platform from which to teach and learn fieldwork (Smith, 2008). However, few of the increasing number of youth expedition providers still include traditional science and fieldwork in their programmes, with those that do tending towards the descriptive survey and mapping of landforms approach taken by early explorers, and only a few undertaking process-based fieldwork. Smith (2008: 4) reports that, 'according to records kept by Geography Outdoors, the centre supporting field research, exploration and outdoor learning at the RGS-IBG, the proportion of youth expeditions undertaking field projects has fallen to one in ten'. This may be due to the growth of commercial providers of expedition experiences that organise adventurous activities and community projects with the expressed aim of 'putting something back' into the host country, while often neglecting science and fieldwork. However, if commercial providers are responding to their clients' demands, it follows that the clients (usually school groups) may not be asking for science and fieldwork in their expedition programmes, perhaps because it might make them appear 'too much like school' for the students. Obviously, if teachers do not ask for science and fieldwork to be included in the programmes, then this decline will inevitably continue.

There has also been a reduction in fieldwork provision in many schools and universities, probably because it is costly to provide and manage in terms of both time and money. As the impact of this reduction has fed through to the current generation of young adults, the resultant loss of fieldwork experience and expertise may have had an impact on teachers, expedition providers and volunteer leaders with the confidence to take on expedition field projects. Another factor has been the increasing popularity of adventurous activities in exotic locations. The appeal of kayaking, scuba diving and even bungee jumping to potential expedition members is obvious, but such activities tend to focus on the personal growth and skills of participants, rather than on exploration of the world around them. The fact that this is happening at the same time as a growth in numbers participating in youth expeditions means that the huge and increasing potential of using youth expeditions as an informal global classroom is perhaps not being fully exploited.

In the state education sector, there seems to be an increasing emphasis on the value of enrichment activities outside the classroom, reinforced in the UK by the government's publication of a 'Manifesto for Learning Outside the Classroom' and the appointment of educational visits coordinators (EVCs) in schools and colleges. In light of the increasing popularity of youth expeditions, it seems that youth expedition providers are ideally placed to make important contributions to this education outside the classroom and to embrace the national concern about the decline in fieldwork opportunities in schools and universities. Research into learning on youth expeditions (Stott and Hall, 2003; Beames and Stott, 2008) suggests that expeditions are very effective means for developing understanding, setting priorities, achieving goals, solving problems and managing time efficiently, organising others, leading through consultation and developing confidence. Perhaps most importantly, this research has shown statistically significant changes in participants' self-reported enthusiasm, so expeditions seem to enhance their interest, motivation and inclination to learn more.

Following inspirational fieldwork experiences on expeditions, some young people go on to study related degrees in geography or earth, biological or environmental sciences, and/or pursue careers in geography, environmental sciences and conservation. So youth expeditions can help to develop young people's field skills, negate the decline in school and university fieldwork, and contribute to the next generation of field scientists and explorers. They can provide practical field experience, such as animal and plant identification, that participants no longer gain at school or university. Finally, and perhaps most importantly, fieldwork raises young people's environmental awareness. Expeditions often travel long distances to work in environmentally sensitive locations, meaning that their environmental

198

Pete Allison et al.

costs can be relatively high. Such costs are now measured in terms of ecological footprints or carbon tariffs. But these costs are mitigated, at least to some extent, by increasing the environmental awareness of the expedition members, which may help to change the way that young people see and value the world. Well-designed field projects can increase understanding of environmental problems and lead to lifelong changes in the values, attitudes and behaviour of participants, which should offset some, most or all of the environmental costs of the expedition over the long term. We believe that longer expeditions are more justifiable than short ones (as the carbon cost per day is normally lower), and their positive impact potential is very high. Certainly, if the carbon costs of expeditions are compared with those of business travel or academics flying to conferences, we feel that they are far more justifiable. Furthermore, most of the climate-change arguments against expedition travel are put forward by people who have enjoyed the benefits of world travel earlier in their lives – a case of 'do as I say, not as I did'!

We want to caution against overseas expeditions and local journeys being dichotomised and set against each other as an 'either/or'. Rather, we see them as complementary elements of a rich education to which all young people should be entitled and as mechanisms that enable people to engage in exploration of places near and far. Indeed, undertaking self-sufficient journeys early in life may encourage and support young people seeking more adventurous travel further afield as they get older as well as a spirit of enquiry and enthusiasm to learn about the world in which we live.

Psychological considerations

Expeditions present a number of complex and varied challenges that inevitably evoke a range of psychological responses. This aspect of expeditions has received increasing attention, and the field of wilderness therapy has sought to address the learning from, and management of, these unavoidable psychological responses. Some responses are considered positively and are associated with learning (e.g. awe and inspiration, reflecting on past experiences, learning how to interact with others), while others have more negative connotations (e.g. homesickness, psychosocial challenges, eating disorders). Furthermore, the responses to such experiences occur not only during expeditions but when participants return to their home communities. It is helpful to consider three psychological areas.

The first of these is learning in a safe (physical and emotional) environment. Taking people on expeditions is often motivated, to some extent, by trying to trigger some kind of psychological or emotional response to various aspects of the experience. For some, this may be about developing themselves, understanding themselves and others, and exploiting the opportunity to reflect on their lives, behaviour and relationships – past, present and future. For others, the expedition may be a time when reflection brings to the fore difficult issues that may previously have been suppressed, such as confidence issues, dysfunctional relationships, existential challenges and a lack of life direction. Clearly, leaders need to be

199

appropriately prepared to deal with such issues. To this end, planning prior to an expedition, including reviewing applications and holding interviews, gaining medical information, writing clear marketing material, and conducting thorough training weekends are crucial in minimising psychological difficulties.

Second, post-expedition responses are often difficult to gauge, and until relatively recently had not been studied at all. The phenomenon can be understood as similar to 'the blues' felt when returning from a holiday or to a process of mourning (for the wilderness, for friends, or for the simplicity of expedition life). For many young people, going on an expedition for the first time can be life changing. It is often their first visit to a distant place where they will experience a culture very different from their own. As such, returning to everyday life (school, home, university, employment) is often rather awkward. People commonly report difficulties sleeping inside or deciding what to eat, and they miss the intimacy of the relationships they forged on the expedition. Some post-expedition adjustment will therefore be evident in the majority of people. Should there be no signs of post-expedition adjustment, we might question if there had been any changes or examination of values during the expedition experience. Three main themes are evident from our initial work on post-expedition adjustment: a sense of isolation; extending the lessons of group; and using the group as a compass for the future.

The third psychological area that expedition leaders need to address concerns managing threats to the learning environment. When people do experience the challenges outlined above – such as adjustment problems (to and from the expedition), illness/accidents, crises (emotional and otherwise) – it is vital that leaders have the skills to recognise them, decide on a course of action, manage and remedy them. And, unless these problems are deemed to be desirable (rarely the case), they must take steps to avoid their recurrence. Our advice on how to recognise these problems is to get to know expedition members as well as possible so you can identify any changes in their behaviour sooner rather than later. These processes are explored in more detail by Berman and Davis-Berman (2002), Berman *et al.* (1998), Davis-Berman and Berman (2008) and the classic study in this area by Kaplan and Talbot (1983).

Regulating practice in the UK and beyond

Many of the expeditions taking place in the UK that involve participants under the age of 18 are regulated by the Adventure Activities Licensing Service (AALS) (formed after a kayaking tragedy in 1993) and the subsequent Young Persons' Safety Act (1995). However, it is important to note a crucial exception to AALS regulations: expeditions for those under the age of 18 in Britain are not licensable under the AALS if the expedition leader is unpaid (e.g. a teacher leading a student expedition). Once the expedition leaves the United Kingdom, regulation becomes less clear, as there is no statutory obligation for providers to operate at a given standard or for leaders to be qualified.

However, since 1972, the YET has approved expeditions through its national evaluation system. This process was designed and developed as a means of supporting expedition organisers and leaders, and improving the quality of provision. The YET also offers a small grant system to support approved expeditions that are in need of financial support. In 2008, the YET screening process incorporated British Standard 8848 to become the YET Evaluation Process.

British Standard 8848 (published in 2007 and reviewed and updated in 2009) is the closest the sector has come to regulating the practice of overseas ventures. It is not limited to expeditions, but rather covers all visits, trips and fieldwork outside of the UK (British Standard 8848, 2007). Its principal goal is to minimise injuries and illness during such ventures. The onus to follow the practices outlined in BS 8848 is placed squarely on the 'venture provider'. Third-party employees (such as bus drivers and mountaineering instructors) may be used by the venture provider as long as the standard's specifications are being followed. At the time of writing, expedition companies are not required to adhere to the standard, but it is safe to assume that they gain credibility in the eyes of the public if they do.

All of these systems (AALS, YET and BS 8848) are concerned with a systems approach – accrediting organisations rather than certifying individuals. This approach has been developed in response to the increasing number of overseas expeditions, in a wide range of environments, with a broad spectrum of aims. In these varying circumstances, specifying individual leader certifications may be too complex to manage. Compare the leadership skills that are needed for a small school group going on a two-week summer expedition to the Swiss Alps with those that will be needed for a three-month expedition to Kenya that will entail kayaking, implementation of service-learning projects and visits to game reserves. To account for such differences, the evaluation system for BS 8848 (which is administered through the YET) offers a flexible approach that considers the specific expedition aims, location and context in a descriptive rather than a prescriptive manner. This encourages organisations and individuals to focus on managing the multitude of situations they may encounter on expeditions, rather than burdening them with reams of paperwork.

Although we have specifically focused on the UK context in order to provide some depth and context to the issue of regulating practice, other countries are currently facing similar issues.

Accessibility

Of course, there are inequalities with respect to different people's access to society's resources, including such essentials as food, education, medical treatment and property. Historically, in the UK, educational expeditions have been dominated by upper- and upper-middle-class white people (e.g. the early expeditions run by the PSES). However, from the mid-1980s to the mid-1990s, the British overseas youth expedition was transformed from a product that catered exclusively to the socio-economically privileged to one in which a wider range of children of varying social backgrounds and academic ability could participate. The Next Generation scheme, offered by the British Schools Exploring Society, has contributed to this change.

Nevertheless, although there are more opportunities for marginalised people to join expeditions – be it in the Duke of Edinburgh scheme or on a summer-long research trip to the Arctic – a fundamental demographic discrepancy remains. For example, in Scotland, where students from the bottom 20 per cent of the socio-economic spectrum are seven times more likely to be excluded from school than those in the top 20 per cent (Scottish Government, 2009), one can reasonably speculate that expedition opportunities for the former will come from some sort of youth-at-risk programme. Conversely, those in the top 20 per cent will usually have to rely on their parents to fund their trip. If the parents are unable or unwilling to pay directly, they may raise the money through their social and business networks.

Beyond financial matters, it is quite likely that young people from low-income families will not be interested in joining an expedition because no family member or friend will have done so. Conversely, teenagers attending an independent school with a strong tradition of expeditioning might feel stigmatised if they are denied an expedition opportunity. Consequently, by choosing to participate in an expedition, they might merely be 'going with the flow' and following dominant social forces.

Of course, practitioners in all countries and cultures should work towards making the benefits of expeditions available to all, irrespective of wealth, physical ability, sex, gender, age, religion or ethnicity.

In June 2008, the 360° on Overseas Expeditions conference brought together academic researchers, expedition organisers and policy-makers to discuss viewpoints and share knowledge, experiences and practices. The event was organised by one of the authors of this chapter (Pete Allison), with funding provided by the Economic and Social Research Council. Around fifty participants attended and a number of key themes emerged:

1   The relatively little (recent) academic research carried out on the educational benefits of overseas expeditions for young people was generally unknown and inaccessible to expedition providers. Therefore, it was agreed that steps should be taken to make this research more accessible to the general public and especially expedition providers.
2   A number of key issues were highlighted as potential research topics, and the methodological challenges to conducting 'good' research were highlighted. Both participants and staff acknowledge that there is inadequate dissemination of research to the wider expedition field and an absence of dialogue between academics and the other sectors involved in overseas youth expeditions.
3   The conference provided an opportunity for dialogue between the various sectors involved in overseas youth expeditions and enabled participants to increase their

202

Pete Allison et al.

knowledge and understanding of the inner workings of the field from a holistic perspective. The presentations developed participants' understanding of key policy, research and practice issues.

4   People's attitudes and ideas towards research were not changed substantially by the conference. Rather, their views were confirmed and strengthened.

5   Since the conference, many participants (over half of those interviewed) have incorporated knowledge that they gained at the event into their own practices and policies.

CONCLUSIONS

UK expeditions have a long history that can be traced back to exploration for geographical purposes. In the past twenty years, expeditions for young people have gained remarkable popularity. This growth has occurred over a broad spectrum of provider organisations and expedition models. However, a small and diminishing proportion of these expeditions follow the tradition of self-sufficient structured scientific fieldwork in a wilderness setting. Rather, a large and increasing proportion offer expeditions designed with personal development as the sole or primary learning outcome. These expeditions often concentrate on adventurous activities or service learning as the vehicles for this personal development.

Overseas expeditions carry some significant psychological risks that can be minimised only by a skilled leadership team for whom the welfare of all expedition members is paramount. This same leadership team must also take care to ensure that the deep metaphysical and personal questions that arise for expedition members are dealt with in an appropriate manner.

Other possible problems include poor accessibility at home due to the prohibitively high cost of these expeditions. In the destination country, social problems can occur through poorly conceived community projects and a lack of cultural sensitivity.

With so many potential pitfalls, today's expedition providers, regulators and researchers have to consider carefully the costs and benefits of launching each new overseas expedition. The commercial demand for expeditions is certainly increasing, but this, in itself, is insufficient reason to continue as before.

There is a growing recognition of the educational benefits that all members of an expedition may derive from either participation or leadership roles. Specifically, immersion in wilderness can inspire young people towards stewardship of their own natural environment. Meanwhile, acting as a member of a team almost always generates benefits in terms of personal and social development.

However, the learning outcomes of each expedition vary enormously, depending on the provider. At the moment, the nascent regulatory framework seems to be doing a good job of promoting safety and learning whilst not stifling creativity. There is no requirement that all expeditions must conform to the same standard as far as expedition design is concerned.

Most providers are also striving to increase access to participants from all social and economic backgrounds, meaning that high-quality, safe provision is becoming available to a greater range of young people.

The advantages that make today's overseas expeditions such powerful experiences hark back to the beginnings of the British outdoor education movement. These same advantages provide a significant counterbalance to modern-day concerns, so expeditions that concentrate on adventurous activities at the expense of Levick's 'serious purpose' sacrifice a great deal. There is little doubt that overseas expeditions will continue to grow in popularity, but key challenges remain: to make them accessible to as many people as possible; to ensure they are of the highest possible quality; and to develop an understanding of the great significance of these experiences to their participants.

ACKNOWLEDGEMENTS

Some parts of this chapter have been previously published in various publications by the individual authors. The section on the PSES and the BSES drew on writings by Ian Ashwell of the BSES, Bob Headland of the Scott Polar Research Institute and George Murray Levick that are now held in the BSES archive. They were accessed with help from Justin Warwick.

REFERENCES

AALS (n.d.) *The Scope of the Regulations.* Available online at: http://www.aals.org.uk/faqs.html#scope.
Allison, P. and Higgins, P. (2002) Ethical adventures: can we justify overseas youth expeditions in the name of education?, *Australian Journal of Outdoor Education,* 6 (2): 22–26.
Allison, P. and Pomeroy, E. (2000) How shall we 'know?': epistemological concerns in research in experiential education, *Journal of Experiential Education,* 23 (2): 91–97.
Allison, P. and Stott, T.A. (eds) (2009) *South West Greenland 2009: Expedition Report.* London: BSES Expeditions.
Andrews, J., Kneale, P., Sougnez, Y., Stewart, M. and Stott, T.A. (2003) Carrying out pedagogic research into the constructive alignment of fieldwork, *Planet,* Special Edition: *Linking Teaching and Research and Undertaking Pedagogic Research in Geography, Earth and Environmental Sciences,* 5: 51–52.
Beames, S.B. and Stott, T.A. (2008) Raleigh International pilot study report: summary of findings on how participants benefited from a 10-week expedition to Costa Rica, report presented to Raleigh International, March.
Berman, D. and Davis-Berman, J. (2002) An integrated approach to crisis management in wilderness settings, *Journal of Adventure Education and Outdoor Learning,* 2 (1): 9–17.
Berman, D., Davis-Berman, J. and Gillen, M. (1998) Behavioural and emotional crisis management in adventure education, *Journal of Experiential Education,* 21: 96–101.
Biggs, E. (2009) Mapping glacial retreat in the Tasermiut Fjord region of SW Greenland using GPS and remotely sensed imagery, in Allison, P. and Stott, T.A. (eds) *South West Greenland 2009: Expedition Report,* London: BSES Expeditions.
British Standards 8848 (2007) *Specification for the Provision of Visits, Fieldwork, Expeditions, and Adventurous Activities, outside the United Kingdom,* London: BSI.

Davis-Berman, J. and Berman, D. (2008) *The Promise of Wilderness Therapy*. Boulder, CO: Association for Experiential Education.

Evans, E.R.G.R. (2006) *South with Scott*, Gloucestershire: The Echo Library.

Jacoby, B. (1996) Service learning in today's higher education, in Jacoby, B. (ed.) *Service Learning in Higher Education: Concepts and Practices*, San Francisco, CA: Jossey-Bass.

Jakubowski, L.M. (2003) Beyond book learning: cultivating the pedagogy of experience through field trips, *Journal of Experiential Education*, 26 (1): 24–33.

Jones, A. (2004) *Review of Gap Year Provision*, DfES Research Report 555, London: Department for Education and Skills.

Kaplan, S. and Talbot, J.F. (1983) Psychological benefits of a wilderness experience, in Altman, I. and Wohlwill, J. (eds) *Human Behavior and Environment: Advances in Theory and Research*, New York: Plenum Press.

Kendall, J.C. (1990) Combining service and learning: an introduction, in Kendall, J.C. *et al.* (eds) *Combining Service and Learning: A Resource Book for Community and Public Service*, Vol. 1, Raleigh, NC: National Society for Internships and Experiential Education.

Levick, G.M. (*c.* 1939) *The Story of the Public Schools Exploring Society*, London: BSES archive.

Lonergan, N. and Andersen, L. (1998) Field based education: some theoretical considerations, *Higher Education Research and Development*, 7: 63–77.

Macklin, D. (1991) Footprints forever: impacts of expeditions, *Geographical Magazine*, July: 40–44.

Maslow, A.H. (1968) Some educational implications of humanistic psychologies, *Harvard Educational Review*, 38 (4): 685–696.

Nuttall, A. (2009) Melting of an outlet glacier of the southern Greenland ice sheet, in Allison, P. and Stott, T.A. (eds) *South West Greenland 2009: Expedition Report*, London, BSES Expeditions.

Rowe, M. (2008) The credibility gap, *Geographical*, 80 (8): 46–53.

Scottish Government (2009) *Exclusions from Schools 2007/2008*, Statistics Publication Notice: Education Series, ISSN 1479-7569. Available online at: http://www.scotland.gov.uk/Publications/2009/01/23135939/35.

Simpson, K. (2004) 'Doing development': the gap year, volunteer-tourists and a popular practice of development, *Journal of International Development*, 16 (5): 681–692.

Smith, M. (2008) *Exploring a Changing World: A Guide to Fieldwork for Youth Expeditions*, London: Young Explorers Trust.

Stott, T.A. (2009) Suspended sediment dynamics and yields in a glacial fed river, Tasermiut Fjord, SW Greenland, in Allison, P. and Stott, T.A. (eds) *South West Greenland 2009: Expedition Report*, London: BSES Expeditions.

Stott, T.A. and Hall, N.E. (2003) Changes in aspects of students' self-reported personal, social and technical skills during a six-week wilderness expedition in Arctic Greenland, *Journal of Adventure Education and Outdoor Learning*, 3 (2): 159–169.

Thomas, G. and Pring, R. (eds) (2004) *Evidence-based Practice in Education*, Maidenhead: Open University Press.

Warburton, J., Higgitt, M. and Watson, B. (1997) Improving the preparation for fieldwork with IT: preparation tutorials for a remote field class, *Journal of Geography in Higher Education*, 21 (3): 333–339.

Warren, K. and Loeffler, T.A. (2000) Setting a place at the table: social justice research in outdoor experiential education, *Journal of Experiential Education*, 23 (2): 85–90.

CHAPTER ELEVEN

VALUES IN ADVENTURE EDUCATION

HAPPY AND WISE THROUGH HANDS-ON LEARNING

*Pete Allison, Malcolm Thorburn, John Telford
and Aaron Marshall*

INTRODUCTION

In this chapter, we use some sharp thinking from the past to consider possibilities for the future. Essentially, we explore values and how they impact on adventure education. You might think that values have little to do with adventure education, but we hope that by the end of this chapter you will have changed your mind. We suggest that without under-standing the role of values, at least at a cursory level, adventure education is destined to be an ill-informed enterprise. We also suggest that one of the main ways to make the most of adventure education opportunities is to adopt a constructivist approach to learning. We explore some of the claims regarding aims and objectives that are often associated with such an approach. This is where the sharp thinking from the past comes into play. By adopting Aristotle's three kinds of practical knowledge, we propose that adventure education should be concerned with learning about the environment, climate change, or other related purposes such as health and wellbeing (*episteme*) as well as with skill development (*techne*). If this coupling is achieved we consider that students can develop practical wisdom (*phronesis*) based on a clear appreciation of what is of real significance and worth in human affairs. Finally, we offer suggestions for how you might incorporate this into learners' adventure education experiences.

VALUES

Values are inherent in the choices we make, and we all have to make choices in our lives every day. Built on beliefs, and bearing significant emotional attachment, values play a crucial role in shaping our approach to decision-making. Some choices we face are small, such as what to eat, while others are larger, such as what kind of job we want to have. A large part of growing up and becoming an active member of society involves developing our abilities to make value-driven choices – and preferably 'good' choices. To complicate matters, some large choices, prior to reflection, may appear small – and vice versa. For instance, deciding what to eat can be a big choice as it demonstrates specific values about our bodies, others and the environment. Asking ourselves if the food is good for us, from a sustainable source, or organic are three of the most obvious choices that face us in a supermarket. Furthermore, simply purchasing food at a supermarket represents a fourth choice that reflects our values – where we choose to shop.

When working with groups, we have often been interested to observe clothing and equipment. Adventure educators often distribute waterproof clothing at a centre (well worn and not particularly comfortable or stylish) and then don their own designer, high-specification kit, which, even to the untrained eye, is very different. Distribution of other equipment often follows a similar pattern: rusty mountain bikes are handed out to the participants before the educator climbs aboard a top-of-the-range model; students are given bashed pairs of skis whilst the instructor uses high-quality brand-name race skis that make demonstration activities look easy!

Similarly, education (formal and non-formal) comes complete with choices, ranging from which school to attend, whether to opt for private or state education, what subjects to specialise in and which, if any, extracurricular activities to pursue. For example, in adventurous education contexts, coherent and considered decisions need to be taken about whether it is acceptable to light fires when wild camping, make quick scree-run descents of hills, mountain bike on particular types of terrain, and travel long distances simply to experience adventurous activities in the first place. Thus, teachers and leaders in education are faced with choices regarding the philosophies of education to which they subscribe, and how to conduct their everyday lives in accordance with these values (Pring, 2005).

The educator, then, faces the challenge of recognising and reflecting on their own values. Because values often rest on our beliefs and bear an emotional attachment, we do not tend to think about them unless our attention is drawn to them. Without intending to, we act, unaware of many values that drive our decision-making. If the development of good decision-making rests on value-based choices, it is imperative that adventure educators intentionally reflect on and locate their own value sets. This awareness deeply impacts on approaches to teaching and expectations for students as we strive to help them reflect on and develop their own values.

Before developing these ideas further, and drawing on the ideas of Aristotle for assistance, it may prove helpful to examine constructivist learning.

CONSTRUCTIVIST LEARNING

Here, we offer a brief outline of constructivist learning, or what Grandy (1998) identifies as cognitive constructivism. Constructivist learning is the teaching approach (or pedagogy) that adventure education literature commonly espouses. The philosophical foundations of this view suggest that humans generate meaningful mental representations, or mental maps, based on their prior and current experiences to build their views and understandings of the world – including developing beliefs and associated values. The theory was initially proposed by Jean Piaget and then developed by John Dewey, amongst many others. Dewey was from the pragmatist school of philosophy, which is concerned with what works in any given situation (in contrast to those who are concerned with proving how the world 'is' or 'should be'). This school, and specifically Dewey's work, is very helpful for adventure educators and is often referred to in texts relating to outdoor education, adventure education and experiential learning. Dewey was primarily concerned with developing a philosophy of education based on the nature of experience. He held a dynamic, wide view of knowledge as a changing phenomenon, and accordingly believed we should educate to widen the area of shared concerns by emphasising participation and cooperation. This idea is equally evident within adventure education literature.

Two of Dewey's central educational principles are useful in exploring and developing ideas of constructivism. First, he developed a principle of *continuity*, which he summarised as 'every experience both takes up something from those which have gone before and modifies in some way the quality of those which come after' (Dewey, 1938: 27). Second, his principle of *interaction* tells us that experiences result from an interaction between a student and their environment (in a broad sense), so educators need to consider elements of experiences that are internal to the student and 'objective' aspects of the learning environment. Thus, Dewey's principle of interaction is concerned with student perception, reactions, attitudes, beliefs, habits and emotions, and the way they interact with the learning environment. Together, these two principles are described as longitudinal (continuity) and lateral (interaction) aspects of experience that may intercept at any given time (Dewey, 1938: 42).

In the context of adventure education, this basically means that as an individual takes part in the programme he or she will bring the benefits (and disadvantages) of previous experiences into the present moment. Every individual will bring something slightly different to the 'mix'. These very individual previous experiences will then combine and interact with the particular aspects of the learning environment to have an effect on how the individual experiences that present moment and what learning he or she takes from it. For instance, the sight of a swan swooping low overhead when canoeing on a lake could be interpreted in several ways or ignored completely. The swan, unless it has aspirations to be a fighter pilot, is probably making a demonstration in order to protect its territory. For the students in the canoe, however, the combination of previous experiences and knowledge, level of confidence regarding being on a lake, the way the group is interacting and any number of other factors could result in the experience inspiring (among many other things) a lifelong interest in birds or a deep-seated fear of birds.

Dewey's model identifies these connecting points of continuity and interaction as central to understanding the way that learning occurs (is constructed) in different ways for different people depending on the specifics of their previous experiences and the specifics of the present learning environment. An awareness of this, as opposed to assuming that all students are experiencing everything in more or less the same way, can allow the teacher to relate to students individually rather than treat them all exactly the same. It also allows the teacher to nurture the interests of individual students in ways that are helpful for those individuals and to create space for them within adventure education experiences to practise value-driven decision-making.

We have often found Dewey's principle of continuity to be interesting when we visit outdoor centres that offer five-day programmes. Some centres we visit have aimed to 'deliver' the same programme every week, regardless of the backgrounds or histories of the group members. This seems to ignore the principle of continuity and treats all people as the same. Our experience is that this is unhelpful when trying to increase quality and maximise the benefits of adventure education for all people. Rather, we prefer to take an approach where we might plan the first day when working with a group but then rapidly engage the group in deciding what they want to do and designing a programme for the rest of the week. Of course, this needs lots of support and advice, and it can be logistically complex, but we have found that it makes for a much richer learning experience and enhances the education in adventure education.

Dewey's prolific writings are far-reaching and considerably more complex than presented above, but these two principles offer an insight into the subtle considerations that adventure educators can benefit from appreciating and understanding. In order to operationalise his philosophy, Dewey developed a model that he calls the 'pattern of inquiry'. The essential elements of this model are, first, that the student has

> a genuine situation of experience – that there be a continuous activity in which he is interested for its own sake; secondly, that a genuine problem develop within

Figure 11.1 Dewey's principle of continuity encourages working with participants to plan a programme

this situation as a stimulus to thought; third, that he possess the information and make the observations needed to deal with it; fourth, that suggested solutions occur to him which he shall be responsible for developing in an orderly way; fifth, that he have opportunity and occasion to test his ideas by application, to make their meaning clear and to discover for himself their validity.

(Dewey, 1916: 163)

Thus, by viewing the student's learning as a journey that began long prior to the present experience, and recognising that the present experience will be incorporated into that larger history of meaning representations, the adventure educator creates a space for students to develop greater inquiry habits, problem-solving and decision-making at both the personal and the social level.

Another figure who practised a constructivist approach to learning and was influential in the development of adventure education was Kurt Hahn. Among many other achievements, he inspired Outward Bound, Round Square Schools, United World Colleges and the Duke of Edinburgh Award (Veevers and Allison, 2010). His vision of education has continued beyond his lifetime in these four organisations, all of which epitomise his values in their philosophies, objectives and everyday practices. Hahn's four pillars – physical fitness, an expedition that provides challenge and adventure, a project that develops self-reliance and self-discipline, and a sense of compassion through service – encompass the values he believed to be vital. He strongly believed that the type of education he advocated should be available to as many people as possible. This was demonstrated throughout his life, from the scholarship scheme discussed before the opening of Salem School in the 1920s and introduced at its inception to the similar scheme that continues today at Gordonstoun. There were also his successful attempts to bring this type of education to a UK-wide audience. These two themes of inclusion and expansion run throughout his philosophy and life.

While there are certainly differences in the philosophies developed by Dewey and Hahn, there are many similarities, too. Perhaps the most striking is that they both believed in students learning through experience, through problems and projects that arose out of their interests and passions. In subscribing to the philosophies espoused by Dewey and Hahn and others in this tradition, it is impossible to escape the approach to learning they represent: we are concerned with enabling students to construct their own knowledge and learning in any given context. This means that the educator's role shifts from teacher or instructor to facilitator or co-learner (Allison and Wurdinger, 2005). Thus, the student actively engages the process by encountering choices and reflecting on the values that shape their decisions. The educator assists that process through support and facilitation as a co-learner.

This pedagogical shift has some significant consequences for the educator, not least of which is that it makes it challenging to identify learning outcomes and remain true to

210

cognitive constructivism. For example, when organisations espouse a constructivist learning philosophy and concurrently claim that participants will learn about the significance of climate change and their role in contributing to it, we are suspicious that some kind of neo-colonial indoctrination is taking place. Telling people what they are going to learn prior to an experience at best contradicts and at worst negates their opportunities to construct meaning from the experience and construct knowledge on their own terms. We do not doubt the importance of climate change and the associated debates, but offer the example as an illustration of the inconsistency and contradictions that are present in some adventure education contexts today.

There are, of course, potential limits to any philosophy and associated approaches to education. Therefore, it is important, for precision's sake and to keep constructivism from being considered a peculiarly elastic approach to teaching and learning, that we briefly outline three of the more readily acknowledged limits of constructivism. First, pragmatically, a degree of trust between teachers/leaders and learners is required for constructivist teaching approaches to work well. Unsurprisingly, if trust is problematic due to, for example, poor behaviour, limited attention span or excessively large student groups, then a retreat towards more traditional teaching approaches is likely, rather than yielding further decision-making responsibility to learners. Second, excessively adventurous activities are likely to result in the same outcome. If teachers and leaders are preoccupied with safety concerns, it will be difficult to focus on constructing problem-solving learning environments. Third, conceptually, difficulties may arise when adventure education programmes framed on constructivist learning principles are required to articulate with precise learning outcomes, such as those documented in the National Curriculum. In these circumstances, it is often difficult to match the authenticity of learners' learning experiences with the requirement that they must attain certain age and stage outcomes.

It is particularly interesting to view these constraints on cognitive constructivism from the educator's perspective. In terms of developing trust, the educator should be aware of their own values, and the bias those values will generate. A trusting relationship framed within a constructivist approach to learning suggests the educator will allow students freedom to develop their own meaning from the experience personally and socially within the context of the experience and associated reflections. Thus, educators who are aware of their own bias can constrain their views appropriately, allowing students the space to develop their own views thoughtfully. Second, risk-management issues may not allow for student decision-making. In safety-related situations, the decision-making of the educator will be on display for the group and can still play an influential role in developing student decision-making if the educator is willing to allow students open reflection over the benefits and disadvantages of the educator's decision within the social context of the group after the decision has been made and safety restored. Finally, facing the challenge of learning outcomes, educators can develop broad outlines within which varied groups and varied activity interests will flourish. Examples include outlines that emphasise personal and social development, problem-solving and practice that increases 'good' judgement.

211

One of us often employed initiative games and ropes courses when working with groups. One member of staff at the centre was full of enthusiasm (so much so that it could become irritating), and would talk a great deal when working with groups. At the start of one day when he was co-facilitating with us, he introduced himself and the first activity and proceeded to tell the group extremely detailed rules. He also explained how people had completed the activity in the past. On listening to him, the messages were very clear: I am the most important person here, so you have to listen to me; and I have decided that there is a right and a wrong way to do this activity. Any potential creativity in the group was immediately crushed, which left us with some serious dilemmas. We chose to confront the issue head on. So, after starting the group on their next exercise, we explained to him that he would be shadowing during the next few activities, and we would talk over lunch. The group quickly adjusted to the different style and exploited the space they had been given. They developed their own meanings through the activities and explored some values. However, the learning climate was crucial, and we had certainly set off on the wrong foot!

This illustration demonstrates that mere use of the prefix 'co', as in 'co-learners', does not automatically guarantee that a new, democratic set of practices is in place. Existing hierarchies and agendas for perceived efficiency and effectiveness can mean that the status quo remains almost wholly intact. For these reasons, teachers and leaders might like to run through some self-check questions when planning and reviewing their adventure education practices (see Figure 11.2).

ARISTOTELIAN ADVENTURE EDUCATION

Suggesting that adventure education is couched in values is not a particularly new or indeed controversial idea. However, an emphasis on values and choices that is much more 'front and centre' helps to conceptualise adventure education as an educational and thus moral endeavour. This may seem self-evident, but it is worthy of further exploration. Looking back to Aristotle can help us to look forward and improve our practices on a daily basis.

Making choices and decisions requires us to weigh up options and balance the advantages of different courses of action, which requires thinking and considering the processes and outcomes of various pathways. When decisions need to be made about serious things, they usually require some deliberation – they are rarely straightforward and are not normally measured on one scale, but more typically through a complex tapestry of multidimensional scales. Hunt (1990) offers a seminal overview and discussion of these complexities from an ethical perspective in the context of experiential learning. These options, it can be argued, are ways in which we are empowered as consumers and more generally as individuals in society with increasing degrees of autonomy and self-determination. For example, Taylor (1991) highlights the importance of choices in understanding ourselves and others. He suggests that relationships with others are crucial in understanding the choices that we make and their consequences as we search for ways to construct full and valuable lives.

Learning

- Were learners aware of the aims of activities and scheduled learning experiences?
- Was there a regular ongoing overview of learning aims?
- Were the learners actively involved in constructive dialogue with other learners?
- Did learners assume some 'active' responsibilities for their own learning?
- Could learners begin to see problems from different perspectives?
- Could learners merge reason and feelings?
- Did facilitating learning lead to some learners appearing unduly lost?
- Could learners be trusted to remain on task?

Teaching

- Were you aware of the values you brought to the learning setting?
- Were you aware of the implicit values conveyed by the learning setting?
- Were you confident in your ability to set up learning tasks?
- Could you adapt to teaching in more uncertain teaching and learning environments
- Were you able to limit the amount of time you talked to the whole group?:
- Could you cater for most individual learner differences?
- What types of questions did you ask: e.g. convergent, divergent? Were these appropriate?
- Were you able to trust learners and 'wait' for real learning gains to occur?

Figure 11.2 Self-check questionnaire for reviewing some of the main features of constructivist-informed learning and teaching

Awareness of the options that are open to us as moral agents is also important. We must appreciate that a range of options is available and should recognise that other people select different options from our own. In other words, other people express different preferences through the choices they make. As we become aware of such differences, we will take less for granted and will make fewer assumptions. While we might still select the same options, we will see them in a different light and recognise that they are not the only, or the only right, options (Haydon, 2005).

This shift – from seeing situations as having one clearly defined, 'correct' solution to appreciating the messiness of a larger set of appropriate or equally right options – is a real struggle for many students. On a recent camping residential experience, we noted how one girl initially struggled to accept that there were different ways of cooking relatively common meals. However, there was a visible breakthrough when she discovered that eggs did not have to be fried – that they also tasted really good when they were boiled. Thereafter, she was interested in discovering different ways of doing many other things, such as packing

213

her belongings, working out which belongings to bring on an expedition, and so on. To explore their values, participants in adventure education need to be given opportunities to make choices and decisions as well as the space to deal with the associated consequences.

At this point, it may be worth looking into the philosophical presuppositions of these general educational points. We find it useful to refer to Aristotle, who distinguished between several different types of knowledge, enquiry and understanding. He identified three key modes of practical knowledge: *techne*, *episteme* and *phronesis*. Whereas *episteme* is the knowledge of much academic instruction, and *techne* is the knowledge and skill of vocational and other training, the deliberative capacities of *phronesis* are directed more towards clear appreciation of what is of real significance and value in human affairs, moral and otherwise. Thus, while we might well become knowledgeable, skilled or 'clever' through academic and technical learning, we may not become wise. Aristotle places the greatest value on the development of this latter quality. This is relevant when thinking about people who work in adventure education. We might have all kinds of skills, but if we do not know which knot to tie on which rope at the right time, we will rapidly find ourselves in trouble. Similarly, if we do not make a good route choice (which is much more than a technical skill, given that we need to consider educational objectives, the characters in the group and other information), we might find ourselves walking much further than anticipated or camping in less than ideal locations.

According to Aristotle, distinctions between these types of knowledge cannot be fully appreciated without understanding certain differences in how they are acquired. First, whereas theoretical or academic knowledge may be learned best via books and/or direct instruction, forms of practical knowledge – whether *techne* or *phronesis* – usually require a more 'hands-on' approach, which in turn demands some sort of non-academic experience. (This is usually appealing to adventure educators.) However, *phronesis* also differs crucially from *techne* in that it involves the cultivation of a repertoire of moral, context-specific sensibilities that are not subject to codification as mechanically applicable rules: in short, the appreciation and understanding of *phronesis* exhibited in good or wise judgement are more effective than mere recall or technical routine. While adventure education might include skills development (*techne*) and learning about the environment, climate change, health and wellbeing (*episteme*), primarily it should be concerned with developing practical wisdom (*phronesis*). The connections between constructivist approaches to learning, experiential education and Aristotelian notions of practical wisdom are enhanced when noting the value Aristotle places on the deliberative process, wherein *phronesis* greatly benefits learners working constructively together on tasks that tease out human virtues. This is captured in the following extract from a Scottish study:

> [Teachers] conceive outdoor learning more in terms of open enquiry into moral and other issues and values than as the acquisition of skills (*techne*) or of academic facts or information (*episteme*). The most prominent theme to emerge during the visits was that development of the good judgement of practical wisdom (*phronesis*)

214

is more conducive (than learning facts or skills) to assisting pupils to live a meaningful life – or to achieving (though this term was not used in discussion) what
ancient Greek philosophers referred to as *eudaimonia*.

(Allison, Carr and Meldrum, forthcoming)

PUTTING IT INTO PRACTICE

Turning now to practice, we will address how an educator might aim pupils towards
developing *phronesis* in an adventure education context. Here, again, Aristotle has much
to contribute. He argues that students lack practical wisdom because they lack experience.
As students gain experience, they have opportunities to make 'good' judgements. Parallel
to Dewey's notions of continuity and interaction, Aristotle recognises the role of deliberation
– both on an individual basis and within a group context – in processing judgements that
have already been made and preparing to make future judgements. He uses the term *praxis*
to denote the process of making progressively better decisions because of experience and
reflection. However, it is possible to accrue numerous experiences while continuing to
make poor decisions. Dewey calls this process 'mis-education', while Aristotle describes
the individual who makes such decisions as 'incontinent'. The incontinent person fails to

Figure 11.3 A group is able to enjoy a happy mealtime as a result of making sound
decisions throughout the day; Aristotle used the term *praxis* to denote the process of making
progressively better decisions through experience and reflection

exhibit *praxis* by failing to adjust their present and future decisions in light of past decisions and their associated deliberation and consequences. In other words, they do not learn from experience.

The adventure educator therefore has a responsibility to generate a multiplicity of experiences that involve choice, individual reflection, group deliberation and consequences. The more opportunities students have to make choices, the more opportunities they will have to make 'good' choices or move towards 'better' judgement. When we work with groups, we are always looking for ways to hand decisions and choices over to the groups. For example, when teaching skiing, we often ask students to navigate to a certain area and then, as the days go by, they take more responsibility regarding where to spend the morning, the day, the next two days, planning different journeys, when to stop for breaks, when to review, when they feel they need technical input, when they want to practise and consolidate their learning, deciding what and when to eat, developing rotas for cooking, washing up and other domestic duties as well as responsibilities when engaged in 'the activity' itself.

A further nuance in Aristotelian thought may be helpful here. Aristotle notes that the range of what is considered a 'good' judgement appears much larger for the inexperienced decision-maker, but can become honed and refined with experience and *praxis*. A mature person with a developed sense of *phronesis* will better understand the subtleties of particular situations, and make 'better' judgements in light of these subtleties. For example, on a recent sailing journey of several days, the subtlety of such judgements were illustrated. After a day of good weather and fine sailing, when the young people were in charge of the vessel, we reached the planned place to anchor. The following day involved a passage through a tidal area that required the full attention of the whole crew before heading into interesting coastline. The group suggested making the passage that evening. (They knew this was possible as they had already checked the tides.) However, they were on a high from a successful day and were exhibiting early signs of tiredness. In discussion with them, we explored the wisdom of 'ending on a high' for the day and getting a good night's sleep at a reliable anchor before attempting the passage the following day. They soon saw the sense in 'not pushing it', had a decent rest, and so were on 'good form' (their phrase) the next day.

There are two important points for the adventure educator to bear in mind here. On the one hand, the educator should allow the student to develop their 'taste' for good judgement by carefully restraining advice and direction as appropriate. On the other hand, the educator's experience and decisions should still be utilised (and reflected upon later) when it is not possible or appropriate to allow full student choice, especially in risky or safety-related situations.

In distilling Aristotle's advice to the adventure educator, then, we can say that *phronesis* is best developed when students are given space for choice, reflection, deliberation and consequence. Further, the educator, presumably equipped with a greater sense of *phronesis*

216

than the students, is equally responsible to employ restraint and good judgement while encouraging student engagement throughout the experience. If Aristotle is correct, as we believe him to be, *phronesis* will grow naturally in students through the accumulation of such experiences.

For example, one of us was working with a group on a twelve-day kayaking expedition. The first two days comprised planning routes, preparing equipment and some training before the group departed. As they came around a headland on a lake, they had a choice of different directions. Rather than consulting the map, they relied on their memories and, unfortunately (for them), they selected a dead end. They paddled for a further six hours before making camp, and it was only in the evening that they consulted the map and started to plan the next day. They quickly realised – amidst much anger and disappointment – that they had no option but to retrace their route and recover the lost time with some longer days. Of course, the leader could easily have interjected and pointed out the error at the point when it was made, but then the group would have missed out on valuable lessons in navigation, attention to detail, group process, deferring responsibility to others, taking personal and group responsibility and many other things. Moreover, because they learned these lessons through their own experience, they still resonate with them today, many years later.

It is worthwhile at this point to return to the theme of the first section of this chapter and consider that the adventure education experience that the educator has chosen for the students will reflect particular values – both implicit and explicit. For example, it may be that during a residential adventure education experience students are encouraged to explore concepts of community and service to others during the daytime hours of 'formal' learning activities. If, however, these concepts are not reflected in the domestic arrangements – perhaps through shared responsibilities for cleaning communal areas (because cleaners are hired to do this), serving food to others (because dining works on a canteen system), and cleaning dishes (because mechanical dishwashers are more time-efficient) – students may well conclude that values of community and service apply only in the structured learning activities. This is evident in some residential contexts at a range of levels, and it seems to us that such an approach deprives students of potentially rich learning opportunities that are genuine and useful in enabling the elusive and sometimes troublesome idea of transfer of learning. At this point the educator needs to consider whether contrasting values are being conveyed. The educator also needs to consider whether the opportunity for direct experience of the realities of everyday living, which need no metaphorical transfer in order to become relevant and applicable to students' lives, is being provided in order to allow students to explore whether there is meaning in service and community and to develop practical wisdom in these areas.

As highlighted earlier, the focus in evaluating planning and practice is on teachers and leaders reviewing through a self-check approach. The key stages of this self-check ensure that a philosophy of intention articulates clearly with a psychology of learning. In this chapter we have presented a framework of Aristotelian-informed adventure education whereby the intention to improve learners' practical wisdom of *phronesis* is cultivated by experientially merging a focus on both cognitive and emotional domains of learning. This provides a means by which teachers and leaders can provide adventure education experiences that are consciously grounded in value judgements that reflect a linking of reason and feelings.

ACKNOWLEDGEMENTS

Some parts of this chapter have been previously published in various publications by the authors.

REFERENCES

Allison, P., Carr, D. and Meldrum, G. (forthcoming) Potential for excellence: interdisciplinary learning outdoors as a moral enterprise, *Cambridge Journal of Education*.

Allison, P. and Von Wald, K. (2010) Exploring values in the wilderness: PSD on educational expeditions, *Pastoral Care in Education*, 28 (3): 219–232. doi:10.1080/02643944.2010.504222..

Allison, P. and Wurdinger, S. (2005) Understanding the power, promise and peril of the experiential learning process, *Teacher Education and Practice*, 18 (4): 386–399.

Dewey, J. (1916) *Democracy and Education*, New York: Free Press.

Dewey, J. (1938) *Experience and Education*, New York: Macmillan.

Grandy, R.E. (1998) Constructivisms and objectivity: disentangling metaphysics from pedagogy, in Matthews M.R. (ed.) *Constructivism in Science Education: a philosophical examination*, Dordrecht: Kluwer Academic.

Haydon, G. (2005) *Impact No. 10: the importance of PSHE: a philosophical and policy perspective on personal, social and health education*, Salisbury: Philosophy of Education Society of Great Britain.

Hunt, J. (1990) *Ethical Issues in Experiential Education*, Boulder, CO: Association for Experiential Education.

Pring, R. (2005) *Philosophy of Education*, London: Continuum.

Taylor, C. (1991) *The Ethics of Authenticity*, London: Harvard University Press.

Veevers, N. and Allison, P. (2010) Introduction: the philosophy of Kurt Hahn, in Zelinski, M., *One Small Flame: Kurt Hahn's vision of education*. Ontario: From the Heart.

Pete Allison et al.

CHAPTER TWELVE

INCLUSIVE ADVENTURE EDUCATION

BETTER OPPORTUNITIES FOR PEOPLE WITH DISABILITIES

Joseph Gibson

INTRODUCTION

The general growth in the number of people engaged in adventure education is encouraging, as is the increase in the diversity of people who now benefit from it. Whilst there is still much to do, there are encouraging signs that a more inclusive philosophy is being embraced within adventure education, despite some of the obvious (and indeed less obvious) challenges that it might bring. This chapter looks at embracing inclusivity by focusing on the practice of adventure education with people who have disabilities.

There are many issues to contend with, but I will start by examining the basic framework of legislation that is relevant in the area and outlining some general concepts relating to disability. The chapter will also examine some of the ways of working in the outdoors with people with disabilities and suggest some of the benefits that adventure education may offer them through a brief review of the literature. Finally, a case study will present the outdoors experience of an individual who is congenitally deafblind.

This chapter is by no means an exhaustive manual for how to work in the outdoors with people who have disabilities. Nevertheless, I hope that it will offer an introduction to the area and provide a guide to further reading and information. Finally, and perhaps most importantly, I hope to stimulate your thoughts regarding just who could, and indeed should, benefit from the vast opportunities afforded by adventure education.

LEGISLATION

The Disability Discrimination Acts (1995 and 2005) and more recently the Equality Act (2010) have turned what was once a *moral* obligation into a *legal* requirement for all service providers, including outdoor centres, to offer their services to all people, regardless of disability, and to make reasonable adjustments where necessary. This means that a person with a disability can approach *any* outdoor provider and insist on their legal as well as their moral right to receive 'appropriate services'. However, this is largely a specialist area, and

219

a number of outdoor providers – the 'Adventure for All' centres – cater specifically for people with disabilities. They have specialist equipment and expertise in facilitating activities for people with disabilities, and their residential facilities have also been adapted to make them fully accessible. That said, education is an inclusive community and it is common for visiting groups to include participants from a wide range of backgrounds.

RANGE OF DISABILITY

People with disabilities are in no way a homogeneous group; indeed people with the same disability are not all the same. However, it may be useful at this point to look at the different types of disability and some broad categories.

Disabilities can be divided into two main groups: physical disabilities, which affect the physical functioning of the body; and learning or cognitive disabilities, which affect the cognitive functions. The limits of space preclude examination of all types of disability here, but two continuums are useful for facilitators seeking to determine whether a participant's disability is physical, cognitive or both. The first concerns the severity of their impairments, which can range from mild to severe (sometimes called 'profound' with respect to learning disability). The second relates to whether the disability is congenital or acquired: whether it has been present since birth or manifested later in life.

While these continuums offer a guide as to the nature of a participant's impairment, individual assessment of ability, as with any participant, is a more useful approach. Asking questions and making assessments about a participant's functional abilities are of much more practical use than merely knowing the name of their disability, particularly with respect to physical disabilities. Finding out if someone can stand unaided, bear weight on their legs or possess significant grip strength, for example, can guide an instructor towards any adapted equipment that may be required and to an appropriate starting-point for activities. Knowledge of a participant's cognitive understanding will allow you, as facilitator, to assess how you might break down an activity into easily understood segments that can then be scaffolded (built up) towards the final activity.

It is worth looking a little deeper into some considerations facilitators may make or questions they may want to ask for/of people with different types of disability. I will not discuss the types of disability here, but rather offer some of the functional considerations by briefly looking at people:

- who are ambulant with a physical impairment
- who use a wheelchair for moving around
- who have visual impairments
- who have hearing impairments
- who have multi-sensory impairments
- who have a learning disability.

220

Joseph Gibson

For people who are ambulant with a physical impairment, you may wish to ask a number of questions, such as:

- Does the participant use any aids to walk (crutches or sticks)?
- Do they sometimes use a wheelchair for long walks or rough ground?
- If they wear a prosthesis (false limb), is the participant prepared in case of blisters/stump soreness?
- What is the participant's level of grip?
- Do they have a preferred side for holding things?
- Finally, consider pace, length, surface and gradient of the routes to and from activities and whether regular rest points are required.

For people who use a wheelchair for moving around, the primary consideration is whether they self-propel and control their own chair or need to be pushed. Again, you will need to consider pace, length, surface, width and gradient of the routes. Access can become an issue when encountering gates, styles and other road/path furniture. You may wish to check procedures for such problems as punctures and battery failure. You should also ask whether the participant can bear weight at all and assess how easy it is for them to get in and out of their chair. A hoist may be required. Some participants may have only one chair that they are reluctant to use on rough ground, while others may be keen to move over rough terrain either independently or with help. (Beware: electric chairs are usually much heavier than manual ones!)

When working with people with visual impairments, you first need to ascertain the level of their impairment. You will need to establish if they require a guide or a guide dog, or whether they can move about independently. Different lighting conditions might also affect their level of vision. You may want to find out if the participant's condition is congenital or acquired. (If the person had sight at some point in their life, they will be able to form visual images more easily than someone who has never had sight.)

When dealing with people with hearing impairments, you need to ascertain the level of their hearing loss and establish whether they routinely use a hearing aid. You will also need to learn the participant's preferred method of communication (lip-reading, sign language or finger spelling). Ensuring information is passed on successfully is a big issue, whether it be the time of breakfast at a centre, the location of toilets or the instructions for an activity. Particular care should be taken in activities when the hands are essential for safety (such as belaying) because participants who use sign language as their main form of communication may sign instinctively and put themselves at risk by doing so. Methods for gaining participants' attention at a distance may also need to be considered.

For people with multi-sensory impairments, the nature of the impairments – acquired or congenital – is a key factor. Having had any level of vision and/or hearing is a huge benefit for those whose impairments are acquired. You will have to think in a tactile way, as this is how those with multi-sensory impairments experience the world. However, many people

221

with multi-sensory impairments do have some degree of useful vision or hearing. Utilising any residual hearing or vision will greatly aid their understanding.

For people with learning disabilities, the manner in which information and instructions are given is central to generating understanding, so try to avoid technical jargon, at least initially. The learning process can sometimes be made more effective by using pictures and demonstrations. Such information as times and distances could be given in a different format. When you are giving safety information, ensure that this is completely understood by asking for confirmation from every member of the group.

ADAPTED OUTDOOR EQUIPMENT

Adapting equipment for people with disabilities has a long history (see Croucher, 1981; Laurence, 1988; Swiderski, 1989a, 1989b, 1989c; Thompson and Hitzhusen, 1980). More recently, organisations such as Equal Adventure have developed adapted equipment such as the Kite Harness, Aquabac, Cango and the Field Toilet for general use as well as equipment designed for individuals such as the 'snap snowboarding foot'. Meanwhile, a basic internet search for 'cross-country' or 'all-terrain' wheelchairs shows the plethora of specialist equipment that has greatly increased the potential for independent access to the outdoors for people who use a wheelchair. There is also a wide range of adapted cycles, including tricycles, hand-cycles, side-by-side and duet bikes, enabling people with many types of physical disability to enjoy cycling.

Various national governing bodies have also produced literature and provide specialist training in their own areas. The International Orienteering Federation has led the way, with Trail Orienteering (Trail O) recognised as one of four orienteering disciplines. More recently, the British Mountaineering Council's Climbing for All: Disability Awareness in Rock Climbing initiative has been supplemented with a training course, and the British Canoe Union is planning a similar course for canoeing and kayaking.

VIEWS OF INCLUSION

In 1987, Joseph Winnick published an 'Inclusion Continuum' that outlined five strategies for including disabled children in physical activity programmes, ranging from fully inclusive activities to those where children participate in a segregated environment. In the 1990s Ken Black and others refined this concept to develop the 'Inclusion Spectrum' (Figure 12.1), primarily to move away from the original continuum's hierarchical structure. Now each strategy is valued equally, rather than being presented in a hierarchy.

While the Inclusion Spectrum is useful for outdoor practitioners who work with people with disabilities, taking time to consider the flexibility of outdoor activities themselves is beneficial in this context. If we consider climbing as an example, people of all abilities participate at

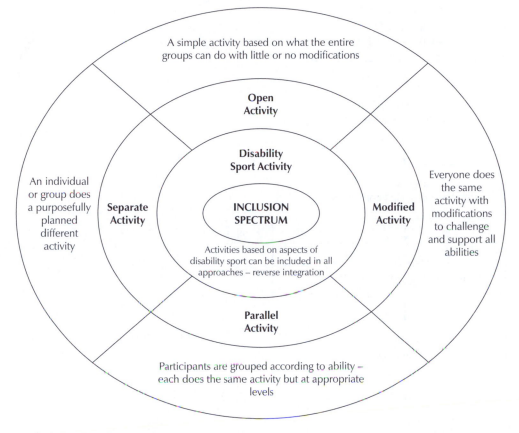

Figure 12.1 Inclusion Spectrum

Source: Black, 2009

a variety of levels in everything from bouldering to Himalayan expeditions, each with their own set of rules and ethics (see Tedja-Flores's (1995) entertaining discussion of 'climbing games'). A beginner climbing a 'moderate' graded route up a roadside crag can experience the same exhilaration as a more experienced and competent climber ascending an E4 in the Scottish Highlands or a world leader establishing a new route up a previously unclimbed tower in Patagonia.

Specifically within the field of adventure education, Sugarman (2001) discusses the concept of inclusive facilitation and offers a model (Figure 12.2), which is of use to facilitators preparing to work with people who have disabilities.

More recently, Paul (2010) has placed people at the centre and highlighted four areas (environment, equipment, practice and planning) that may be barriers to participation for people with disabilities (Figure 12.3). An outdoor provider will need to consider each of these carefully and devise methods to overcome them.

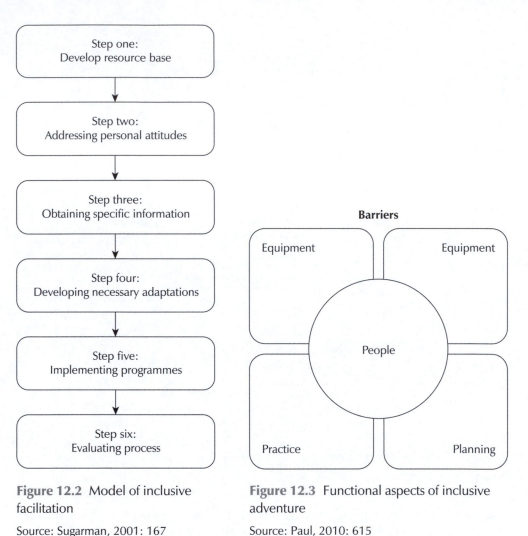

Figure 12.2 Model of inclusive facilitation

Source: Sugarman, 2001: 167

Figure 12.3 Functional aspects of inclusive adventure

Source: Paul, 2010: 615

REVIEW OF THE LITERATURE

A limited amount of adventure education literature and research focuses specifically on disabilities. Much information in this area tends to be anecdotal, but there have been some more reliable, empirical accounts that would be of use to those wishing to develop greater knowledge and skills in this growing filed. This section illustrates the evolving nature of research in this area and discusses some of the literature.

Lamb (1990) provides a case study of deaf children participating in outdoor activities as part of the Duke of Edinburgh Award Scheme. McRoberts' (1992) case study concerns a mountaineering expedition including four climbers with learning disabilities who successfully

Joseph Gibson

climbed Mount Elbus in 1991. The report discusses the aims of the Gateway Organisation, the activity arm of the Royal Society for the Mentally Handicapped (MENCAP), and gives anecdotal evidence of the benefits of the expedition, with integration offered as the greatest achievement. Cooper (1992) identifies the benefits of a general range of outdoor activities for people with more severe and profound learning disabilities, and some degree of challenging behaviour, when implemented within the community at a more therapeutic level. According to Cooper, these activities can have diagnostic benefits, and might also improve self-image, pride, confidence and independence among participants.

Rose (1990) looks at the general history of adventure education, particularly in the area of special needs, and discusses a range of benefits, as well as techniques for measuring some of these, observed during activities at the Basingstoke Outdoor Pursuits Club. The benefits include:

- immediacy
- involvement and participation
- risk and uncertainty
- challenge
- respect and presence (Rose, 1990: 14–16).

Massey and Rose (1992) report on the need for and the creation of a new service delivery package for their clients. They discuss the ways in which everyone can benefit from outdoor activities alongside five areas where normalisation principles, which are particularly appropriate for their client group, could be applied:

- community presence
- community participation
- competence
- choice
- respect (Massey and Rose, 1992: 1416–1417).

The authors offer an example programme to illustrate aims, objectives and outcomes. They utilise a wide range of sources, in contrast to their article that appeared the following year in *Mental Handicap Research* (Rose and Massey, 1993), which is far more specific. It concentrates upon an expedition to the French Alps in which the results are compared to those of a previous expedition to Mount Kilimanjaro. The article looks at the issue of exclusion and some of the constraints placed upon the target group. Using the two expeditions as case studies, the perceived benefits to the group were examined and compared. The authors' methodology in gauging the benefits for the target group are also explained: they conducted interviews and reviewed diary observations and holiday video footage to measure 'levels of engagement' (Rose and Massey, 1993: 292). Table 12.1 lists the benefits of the two expeditions.

Table 12.1 Comparing the benefits of two expeditions

Kilimanjaro	Alps
• Sense of achievement • Enhanced understanding • Hygiene and dressing • Role reversal	• Sense of achievement • Cooperation • Fitness • Role reversal • Self-esteem • Trust • Deeper understanding • Problem-solving skills

Source: Rose and Massey, 1993: 292–296

Levi (1994) also provides a case study about deaf children, although younger than those in Lamb's (1990) study. The group also differed in that it was integrated, and some of the problems and benefits of the integration are discussed, with communication being highlighted.

Rose and Jones (1995) present a case study of the Red Ridge Centre in which they describe the benefits that adventure education affords its clients, before going on to discuss the current state of research, the research techniques they used and the positive early indications from some longitudinal studies. However, they admit, 'Research into the benefits of adventure for people with learning disabilities is still in its infancy' (Rose and Jones 1995: 16).

Allison (1995) offers practical suggestions for facilitation and some justifications for researching the area. Later, he discusses (Allison 1997: 6) two methods of programme design that can help provide inclusive adventure programmes: compensation, where programmes are adapted in order to be inclusive; transcendence, where programmes are specifically designed around the abilities of the participants.

Hunt (1990) outlines the benefits of adventure education for people with special needs, using anecdotal evidence, and gives a brief history of the centre-based provision of adventure education for this group.

Hopkins and Putnam (1993: 165–166) briefly discuss the relative merits of specialised or mixed courses. They suggest that while there may be benefits for all participants in mixed courses, those with more complex disabilities might benefit more from courses that have been tailored to their individual needs. Woodyer (2000) takes this point further by raising the possibility of negative impact on those with special needs in mixed-ability groups, as the able-bodied participants take the lead.

Barret and Greenaway's (1995) review of outdoor research, the treatment of the target group and special needs groups in general is disappointing. It concedes that it is based primarily on examples of practice and is not research based. They do, however, state, 'The main value of outdoor adventure for disadvantaged groups may be the breaking down of barriers, both psychological and social' (Barret and Greenway, 1995: 15).

Woodyer (2000: 191–193) uses anecdotal evidence in his discussion of the value of adventure education for those with special needs to highlight its role:

- in personal development
- in confidence building and independent living
- as building blocks
- as a stimulus
- to change attitudes.

He also recognises the importance of the relationships and questions the need for research:

> There is a definite surge of energy and emotion from the instructor/carer transmitted towards the person with the disability when an activity/exercise is achieved . . . If it encouraged the carer to continue caring in a positive way for the client and it encouraged the instructor to carry on being positive about their job, does it have enough values so that we don't need to know whether or not it has value for the participant.
>
> (Woodyer, 2000: 189)

From America, Havens (1980) provides an early consideration of the use of adventure education with people who have special needs. The ways in which adventure education can address the problems inherent in special education are outlined. Robb (1984) continues this theme, highlighting the way in which the outdoors can be used in the special classroom, while Roland (1982) provides examples of suitable activities and the possible outcomes they can achieve. Robb and Ewert (1987) discuss the use of risk recreation with people who have disabilities and outline the research in the area. They go on to discuss the difference between the perception of risk and actual risk, and highlight self-concept as a possible area for research (Robb and Ewert, 1987: 61).

Sugarman (1988) provides a brief history of people with special needs participating in adventure education and outlines the benefits for those with physical, cognitive and psychological disabilities. Gray (1980) gives an early case study of a group of adults with severe and profound learning disabilities during a camp. Brannan et al.'s (1984: 3–4) discussion of current issues at the time in adventure education still has relevance today for people with disabilities. They suggest three areas that require attention to ensure successful courses:

1 Continued after course follow-up.
2 Sequential approach to experiences.
3 Focus on process rather than product.

Rynders *et al.* (1990) focus on the feasibility of integrating children with severe disabilities for intensified adventure education. The social interactions and attitudes of the staff and campers were measured using attitudinal tests and a variety of observational methods. The limitations of the study are discussed (need for larger numbers, more work on transferability and generalisation) and further areas of research are identified. This study also makes some important discoveries regarding the outcomes of integrated experiences and day-to-day socialisation of the target group with their peers. Also from America, a special issue of the *Therapeutic Recreation Journal* focused on camping and outdoor programming for people with disabilities. It contains three relevant articles (Johnson, 1992; McCormick *et al.*, 1992; Sable, 1992) as well as a book review of Havens' *Bridges to Accessibility* (1992), which provides practical and pedagogical advice on providing adventure activities for people with disabilities.

Johnson (1992) explores the links between ropes courses and wilderness experiences, and discusses the therapeutic benefits and transferability of both types of experience. The author also draws attention to the positive, influential power that witnessing the participants' experiences and their benefits has on their therapists' perceptions. McCormick *et al.* (1992) investigate the perceptions of the parents of children with 'mental retardation' towards the benefits of summer camp. The parents completed a questionnaire that included such topics as:

- skill development
- social competence
- respite care
- cognitive development
- expressive development
- physical competence (McCormick *et al.*, 1992: 33).

Sable (1992) discusses and evaluates integrated camping experiences. Inclusive courses were found to offer new appreciation for the accomplishments of disabled peers and respect for fellow-participants who may have endured similar experiences. The positive long-term impact for society of integrated experiences is also highlighted.

Thompson (2002) examines the concept of inclusion, terming it 'mainstreaming', and highlights the possible negative outcomes of 'excess baggage' syndrome, where people with disabilities depend on their able-bodied peers to complete a course. An alternative view is offered by Borgman (2002), who highlights the positive aspects of integrated adventure programmes, with social integration offered as a key element.

The term 'challenge by choice' is another concept that is often employed in the therapeutic use of the outdoors. Carlson and Evans (2001: 59) outline three core values of challenge by choice:

1   Participants set their own goals on each element: 'Success is not in completing the entire element as it was built, but in reaching one's own predetermined goal.'

2   Participants must be able to choose how much of an element they will experience: 'They must be able to determine when the ending of their journey on an element arrives.'

3   Participants must be able to make 'informed choices'.

More recently, Brodin (2009) has discussed inclusion through adventurous activities in a research project based in five countries across Europe. Brodin notes that full inclusion still has some way to go (for adults in particular) and that health is of prime importance to the target group.

Research has invariably found that people with special needs benefit from adventure education. However, thus far, there has been minimal discussion of the participants' specific experiences and little explanation of how particular benefits might be achieved. Recently, though, we have witnessed a positive development in that greater distinctions have at least been drawn between different participant groups. Adventure education research always should strive to avoid viewing 'people with special needs' as a homogeneous group, as Hopkins and Putnam (1993: 165) point out: 'It is now widely recognised that through careful focus on the precise characteristics or requirements, people who might formerly have been regarded as unsuited to adventurous experiences may also gain considerable personal benefit by participating.'

THE BENEFITS OF ADVENTUROUS ACTIVITIES FOR PEOPLE WITH DISABILITIES

People with disabilities enjoy precisely the same benefits from adventurous activities as anybody else does. However, research has highlighted some additional benefits, too. In this context, I find it useful to use a continuum developed in the mental health sector (Gilliam, 1993; see Figure 12.4).

At the left of the continuum, the reasons for participation are recreational. This area is often neglected when dealing with people with disabilities, because almost all of the focus tends to fall on therapeutic or educational benefits. However, it is probably the primary reason why every person reading this book does the job they do, and it is the case that people with disabilities have as much right as anyone else to participate in activities purely for the sake

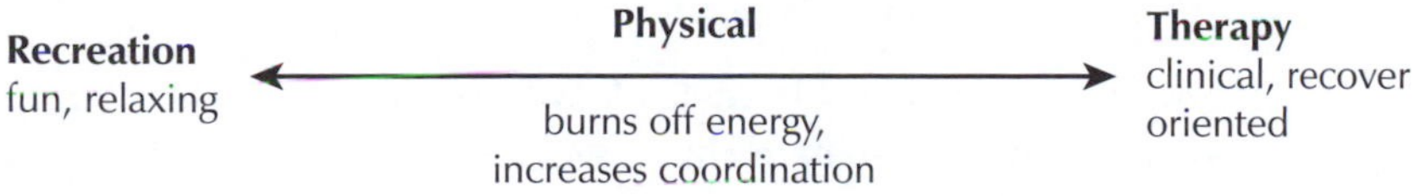

Recreation	Physical	Therapy
fun, relaxing	⟵————————⟶	clinical, recover oriented
	burns off energy, increases coordination	

Figure 12.4 Gilliam's continuum of how adventure therapy is perceived

Source: Gilliam, 1993: 212

of enjoyment. In the middle of the continuum, there are the physical benefits. Whilst often a powerful developmental medium, adventure education is not going to 'fix' someone's physical disability. It can, however, offer alternative activities to develop and maintain fitness and challenges that can aid in motivation to exercise. (People with learning disabilities tend to lead relatively sedentary lifestyles.) In short, adventurous activities can offer ways of exercising without the focus being on the exercise itself. Such activities can also help with those who have attention deficit disorder or disturbed sleep patterns, whilst both gross and fine motor control and balance can be developed through participation. Finally, the right end of the continuum focuses on therapy (it should be remembered that it was developed in a clinical mental health context). There are many therapeutic opportunities for people with complex, multiple disabilities through participation in adventure education (the following case study outlines this in respect of an adult with congenital deafblindness). A range of educational opportunities, especially for people with learning disabilities, are also best addressed in the natural environment.

CASE STUDY

This case study centres on an individual whom I shall name Fred. He is congenitally deafblind (cdb) and 40 years old. He spent his early life in a long-stay hospital and now lives in a housing-support project within the community. Being congenitally deafblind, Fred's principal challenge is communication. He has no speech and communicates through a variety of standard and idiosyncratic hand-over-hand (HOH) and on-body signs that are generally understood as being imperative rather than declarative: that is, his communication is usually understood to be grounded in the here and now (imperative) rather than relating to the past or the future (declarative).

Practitioners in the field of congenitally deafblind communication development have striven to help develop declarative communication with their cdb communication partners, with much of the early work done with young children through interactive tactile games. Outdoor activities found in adventure education have much in common with such games (and, of course, have a host of other benefits too, as outlined above). There can be a storyline to the activities, with moments of high drama. The activities are tactile in nature, with large physical movements and different equipment used. And we can do the activities together, thereby sharing the same physical impressions. This case study will examine how directed outdoor activities with Fred have deepened his understanding of the world and developed his declarative communication.

Fred had three outdoor/adventure sessions each week. He was part of a hill-walking group including some of the people with whom he shared his house and other adults with various degrees of multi-sensory impairment from other housing-support projects in the local area. This was a group session with the broad objectives of offering a chance to explore various environments, improve and maintain fitness and develop social relations with peers. The other two 'outdoor' sessions were a one-to-one environmental exploration session and a weekly visit to the climbing wall, sometimes with one of the men who shared Fred's house. These two sessions were complemented by follow-up 'communication sessions' and were more focused to Fred's individual needs.

The weekly visit to the climbing wall came about after a successful visit to Bendrigg Lodge in 1998. Bendrigg Lodge is an outdoor education and activity centre that has a long history of working with a vast range of groups with particular needs. During Fred's visit, he climbed successfully on an outside crag. We had built up to this by first climbing up grassy slopes together, then scrambling over very small rocky outcrops. We next spent an evening exploring and playing with the climbing helmet and harness. Finally, before the actual climbing session, we climbed up and down a ladder with the harness and helmet in place, and used the rope to give Fred an idea of how the system might protect him. The first climb on the crag itself was a significant moment for all concerned. It opened up a range of conversations with Fred alongside areas for further research regarding practice (see, e.g., Gibson and Ask Larsen, 2009).

Prior to the climbing, we had some concerns about how Fred might react to wearing the harness and helmet, due to his history of having been restrained and made to wear a padded helmet while in hospital. We thought the harness and helmet might remind him of these negative experiences. Reviewing video footage of the climb, it is clear to see Fred's interest in his helmet (he stops to investigate it during the climb), although this was not noticed at the time. In the follow-up 'conversation sessions', we investigated all the climbing equipment (helmet, shoes, rope and harness), but Fred remained most interested in the helmet. At first, he put the helmet on but would not let go of my hands; next, we put it on and buckled it up, although he still held my hands. Later, this developed into putting the helmet on, buckling it up and letting go of my hands for a short period before getting me to unbuckle it. This was very interesting at the time, and on reflection it might have signified Fred reassuring himself that this was not the same as the hospital helmet and he could control when it came off. I was keen to develop this concept of control, so during subsequent visits to the climbing wall, whenever Fred brought my hands to his helmet buckle, we would come down from the climb and take off the helmet. Eventually, this developed into Fred's way of expressing that he wanted to come down from a climb.

Over the years, the environmental sessions with Fred were held in a variety of locations in all weather conditions imaginable (the weather can be a great topic of conversation). The challenge lies in trying to find ways to explain things in a way that is meaningful to Fred (the rain is like a shower, for example). Many of the sessions focused on a particular park local to Fred and followed a particular routine (see Hart (2008) for a further description of such environmental sessions). We would follow a path up to a holly tree that we would carefully examine. From here, we would move into the woods, and specifically to the 'over–under tree'. This was a large horse chestnut with two branches that drooped down to the ground. We would climb over the first branch and then under the second – hence the name. We would then set out on a route that took in certain things every week: an old tree covered in moss, a passage through a rhododendron bush ('tree wall way'), a fallen tree with its roots exposed ('fallen tree with feet') and so on. We would stop and explore at each of these points, and I would try to explain them to Fred. We would also explore new or different things each week – such as feathers, a pine sapling or a rabbit hole.

Eventually, we would make our way back to the over–under tree, where we would first have a drink from our flask and then 'talk' back through the walk we had just taken. The regular routine of the sessions allowed us to follow a storyline, with gaps left for the new or different things we found or explored that week. This allowed me to ask what Fred could remember of the walk. The tactile nature of the natural environment and the objects we collected helped him recount his experiences; and because we had shared the experience, I had a good chance of interpreting his gestures when he did not use regular signs.

An example of Fred communicating declaratively occurred after we had met a horse and rider on one walk. Fred and I explored the horse, which at one point nuzzled into his hand. When we were back at the over–under tree, discussing the walk, I signed to Fred: 'You remember horse?' He responded by sniffing, blowing and licking his hand, as if to say, 'The thing that felt like this.'

This case study shows how adventurous activities can be used with someone who has complex, multiple disabilities to achieve both specific and general objectives. It highlights the importance of tailoring activities to the needs of an individual and the benefits that this approach can bring. It also shows how activities such as climbing can be broken down into very simple stages, which can then be built back up (scaffolded).

SUMMARY

I hope this chapter will help those who wish to work with people with disabilities and that it piques the interest of those who are still searching for their niche in the world of adventure education. I am writing this summary at Glenmore Lodge, where I am taking part in an event that has brought together people with the full spectrum of disabilities – congenital and acquired, mild and severe – for a weekend of inspiring lectures and competition. This event has exemplified the fact that it is our job as practitioners in the field not only to support the 'elite' disabled adventurers or merely offer taster sessions to beginners, but to provide all people with disabilities the full spectrum of adventurous educational activities.

REFERENCES

Allison, P. (1995) Inclusion of people with disabilities in challenge education, *Journal of Adventure Education and Outdoor Leadership*, 12 (3): 10–12.

Allison, P. (1997) Inclusive adventure programs: the ripple effect, *Teachers of Experiential and Adventure Methodology*, 13: 6–7.

Joseph Gibson

Barret, J. and Greenaway, R. (1995) *Why Adventure? The role and value of outdoor adventure in young people's personal and social development*, Coventry: Foundation for Outdoor Adventure.

Black, K. (2009) The Inclusion Spectrum: a model for including all young people in physical activity and sport, *International Council of Sport Science and Physical Education Bulletin No. 55*. Available online at: http://www.icsspe.org/bulletin/bulletin.php?v=577&kat=4&No=55&l=2&par=1.

Borgman, M. (2002) Social integration through adventure programming, *New Zealand Journal of Outdoor Education*, 1 (1): 14–23.

Braggins, A. (1993) *Trail Orienteering: an outdoor activity for people with disabilities*, Perthshire: Harvey Map Services.

Brannan, S.A., Rillo, T., Smith, T. and Roland, C. (1984) Current issues in camping and outdoor education with persons who are disabled, in Robb, G. and Hamilton, P.K. (eds) *The Bradford Papers*, Vol. 4, Bloomington: Indiana University Press.

Brodin, J. (2009) Inclusion through access to outdoor education: learning in motion, *Journal of Adventure Education and Outdoor Learning*, 9 (2): 99–113.

Carlson, J.A. and Evans, K. (2001) Whose choice is it? Contemplating challenge by choice and diverse-abilities, *Journal of Experiential Education*, 24 (1): 58–63.

Cooper, M. (1992) The use of outdoor activities as a therapeutic approach to mental handicap, *Journal of Adventure Education and Outdoor Leadership*, 9 (1): 37–39.

Croucher, N. (1981) *Outdoor Pursuits for Disabled People*, Cambridge: Woodhead-Faulkner.

Disability Discrimination Act (1995) London: HMSO. Available online at: http://www.opsi.gov.uk/acts/acts1995/ukpga_19950050_en_1.

Disability Discrimination Act (2005) London: HMSO. Available online at: http://www.opsi.gov.uk/acts/acts2005/ukpga_20050013_en_1.

Equality Act (2010) London: HMSO. Available online at: http://www.legislation.gov.uk/ukpga/2010/15/pdfs/ukpga_20100015_en.pdf.

Gibson, J. and Ask Larsen, F. (2009) *Out of the Comfort Zone: a preliminary analysis of the psychological dynamics of letting go and still being safe – examples from climbing with cdb adults*, Working Paper No. 50, Nordic Centre for Welfare and Social Issues. Available online at: http://www.nordicwelfare.org/outofthecomfortzone.

Gilliam, N. (1993) What happens when ropes courses move from the woods to psychiatric treatment facilities?, in Gass, M. (ed.) *Adventure Therapy: therapeutic applications of adventure programming*, Boulder, CO: Association for Experiential Education.

Gray, M. (1980) Report on the handicapped unbound program for severely and profoundly mentally retarded adults, in Robb, G.M. (ed.) *The Bradford Papers*, Vol. 1, Bloomington: Indiana University Press.

Hart, P. (2008) Sharing communicative landscapes with congenitally deafblind people: it's a walk in the park, in Zeedyk, S. (ed.) *Promoting Social Interaction for Individuals with Communicative Impairments: making contact*, London: Kingsley.

Havens, M.D. (1980) Special education out of doors, in Robb, G.M. (ed.) *The Bradford Papers*, Vol. 1, Bloomington: Indiana University Press.

Havens, M.D. (1992) *Bridges to Accessibility: a primer for including persons with disabilities in adventure curricula*, Dubuque, IA: Kendall/Hunt.

Hopkins, D. and Putnam, R. (1993) *Personal Growth through Adventure*, London: David Fulton.

Hunt, J. (1990) *In Search of Adventure: a study of opportunities for adventure and challenge for young people*, Guildford: Talbot Adair Press.

Johnson, J.A. (1992) Adventure therapy: the ropes wilderness connection, *Therapeutic Recreation Journal*, 26 (3): 17–26.

Lamb, I. (1990) Observations on hard of hearing children in outdoor activities, *Journal of Adventure Education and Outdoor Leadership*, 7 (2): 32–34.

Laurence, M. (1988) Making adventure accessible: innovations in adapted physical education/recreation curricula, *CAHPER/ACSEPL* [Canadian Association for Health, Physical Education and Recreation/ Association Canadienne pour la Santé, l'Éducation Physique et le Loisir] *Journal*, 54 (3): 10–13.

Levi, J. (1994). Signs of the times: an outdoor education project with profoundly deaf and hearing children, *Journal of Adventure Education and Outdoor Leadership*, 11 (2): 23–25.

Massey, P. and Rose, S. (1992) Adventurous outdoor activities: a review and a description of a new service delivery package for clients with learning difficulties who have behaviours which challenge society, *Journal of Advanced Nursing*, 17 (12): 1415–1421.

McCormick, B., White, W. and McGuire, F.A. (1992) Parent perceptions of benefits of summer camp for campers with mental retardation, *Therapeutic Recreation Journal*, 26 (3): 27–37.

McRoberts, M. (1992) Gateway makes history in Russia, *Journal of Adventure Education and Outdoor Leadership*, 9 (3): 17–18.

Paul, J.S. (2010) Inclusive adventure by design: the development of opportunities in outdoor sport for disabled people through co-ordinated people centred research and development in design and coaching, unpublished Ph.D. thesis, Department of Bioengineering, Brunell University.

Robb, G. (1984) Outdoor education: an alternative to learning for children with special needs, in Robb, G. and Hamilton, P.K. (eds) *The Bradford Papers*, Vol. 4, Bloomington: Indiana University Press.

Robb, G.M. and Ewert, A. (1987) Risk recreation and persons with disabilities, *Therapeutic Recreation Journal*, 21 (1): 58–69.

Roland, C.C. (1982) Adventure education with people who are disabled, in Robb, G. (ed.) *The Bradford Papers*, Vol. 2, Bloomington: Indiana University Press.

Rose, S. (1990) The value of outdoor activities, *Nursing*, 4 (21): 12–16.

Rose, S. and Jones, P. (1995) Adventure for all: disability is no handicap, *Journal of Adventure Education and Outdoor Leadership*, 12 (3): 16–17.

Rose, S. and Massey, P. (1993) Adventurous outdoor activities: an investigation into the benefits of adventure for seven people with severe learning difficulties, *Mental Handicap Research*, 6 (4): 287–302.

Rynders, J.E., Schleien, S.J. and Mustonen, T. (1990) Integrating children with severe disabilities for intensified outdoor education: focus on feasibility, *Mental Retardation*, 28 (1): 7–14.

Sable, J. (1992) Collaborating to create an integrated camping programme: design and evaluation, *Therapeutic Recreation Journal*, 26 (3): 38–48.

Sugarman, D. (1988) Adventure education for people who have disabilities: a critical review, in Robb, G. (ed.) *The Bradford Papers*, Vol. 3, Bloomington: Indiana University Press.

Sugarman, D. (2001) Inclusive outdoor education: facilitating groups that include people with disabilities, *Journal of Experiential Education*, 24 (3): 166–172.

Swiderski, M.J. (1989a) Outdoor adventure equipment modifications and assistive devices for people with various handicaps, Part One: Land based activities, *Journal of Adventure Education and Outdoor Leadership*, 6 (1): 20–22.

Swiderski, M.J. (1989b) Outdoor adventure equipment modifications and assistive devices for people with various handicaps, Part Two: Snow based activities, *Journal of Adventure Education and Outdoor Leadership*, 6 (3): 12–14.

Swiderski, M.J. (1989c) Outdoor adventure equipment modifications and assistive devices for people with various handicaps: Part Three: Water based activities, *Journal of Adventure Education and Outdoor Leadership*, 6 (4): 23–26.

Tedja-Flores, L. (1995 [1978]) Games climbers play, in Wilson, K. (ed.) *The Games Climbers Play*, Birmingham, AL: Baton Wickes [London: Diadem Books].

Thompson, A. (2002) Outdoor education for people with disabilities in Aotearoa, New Zealand, *New Zealand Journal of Outdoor Education*, 1 (1): 51–59.

Thompson, G. and Hitzhusen, J. (1980) Canoeing and kayaking with individuals with physical disabilities, in Robb, G.M. (ed.) *The Bradford Papers*, Vol. 1, Bloomington: Indiana University Press.

Winnick, J.P. (1987) An integration continuum for sport participation, *Adapted Physical Activity Quarterly*, 4: 157–161.

Woodyer, P. (2000) The value of and the values within outdoor education for those with disabilities, in Barnes, P. (ed.) *Values and Outdoor Learning*, Penrith: AfOL.

For further information about the use of outdoor activities with the congenitally deafblind also see:

Gibson, J. (2000) Fred outdoors: an initial report into the experiences of outdoor activities for an adult who is congenitally deafblind, *Journal of Adventure Education and Outdoor Learning*, 1 (1): 45–54.

Gibson, J. (2010) The map stick, *Horizons*, 50: 14–16.

ORGANISATIONS' WEBSITES

Adventure for All: http://www.adventureforall.org.uk.

Equal Adventure: http://www.equaladventure.org.

CHAPTER THIRTEEN

ENHANCING PROFESSIONAL DEVELOPMENT FOR THE ADVENTURE EDUCATOR

Paul Gray, Chris Hodgson and Chris Heaney

INTRODUCTION

Some managers can be reluctant to invest in staff development on the grounds that they may then look to move on to 'better' jobs. However, just for one moment, consider this statement which was overheard during a staff development day: 'We can develop our staff and they may leave, but imagine if we don't develop our staff and they stay!' Imagine providing a kayak session on a sheltered inland lake to a novice group of eager and hyperactive schoolchildren or delivering an introductory climbing session. This picture may initially look quite inviting, but what if you were running an identical session for the fourth time in three days. You may wish that you had additional skills, experience or knowledge so your day-to-day work could be more varied. Alternatively, you may have witnessed an emotionally sensitive issue between two young children in your group, or a complex moral issue where a client feels humiliated in front of their peers. Would you feel confident that you have the knowledge or skills to respond in the appropriate way?

Many adventure educators reach a stage where they know they need to increase their experience, knowledge or qualifications if their career is to progress, but they have no idea how to go about this. Some aspire to guide multi-pitch climbing in the Highlands of Scotland, whilst others feel more fulfilled coaching a group of children on a picturesque English river as the climax to a sustained and purposeful educational experience.

Undoubtedly, much can be gained from seeing the development of the participants you have worked with. Being witness to, and having input in, the growth and progress of another human being can be incredibly rewarding. Imagine how proud you would feel having coached or worked with a young person who succeeds in leading their first climb or even securing their first job. While this form of intrinsic reward is a key motivator for those of us sustaining a long career in the outdoors, we should remember that being a coach, mentor or leader is a privileged position, and to fulfil such a role effectively in an adventure context requires us to be both mindful of and responsible with the influence we may have on the individuals or groups with whom we work.

Adventure education can provide a long-lasting and satisfying career. Moving from being the facilitator of quite short and arguably superficial activities to the adventure educator who is capable of taking responsibility for a sophisticated and pedagogically sound adventure programme takes time and, more importantly, planning. We are used to planning activities for clients, but few novice adventure educators appreciate that they need a development plan for themselves if they are going to realise their full potential. Adventure educators are often, by their very nature, quite spontaneous individuals, but one of the key characteristics of adventure-based undergraduates who gain professional awards and credible experience alongside their academic qualifications is planning (Hodgson and Sharp, 2000).

This chapter is designed to arm the neophyte adventure educator, or a manager responsible for developing staff competence and qualifications, with some of the knowledge necessary to draw up just such a plan. It will focus on ideas for getting to know yourself and others through areas of motivation and personality. It will cover self-assessment tools, including personal profiling and SWOT analysis, that can be used to take stock of one's current position and explore how goal-setting can be used in conjunction with other development strategies to guide and enhance development and achieve long-term career goals.

UNDERSTANDING INDIVIDUAL MOTIVATION

A pertinent question is: what makes the difference in the individuals who choose to develop a career providing adventure education opportunities for a wide variety of individuals? If human drive provides an innate, biological force that impels us to behave in particular ways at particular times, motivational (from the Latin *movere* – to move) factors influence behaviour with the intention of bringing about specific outcomes based on social value. As a consequence of motivation, humans will invest energy and effort into achieving a desired outcome that is perceived by the individual to be feasible and beneficial. It is prudent, however, to be mindful of the words of Titus Lucretius, who stated, 'What is food to one is bitter poison to others.'

Although there is undoubtedly something glamorous and romantic about working in aesthetically or climatically pleasing countries of the world, this is only one factor that may influence an individual's commitment to adventure education. Other factors may include social engagement with likeminded people and immersion in the natural environment. Decisions may be based on the type of client with whom you wish to work. An individual's interest may be in social and moral education with young offenders to give them support and address issues that led to their antisocial behaviour. Some enjoy providing introductory canoeing and kayaking sessions to schoolchildren on a local canal, whilst others like off-piste guiding with an expert group in the Swiss Alps. Passing on knowledge-based subjects, such as sustainability, environmental awareness, geography and geology, that can be delivered through the outdoor environment may enthuse another practitioner. The choices within adventure education are vast and will no doubt continue to grow. The motivation behind an adventure educator's engagement is important and provides us with an insight into the direction of their future development needs.

An additional consideration is the issue of career longevity. The chosen employment may form part of a long-term, structured career path or may simply be a bit of fun during a gap year or career break. Given the current culture of qualifications, qualifications and more qualifications, some may seek out employment opportunities with companies that offer national governing body qualifications. Alternatively, some individuals may look for employment that allows them to gain experience working with colleagues who are highly competent in soft-skills facilitation and social development or may wish to work in a more diverse environment, climate or culture.

Below, we outline some of the more common motivations for those working in the adventure education sector.

Personal skill development

Motivation may be partly driven by obtaining higher levels of skill within a specific sport or activity, which may involve achieving a higher grade in climbing or negotiating a more technical rapid in a canoe. This kind of development may contribute to further logbook experience or a national governing body award.

Environmental interaction

An individual may be motivated into embarking on an outdoor/adventure-based career by their fondness for the environment in which it takes place. They may take pleasure from the aesthetic value of the environment or may enjoy seeing others gain an understanding and appreciation of it. Working outdoors might be appealing because it provides an escape from the high-speed, technologically driven society in which many of us now live.

Social interaction

One may feel that this environment and the activities in which we engage draw us closer to people. Or one might simply enjoy being with people who want to learn about themselves and develop skills in specific activities.

Paul Gray, Chris Hodgson and Chris Heaney

Lifestyle

The lifestyle offered by an adventure-based career might be seen as appealing, in that the company of colleagues who also choose this line of work provides benefits to the individual, and there will likely be opportunities to live in parts of the world that provide further advantages that are not available at home. Accepting a job as a raft guide on the Zambezi may afford the individual greater opportunities for personal development in craft handling, safety and rescue than working on an artificial whitewater course in the UK.

Once the individual's motivations have been established, it is possible to begin to structure their goals and personal development activities more accurately, enabling the individual to develop an action plan with aims that complement their motives.

MASLOW'S HIERARCHY OF NEEDS

The human motivation theory of Abraham Maslow (1954) – known as the Hierarchy of Needs – attempts to explain the priority that human beings ascribe to all of their activities, including work and recreation. Maslow suggested that the four lower structures, collectively classified as 'deficiency needs', all need to be satisfied in order to progress to the next level in what is effectively a 'needs ascendency' process. This theory has commonly been applied to workplace and career-based motivation and it can offer some insights in the context of an outdoor/adventure setting.

Physiological needs

These needs are basic biological imperatives, such as maintaining a comfortable thermal balance, satiating hunger and thirst, getting sufficient sleep and so on. Although it may

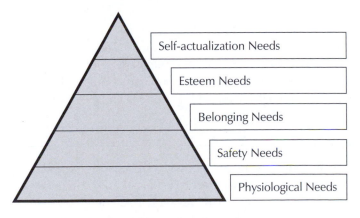

Figure 13.1 Maslow's hierarchy of needs

seem obvious that these essentials must be satisfied, sometimes that does not happen. I (Paul) recall observing seasonal instructors guiding clients on a thirty-kilometre river trip with an overnight camp. The trip involved a lot of physical work and two long working days. Only simple and small amounts of food were supplied to 'fuel' the staff: a bite-size bread roll, a piece of fruit and crisps for lunch, dehydrated meals for the evening meal and more bread rolls for breakfast. This was surely not enough, given the intensity of the work, so in this case even the lowest level of Maslow's Hierarchy of Needs was not addressed. In order to meet their simple need, the staff supplemented their rations with personally purchased items. In this kind of scenario, the adventure educator needs to be able to compensate for the undersupply by increasing their calorific intake; if this opportunity is not built into the programme, then dissatisfaction and disengagement will surely follow.

Safety needs

Within the outdoor/adventure environment, you would expect a focus on safety needs to be second nature, especially in the provision of highly governed activities, such as climbing and mountaineering. However, 'safety' can also relate to feelings of security regarding the human environment. For example, how safe do staff feel about leaving their car within the car park, leaving valuables onsite, or walking back to the staff area in the dark after an evening activity? Other security concerns may revolve around job security and long-term employment. This tends to be more prevalent within a culture of temporary employment and hourly contracts. To alleviate these concerns, some UK-based summer-season employers establish links with winter-season employers. This provides opportunities for employment throughout the summer, winter and following summer, as the summer employers tend to offer attractive re-employment schemes.

Belonging needs

Within any employment or social environment, the feeling of not being accepted, or not being able to 'get on' with others, can have serious detrimental effects. This may have even greater significance for an adventure educator because the camaraderie of a close team can be one of the key intangible benefits of employment and can also contribute to a better-quality service for clients. It is quite likely that living, working and even socialising together will heighten this impact.

> Following the completion of my three-year degree course, I applied for a job with a provider that I thought could offer me a step into adventure education. The interview went well: my academic qualifications along with my vocational experience allowed

Paul Gray, Chris Hodgson and Chris Heaney

me to answer the questions with confidence and my curriculum vitae seemed to impress the interview panel. An invitation to meet the staff for lunch was included as part of the interview process. It was at this point when I noticed that all of the staff had a similar hairstyle. Following lunch, I was offered the role of senior instructor, on the proviso that I visited the local barber and asked for 'a grade one all over'! I declined the offer and left the role to someone who would agree to such 'belonging'.

Paul Gray, former centre manager for Acorn Adventure

Organisations in adventure education often want to establish a strong 'corporate image' and portray a lifestyle to entice applications. Fleeces branded with the company's name are a popular perk of employment. This may also encourage a sense of belonging and cohesion within the staff. However, for others, it might be seen as a uniform and a threat to individuality. Finding the right balance is important, and the individual will need to establish whether the 'fit' is right for them in a particular setting.

Esteem needs

Maslow's fourth layer of needs concentrates on esteem, which can be developed through recognition of good work, contribution to a team and/or increased self-competence. Feedback enhancing esteem can be obtained from a number of sources – clients, work colleagues and line managers, for instance.

Self-actualisation needs

Maslow argues that the four lower (deficiency) needs must be satisfied before higher (growth) needs can be addressed. Growth needs include those of self-actualisation, and individuals at this level tend to focus on incorporating an ongoing freshness and appreciation of life with a concern about personal growth and the opportunity for peak experiences (another of Maslow's concepts that is commonly related to adventure education). Of interest here is the work of Griffiths (2003), who suggests that teenagers (specifically teenage lifeguards) may find it difficult to be self-actualised in their work environment due to the time they will need to progress through the deficiency stages.

Although we may not always be working with teenagers, it is useful to be aware of this when working with a relatively young staff team. Becoming more self-actualised and transcendent promotes wisdom and the ability to problem-solve in a wide variety of situations. These are key features in the outdoor/adventure environment, where the experience is often more valuable than the tangible outcome.

241

HERZBERG'S MOTIVATION AND HYGIENE THEORY

Frederick Herzberg (1968) examined workplace engagement and developed a theory known as the Two-Factor model, with the two factors being 'motivators' and 'hygiene factors'. Motivators are associated with job satisfaction and contribute to staff feeling happy about their jobs. They may include such factors as achievement recognition, responsibility, intrinsically rewarding tasks and the opportunity for professional growth. Hygiene factors, on the other hand, relate to issues that contribute to staff feeling dissatisfied or unhappy at work. These are unrelated to the tasks themselves, and are created by the environment in which the tasks are carried out. They include administration, working conditions, supervision, company policies and salary. All of these hygiene factors are extrinsically linked but individually based, and they must be maintained at a level that is acceptable to the individual, otherwise job dissatisfaction will ensue.

A key point in Herzberg's model is that the satisfiers and dissatisfiers are unipolar and non-compensatory. In other words, even when all of the hygiene factors (dissatisfiers) are addressed, staff will remain in the neutral zone (see Figure 13.2). An improvement in hygiene factors does not increase job satisfaction and ultimately motivation very far. Job satisfaction will occur only if sufficient motivators (satisfiers) are also evident. Equally, if satisfiers are all satisfactory but hygiene factors are not, then job dissatisfaction will prevail. It is therefore paramount for the employer to ensure that all hygiene factors are addressed, whilst always remembering that individuals tend to have different hygiene needs. In summary, addressing hygiene needs can eliminate job dissatisfaction but it does not contribute significantly to job satisfaction and therefore does not encourage self-motivation (Skemp-Arlt and Toupence, 2007); for this to happen, we need to address the motivators.

Hygiene factors

Since hygiene factors have such a profound influence upon workplace satisfaction, let us examine them within an adventure-based environment. First, let us consider administration. In the outdoor/adventure context, this does not necessarily mean 'paperwork'. For example,

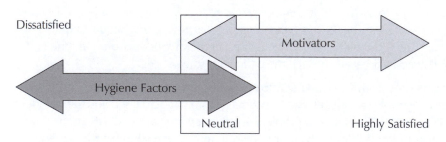

Figure 13.2 The non-compensatory nature of Herzberg's two-factor model

242

Paul Gray, Chris Hodgson and Chris Heaney

it might include the ease and efficiency with which equipment is obtained from the stores. Persistent problems in gaining access to specialist equipment might generate frustration, as might poor maintenance levels. Of course, some problems may be due to genuine limitations and factors out of the employer's direct control, such as reduced budgets, time allocation or staff turnover. However, they will still have a significant impact on the engagement of staff. Other issues on the other hand – such as the early display of weekly staff rotas, which will allow individuals to organise their lives outside of the work environment – should be relatively easy to address at little cost.

At first glance, providing acceptable working conditions may seem to be a simple case of following health and safety regulations. However, we should remember that the working environment includes such things as staff accommodation. If the accommodation is very close to that provided for the client groups, the staff's privacy may be compromised. Noise from the clients might also interfere with the sleep requirements of the hard-working staff. Facilitators and support staff need space away from clients where they know they will not be interrupted when they are off duty. The provision of a staff-only communal area with comfortable chairs, television, radio and kitchen facilities can be seen as a luxury when a facility is pushed for space and cash, but it can contribute to the long-term satisfaction of the teaching team. Easy access to washing machines, microwaves and fridges might also be sufficient to foster sustained motivation.

The location of the workplace can also be important. Rural surroundings might mean increased distances to access local amenities and social networks, generating a feeling of isolation and even entrapment. Increased supervision of and contact with new staff may also be essential in encouraging a sense of belonging. Responsibility for this should not fall wholly on the line manager; for instance, a buddy system is useful in inducting new members of staff into the social network and the workplace.

Although company policy and salaries may be non-negotiable, they should be clearly explained and justified to staff to stop them becoming contentious issues. For example, rather than simply stating the risk assessment for specific activities, why not include staff in the decision-making process for such policies and procedures, and allow staff the opportunity to review these throughout the year.

During my first days of employment within the commercial activity holiday sector, I was based in the South of France. Glorious sunshine filled the sky, the staff team were extremely amiable, laid back, cool instructors (well, at least I thought they were). This was idyllic: kayak in the morning, climb in the afternoon and become friends with a whole bunch of likeminded people. All my motivations for choosing this as a career path seemed vindicated. However, on the morning of my first programmed activity, there was a problem with a 'blockage' in the outflow from the toilet block to the septic tank, situated a hundred metres away. As the new boy, I felt obliged to offer assistance. I will spare you the details, but I can remember standing there thinking: This is not a reason for wanting a career in the outdoors!

Paul Gray, former centre manager for Acorn Adventure

Motivators

There is often an assumption that work in an adventure education context will always be rewarding. However, this assumption can sometimes be shattered by reality. Some clients will prove quite difficult and they do not always appreciate what professionals, including adventure educators, are trying to do for them. So it is important to ensure that all facilitators get a chance to work on tasks where they receive recognition for their efforts and achieve tangible outcomes. It is tempting for a manager to be quite controlling, as this feels 'safe', but such an approach reduces the opportunities for instructors and facilitators to be autonomous. Most adventure educators relish responsibility, so it is important that they get the chance to satisfy this need. Wherever it is reasonable to do so, responsibility and decision-making should be delegated downwards. Given that you are reading this chapter, you have probably already accepted that growth is an important aspect of achieving satisfaction and have recognised that we should plan for growth and advancement as a matter of course. In fact, it would be quite bizarre if we, as educators, did not want to do this!

Motivation can be viewed as having two dimensions: intrinsic and extrinsic. Extrinsic rewards include the external consequences of employment, such as getting paid, achieving status, and receiving free food and clothing. Intrinsic motivation is generally considered as being more powerful. It relates to the product of an experience that is rewarding in itself, and can be divided into motivation for knowledge, accomplishment and stimulation (Vallerand, 2001). Motivation for knowledge is obtaining satisfaction through learning something new and gaining increased knowledge. Training and working alongside more experienced, qualified members of staff may provide opportunities to meet these motivational requirements. Someone who is motivated for accomplishment is interested in mastering a new skill, whilst motivation for stimulation relates to gaining pleasant sensations from activities.

For instance, when leading a climbing session, an individual may be motivated because they have been introduced to a new venue and have just learned a new way to set up a rope system (knowledge). They may also feel that the new crag will give them an opportunity to refine their skills (accomplishment). Finally, they may get pleasure from helping their clients scale a wall for the first time (stimulation).

244

Motivation for knowledge and motivation for accomplishment were both evident during several canoe trips on the Colorado River. Instructors who were motivated for accomplishment saw each trip as a positive and developmental opportunity in which their personal skill could be enhanced. However, those who were motivated for knowledge commented that they were becoming bored and would like to change to another activity where they might learn something new. They should not be criticised for feeling this way. Rather, this story indicates that all adventure educators have their own, individual motivations, and none of these should be ignored.

UNDERSTANDING PERSONALITY

Just as individual motivations differ, so do personalities. Some people relish working with large groups; others find it easier to interact with clients on a one-to-one basis. Some are calm; others are more emotional. Some approach difficulties as challenges; others perceive them as brick walls that cannot be overcome.

Consider two contrasting characters from the *Star Wars* saga: Han Solo is spontaneous, reactive and perhaps overconfident; Luke Skywalker is calm, composed and thoughtful. These differences are immediately apparent, and they are reinforced in a range of situations. However, such character traits must always be assessed in context, taking into consideration the situations and environmental factors in which we find ourselves. For example, a naturally confident, forceful individual who likes to express their opinions might not be the best person to lead a reflective session in which the aim is to encourage individual contemplation. And whilst they might be an ideal companion on a whitewater river trip with friends, they might not facilitate the best learning environment for a group of adolescents on a self-supported canoe journey. Consequently, they might have to adapt their natural behaviour. Of course, this can be very difficult. After all, our personalities are established over many years. But a good facilitator will be able to change their approach to cope with the demands of a specific situation. This is often a learned skill and one that we should try to develop if it does not come naturally.

THE BIG FIVE TRAITS

It is difficult to generalise about an individual's personality. However, psychologists have identified the so-called 'big five' personality traits, and McCrae and Costa's (1987) Five-Factor model is arguably the most popular personality theory in use today. These five factors are:

- conscientiousness
- agreeableness
- neuroticism

245

- openness
- extroversion.

Conscientiousness is the degree to which a person is self-directed, disciplined and prefers to work with a planned agenda rather than an unstructured, spontaneous approach. Staff members who are extremely diligent in their preparation of programmed activity sessions throughout the week may well fell uneasy delivering an unplanned, spontaneous hour of alternative activity. This can be true even when they are an expert in the activity, simply because they are uncomfortable with delivering it in an impulsive, unrehearsed style.

Agreeableness describes the extent a person is understanding and cooperative, as opposed to hostile and distrustful. Imagine discussing new ideas for the delivery of activities with a team. These ideas might be met with open arms and viewed as progressive, or they might be greeted with such comments as: 'Why change, it works fine as it is.' The latter attitude might be generated by worry over a hidden agenda.

Neuroticism is a measure of emotional stability. A neurotic individual might be abnormally sensitive, obsessive or tense and anxious, rather than secure and confident. Such individuals might also be their own worst critics and spend endless hours analysing each reflective session or piece of feedback, causing themselves a lot of stress and anxiety. Consequently, they might need more emotional support and reassurance than others.

Openness describes an individual's curiosity and willingness to embrace a variety of experiences. An individual who has limited openness might prefer consistency and more traditional ideas. Some facilitators will always resist change, no matter how beneficial, preferring to stick to the methods they trust. It can be very hard to overcome their resistance.

Extroversion is a measure of how affable, outgoing and overtly expressive a person is. A more introverted person will display shyness and reticence, and they are likely to be more self-centred. An introverted instructor may need to be coaxed into being more expressive, whilst an extrovert might need help in order to understand when to step back and allow clients to take centre stage.

Mature, experienced adventure educators should not only be able to recognise personality traits in others, but should have a good understanding of their own. We also need to know when to work with or around a trait, and when to challenge one. Working with several colleagues can create opportunities: rather than always working with one person and becoming accustomed to their methods, beliefs and opinions, try to work with other facilitators with different styles.

I specifically remember two members of staff with contrasting personalities. The first was extremely outgoing and spontaneous in their approach, while the other was very

---

246

methodical, organised and diligent with preparation and generally quite reserved in nature. These two members of staff were deliberately programmed together, and although initially both expressed concerns, after discussing the rationale they both decided to give it a go. Some time later, both facilitators approached me and commented on what a valuable experience it had been and how much they had learned about themselves and each other.

Paul Gray, former centre manager for Acorn Adventure

Mentor and buddy systems are useful aids to recognising our own personalities and adapting our behaviour to suit a given situation. Also helpful is placing oneself in challenging situations and planning alternative solutions, instead of relying on one's natural behaviour and instinct.

GOALS

Take time to think about your current role. How did you end up here? Did you follow a structured career path or plan, or was it simply a result of a series of accidental processes?

Having a clear, long-term goal is vital in order to develop ourselves and others. Then subsidiary decisions will serve as steps towards an ultimate achievement, and you will avoid going down a series of dead ends. One might think of this long-term goal as a mission statement. It may be a five-year plan or a twenty-year plan, but it will certainly cover a considerable time period and should provide strategic focus.

A colleague once told me before an interview that a good response if asked 'Where do you see yourself in five years' time?' is: 'Sitting in your chair!' At the time, I thought this was very good advice: it seemed to be a very positive and ambitious statement that would surely seal my appointment by demonstrating my commitment and motivation. Upon reflection, however, I can see problems with it. Although it sets out a very ambitious goal, there is no direction, no idea of how to achieve that goal. It is also a bit of a cop out, as the assumption is that the goals of the interviewer should be the goals of the new employee, and this may well not be the case. (Luckily, I wasn't asked the question!)

Paul Gray, former centre manager for Acorn Adventure

ESTABLISHING A PRESENT POSITION

Once we have established where we would like to be, we need to examine our present position. What skills do we, or the person whom we are helping, already possess that will help us achieve the goal? And what might get in the way or make it difficult? Two analysis techniques might help here: the SWOT analysis and the personal performance profile.

SWOT analysis

The SWOT analysis process, a technique suggested by Albert Humphrey of Stanford University, is often used in strategic planning. It involves looking at the present situation from four perspectives (see Figure 13.3). The first two perspectives are internal and provide opportunities to examine where the individual is in terms of what they bring to a situation. First, list the strengths that the aspirant adventure educator already possesses that will help them achieve the established goal. Next, examine personal weak areas that might stop that goal being realised. Often these are the areas that people are most likely to avoid addressing, yet addressing them can yield the biggest results. Goddard and Neumann (1993) refer to this as the weakest link principle: if we work on the biggest obstacle in the way of our performance, then the same amount of effort should achieve the greatest overall result.

The remaining two areas examine the environment in which we will be working. First, list the opportunities presented by the environment. These might include local geography and facilities; other colleagues and easy access to client groups will add to the relevant experience base. The final perspective comprises the threats contained within the environment. These might impede the successful execution of our plan – either delaying progress or derailing it altogether. Sometimes, these 'threats' might be the same elements that provide opportunities.

A useful exercise is to have a trusted friend complete a parallel SWOT analysis of you and see the extent to which their views agree with your own. Sometimes, individuals will accurately present the positive factors but underplay the negatives (or vice versa), or they

	Positive Factors	Negative Factors
Internal Factors	STRENGTHS	WEAKNESSES
External Factors	OPPORTUNITIES	THREATS

Figure 13.3 The four perspectives of the SWOT analysis

248

will have an accurate internal view but be off the mark externally. The trusted friend can help improve the accuracy of your perception.

Personal performance profiling

The performance profiling approach is based on personal construct theory, developed by George Kelly (1955). It is a way of examining our understanding of the attributes required to be successful in an endeavour and our perception of our abilities relative to these. It is a good way to identify areas for development and the amount of attention each developmental area will require. Moreover, it helps establish areas of strength, where it would be less productive to focus time or energy (to achieve our stated aim).

Step 1 involves establishing the elements that are needed to be successful. At this stage it is best to consider the role in an impersonal way, as if it were to be filled by someone else. This approach helps objectivity. List the components that will contribute to a successful overall performance in the role. These may include physical elements, cognitive elements, affective elements and skill-based elements.

Step 2 entails prioritising these elements. Which of them is most important? Rank them by attaching a score to each element, or just put them in an ordered list.

Step 3 involves establishing a score that relates to a person's present position in relation to the standard required for success in each element. This can be done numerically or pictorially – by shading in a column, where the whole column represents the target and the shaded portion shows the current level of performance in relation to that end point (see Figure 13.4).

The completed profile allows us to understand which attributes are important for success, how these should be prioritised and the size of the gap between one's present position and where one feels one needs to be. As with the SWOT analysis, it is a good idea to compare your own responses with those of a trusted friend or mentor.

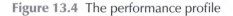

Figure 13.4 The performance profile

The performance profile is a good place to begin when setting development goals and planning a programme that is expected to lead to success.

GOAL-SETTING

A clear goal can provide direction and motivation for a learner. However, if left unmanaged, goals can spiral out of control and lead to a person becoming 'overwhelmed, de-motivated and anxious' by their scale or complexity (Jarvis, 2006: 129). Breaking them down into bite-size chunks will reduce such concerns. The big goals can be called 'outcome goals': they are where we want to end up, but do not specify how to get there.

Outcome goals are often referenced against other people: for example, 'This season, my aim is to climb harder grades than anyone else in the club', or, 'I will achieve higher client satisfaction reports than the other team leaders.' They could relate to gaining status: for example, the achievement of a national governing body award or a particular job post.

However, one might argue that performance goals reap greater rewards than outcome goals. These are self-referenced and based on individual performance. Instead of aiming to climb harder grades than anyone else in the club, you might seek to improve one grade; rather than securing higher client satisfaction reports than the other leaders, you might simply try to improve your own by 10 per cent. Crucially, performance goals are short- and medium-term targets, so they are bite-size and more easily achievable.

It is also important to realise when developing adventure educators that setting goals for certification achievement is only one, small area of development. Martin *et al*. (2006: ch. 9) suggest that individual development should also include the domains of:

- biological/physical (strength, speed, endurance, and so on)
- cognitive/intellect (knowledge of the subject)
- socio-emotional (relationships with others and personal development).

For an adventure educator, it makes sense to set goals for each of these domains and ensure that focus does not rest solely on strengths or favourite areas. The performance profile can help in this respect. For example, one may choose to develop presentation skills in front of smaller audiences (perhaps colleagues and friends) that increase in size over a period of time. It may also be advantageous to record the concerns held by the individual prior to each presentation and see how these concerns dissipate over the time period.

The time allocated to your goals is a key factor. The setting of long-, mid- and short-term goals should allow you to keep focused, as the shorter-term goals will act as 'checkpoints' for progression. A long-term goal may be for an individual to develop their own small business within five years to provide adventure experiences for vulnerable adults. Medium-term goals (typically yearly) will allow this budding entrepreneur to evaluate their progress.

And breaking down these yearly goals into monthly or six-monthly short-term goals will encourage focus and prevent wandering from the structured path that has been established.

To assist in the process of setting goals, George Doran (1981) proposed the use of the SMARTER mnemonic:

- Specific
- Measurable
- Agreed
- Relevant
- Time phased
- Engaging
- Recorded.

The final 'R' (Recorded) is especially important, as this is a step that many adventure educators are very reluctant to take. But there is something much more committing about a written goal. Ideally, record the short-term 'stepping-stone' goals as well, and tick them off to track progress.

Current environment may also determine the time allocated and appropriateness of each goal. As an example, during a goal-setting session with a mentor, he suggested that I should take up sea kayaking to develop my knowledge base within paddle sport more generally. However, he failed to take into account that I lived in Nottingham. There aren't many places in the UK further from a coastline!

THE MENTOR

A very effective strategy for development is mentoring. A mentor can be formally appointed by a line manager, or an informal arrangement can be reached between peers. Megginson and Clutterbuck (2005) suggest that mentoring should be concerned with developing the whole individual and should not focus primarily on skill development. A mentor might be more useful for looking at *what* we do and helping us examine *why* we do it, rather than commenting on *how* we do it. Taylor (2006: 47) suggests that a mentor is someone to 'bounce ideas off, go to for advice and generally use as a sounding board', and that the mentor should allow the mentee to develop their own practice and individual ideas. In essence, a mentor should not aim to produce a 'mini-me', but rather should allow the mentee's individual flair, beliefs and ideas to come to the fore. The mentor acts as a critical friend who can help shape, define and analyse ideas, but they should not stipulate a course of action. The focus could be on any or all aspects of professionalism, including interpersonal skills, career planning and hard-skill goals.

The mentor should guide and encourage understanding rather than procedure. For example, I have witnessed an introductory kayaking session with a group of young children that began with a very prescriptive running order: how to sit in the kayak; what to do in the event of a capsize; how to hold the paddle; and so on. When questioned about why they stuck so rigidly to this format, the facilitators often answered, 'It's what we have been told to do.' The dogmatic following of such fixed systems demonstrates that attending numerous training and induction courses creates a reliance on procedure rather than understanding.

Another example might involve a new member of staff who is finding it difficult to settle into communal living at a centre. In particular, he might be frustrated by excessive noise in the accommodation area keeping him awake at night. This might seem trivial to some of his colleagues, but it could mask a deeper problem. For example, the real issue might be any of the following:

- The mentee feels his concerns are not being treated seriously, and he does not feel respected by other members of staff.
- The mentee finds it difficult to engage socially with certain members of staff, so he withdraws from the team.
- The mentee is homesick and is contemplating resignation.

It would be a shame to learn that a member of staff had departed due to an issue that could have been resolved if they had been encouraged to discuss it. The mentor's role in this case is to bring out the why, what and how of the situation and discuss steps towards a solution. The mentee may offer an appropriate action that will improve their situation, but they should also be encouraged to reflect on how this will affect others. Also, how will it play out over time? Will it seem such an appropriate solution in six months' time as it does now? If not, perhaps they should consider an alternative solution.

Choosing a mentor

The choice of mentor does not need to be based on experience. Although it can be useful to have a mentor who is more experienced than the mentee, there are advantages to having a peer as a mentor, too. For instance, a mentee might be more open to discussing their problems with someone whom they consider an equal, rather than a superior. What is most important, however, is that both the mentor and the mentee feel comfortable with the nature of the relationship.

A good mentor should also be able to recognise when their guidance is no longer being followed and/or when they have no more guidance to offer. A mentee should not feel obliged to remain with a mentor when this situation is reached: if the guidance is no longer helping their development, they should seek a new mentor. A skilful mentor is similar to a good teacher of navigation: they will help interpret the terrain and help shape the skills needed to make route choices based on local and wider considerations, which they recognise can be dynamic, unstable and shifting.

252

COLLABORATIVE STRATEGIES

Collaboration with others is a very effective means of upskilling adventure educators (Hodgson and Sharp, 2000). If people unite to pursue the same goals, their chances of success are greatly increased. Working alongside someone else can produce a sense of camaraderie, and some of the logistics of arranged developmental activities can also be shared. Some skills can be practised on willing peers, and this often reveals problems with a certain approach; scenarios can be run through, and both parties can benefit from any new knowledge that is generated.

Each partner will bring their own strengths to the collaboration and benefit from those of their colleague. If nothing else, it is likely that each individual will be spurred on by the enthusiasm of a training partner and will bolster that partner's motivation when required.

CONCLUSION

Having read this chapter, the neophyte adventure educator (or a manager responsible for developing staff competence) should now know how to draft a personal development plan that will ensure a long and rewarding career in adventure education. To do this, they will need to maintain a meta-perspective of the adventure education sector, and evaluate their place in it realistically, before identifying where they would like to be and planning how to get there.

Whether the aim is staff management, self-development, mentorship of a younger and/or less experienced colleague or working with a contemporary in a peer-support role, applying the principles outlined in this chapter will allow an adventure education professional to focus their mental, physical and emotional energy into satisfying needs and motivators. This will contribute to the individual's personal and professional development, whilst enabling them to sustain a fulfilling career in the outdoor sector. It may also help them avoid frustration by identifying when the time is right to take a new direction.

The choices within the adventure education sector are vast and will undoubtedly continue to grow. Accurately evaluating the motivation behind an adventure educator's engagement is important and provides us with an insight into the required direction of their future development needs in or out of the sector. This should be seen as the foundation of any personal development process. While motivations can, and will, change over time, building a structure on an unstable foundation may result in collapse. It is therefore vital to spend time accurately analysing what drives the individual before building a plan. Once an individual has been able to ascertain what is important to them, and what they want to achieve, they will be able to invest energy and effort (consciously and subconsciously) into reaching their desired outcomes.

Individuals, managers and mentors should be mindful of Herzberg's Two-Factor model. Understanding that we all have our own interpretation of our environment and that this perception may be influenced by the culture of the groups in which we find ourselves will contribute to a positive and fruitful relationship between mentor and mentee. Acknowledging and accepting the perception of another individual should contribute to the development of rapport, a standpoint from which one can begin to understand individual perceptions that provide motivation and limit dissatisfaction. A constructive working relationship can blossom from this rapport, as the mentee is able to take advantage of the trust they have built with the mentor. Common ground is established to promote an understanding of the mentee's intrinsic motivation and formulation of an individualised developmental plan. A good mentor will be able to change their approach to cope with the needs of the mentee, matching and pacing communication patterns, behaviour and individual traits before initiating change, if and when necessary, to promote progress.

Having developed a rapport, a SWOT analysis affords the mentee/mentor partnership the opportunity to explore the mentee's strengths and weakness, automatically highlighting the areas that require development and the established qualities that can be drawn upon when doing so. Looking externally and assessing the positive and negative environmental factors will allow the partnership to shape the plan in response to any opportunities that arise. An honest appraisal allows the mentee to develop personal goals that tally with the SMARTER mnemonic. A recorded document allows periodic reviews to be undertaken and ultimately aids progress.

In order for adventure education to be taken seriously as a profession, and for those within the profession to feel that there are opportunities for continuing personal and professional development, the systematic plan–do–review approach outlined above can provide a model to satisfy personal needs and motivations. We can then take steps towards adventure facilitation that is skilled, informed and better meets the needs of participants. This will contribute on multiple levels to lifelong learning. The question now is: what motivates you?

REFERENCES

Breakwell, G.M. (2007) *The Psychology of Risk*, New York: Cambridge University Press.
Cox, R.H. (2007) *Sport Psychology*, 6th edn, London: McGraw Hill.
Doran, G.T. (1981) There's a S.M.A.R.T. way to write management's goals and objectives, *Management Review*, 70 (11): 36.
Foxon, F. (1999) *Improving Practice and Skill*, Leeds: National Coaching Foundation.
Goddard, D. and Neumann, U. (1993) *Performance Rock Climbing*, Mechanicsburg, PA: Stackpole Books.
Griffiths, T. (2003) *Complete Swimming Pool Reference*, Illinois: Sagamore.
Herzberg, F. (1968) One more time: how do you motivate employees?, *Harvard Business Review*, 46 (1): 53–62.
Hodgson, C. and Sharp, B. (2000) National governing body awards: a strategy for success, *Journal of Vocational Education and Training*, 52 (2): 199–210.
Jarvis, M. (2006) *Sport Psychology: A Student's Handbook*, London: Routledge.
Kelly, G.A. (1955) *The Psychology of Personal Constructs*, New York: Norton.

254

Martin, B., Cashel, C., Wagstaff, M. and Breunig, M. (2006) *Outdoor Leadership: Theory and Practice*, Leeds: Human Kinetic.

Maslow, A. (1954) *Motivation and Personality*, New York: Harper.

McCrae, R.R. and Costa, P.T., Jr. (1987) Validation of the Five-Factor Model of Personality across instruments and observers, *Journal of Personality and Social Psychology*, 52: 81–90.

McMorris, T. and Hale, T. (2006) *Coaching Science: Theory to Practice*: Chichester: Wiley.

McQuade, S. (2003) *How to Coach Sports Effectively*, Leeds: Coachwise Solutions.

Megginson, D. and Clutterbuck, D. (2005) *Techniques for Coaching and Mentoring*, London: Elsevier.

Sharp, B. (2004) *Acquiring Skill in Sport*, 2nd edn, Cheltenham: Sports Dynamics.

Skemp-Arlt, K.M. and Toupence, R. (2007) The administrator's role in employee motivation, *Coach and Athletic Director*, 76 (7): 28.

Taylor, B. (2006) Coaching, in Ferrero, F. (ed.) *BCU Coaching Handbook*, Caernarfon: Pesda Press.

Vallerand, R.J. (2001) A hierarchical model of intrinsic and extrinsic motivation in sport and exercise, in Roberts, G.C. (ed.) *Advances in Motivation in Sport and Exercise*, Leeds: Human Kinetics.

Weinberg, R.S. and Gould, D. (2003) *Foundations of Sport and Exercise Psychology*, 3rd edn, Leeds: Human Kinetics.

CHAPTER FOURTEEN

CONCLUSION

Chris Hodgson and Matt Berry

Adventure education is an exciting and diverse field, and we hope that you have found this introduction both interesting and thought provoking. In our introduction to the book, we suggested that we aimed to support students and professionals alike in moving their understanding forward; and, in doing so, perhaps also improve their career prospects. Remember that this book is an introduction, though: you may feel inspired to look elsewhere to continue to enhance your understanding and practice.

You may also be curious about what the future holds for adventure education and the people who work within the discipline. As professionals ourselves, we often return to this question academically and professionally, as well as individually and socially. It is very common to invest a great deal of our lives and personalities within our chosen field, which means that any change can have a profound impact on us. Obviously, we are no better at predicting the future than anyone else, but as professionals and academics we must endeavour to keep abreast of recent developments and look out for future trends. In some ways, we must take responsibility for shaping the future by actively facilitating change and development. So perhaps we all need to consider what is likely to happen as well as what we would like to see, and whether it is possible to move in a particular direction. In Chapter 1, Pete Bunyan told us of individuals who did just that, and this will continue in the future. One day, a reader of this book may well appear in a history of adventure education. This is an important point, because it illustrates that adventure education will continue to evolve. Our knowledge will never be 'finished'.

Questions about the future in adventure education tend to be concerned with how to achieve particular outcomes, rather than what those outcomes are. Research in this area is developing and future research will endeavour to provide clearer answers. However, it is also likely that unpredicted outcomes will lead to new questions and lines of enquiry. As the sector becomes increasingly professional, there will probably be more emphasis on planning and formalising development in such areas as teaching, learning and facilitation, which in the past have played smaller roles than technical skill sets. It would be nice to think that we will see increased integration between research and professional practice, so these are more frequently viewed as vital components within a single initiative. Perhaps they

256

could even be conducted by a single person. This will move us away from the traditional position of professionals delivering adventure education, and academics writing about it and trying to chart its progress from the outside. We look forward to a time when there is much less of a gulf between theorists and practitioners, and consequently more respect for both understanding and doing. We hope that this will also afford greater opportunities for those who practise to study and greater motivation for those who study to practise. After all, research-informed practice is a key indicator of a healthy profession.

We do not know what the future holds in terms of funding. Recently, though, direct funding from the public purse has become ever scarcer. Organisations have seen their grants reduced and many have lost all of their public funding, leaving them with no option but to switch to charitable status or trade as private concerns. At first glance, this may seem to be a wholly negative situation. However, access to adventure education has actually increased during this period. This austere environment has encouraged providers to be more creative and to focus on the needs of participants and the benefits that they take away with them. This means that we are often asked to demonstrate our 'value' and 'effectiveness'. As a result, the adventure educational professional now needs a broader skill set and a CV that justifies their position through evidenced education, accreditation, experience and training.

If we are adaptable and continue to meet the current and future needs of society, such as recognising the potential of the healthy living agenda, we will always be able to make a difference. As this book has demonstrated, adventure education has much to offer, and it can be used in many creative and exciting ways.

Good luck,

Matt and Chris

257

INDEX

263